# CARRIER AIRCRAFT
## 1917–PRESENT

# THE ESSENTIAL
# AIRCRAFT IDENTIFICATION GUIDE

# CARRIER AIRCRAFT
## 1917–PRESENT

THOMAS NEWDICK

amber
BOOKS

This edition published in 2011 by
Amber Books Ltd
Bradley's Close
74–77 White Lion Street
London N1 9PF
United Kingdom
www.amberbooks.co.uk

A catalogue record for this book is available from the British Library.

ISBN: 978-1-907446-97-9

Project Editor: Michael Spilling
Design: Brian Rust
Picture Research: Terry Forshaw

Printed in China

# Contents

# Introduction

**In the fast-changing world of military aviation, developments in carrier-based aircraft have often been in the vanguard. Designers and operators of these types face a variety of unique challenges, and as developments in warfare and the naval balance of power change, so the aircraft operating from carriers must assume new roles and capabilities.**

THE FIRST MILITARY AIRCRAFT to operate from aircraft carriers were hastily equipped land-based types, with modifications intended to cope with the rigours – and hazards – of operations from decks at sea. However, these early pioneers established the basic requirements for carrier-based aircraft: a robust airframe and undercarriage, and the ability to execute short landing runs at low landing speeds. Before long, drop-down tailhooks and transverse wires had become *de rigeur* in order to effect arrested landings.

As aircraft weights increased, means of assisting take-off began to be introduced, with the catapult or 'accelerator' system borrowed from catapult-equipped cruisers emerging as the most effective. Other early innovations included deck landing officers or 'batsmen' to guide aircraft onto the deck more

accurately, and crash barriers in the event of an aborted landing. Folding wings and elevators allowed aircraft to be stowed more efficiently above and below decks, and permitted an increase in over all air group size. Carriers, meanwhile, soon adopted the flush decks required for practical, routine operations.

By the outbreak of World War II, the aircraft carrier and its embarked air wing had matured to a point at which they could assume the role of arbiter of naval battles from the previously dominant

▼ **Pacific air power**

Carrier air power came of age during the Pacific campaign in World War II. The classic US Navy fighter of the war, the Grumman Hellcat, is seen here: an F6F-3 from VF-5 preparing to take off from USS *Yorktown* (CV-10) during operations in the Marshall Islands in November 1943.

battleship. The aircraft themselves had advanced to such an extent that now they routinely featured monoplane configuration, retractable undercarriage and more powerful armament. The battles fought in the Pacific during World War II were the first in which carrier air power clashed on a large scale, and included the first battles to be fought and decided using carrier air power exclusively. World War II also demonstrated the significance of carrier air power in the war against submarines, while the fighting in the Pacific saw carrier aircraft used in the first practical application of airborne early warning systems.

Coming hand-in-hand with the emergence of the first carrier-based jet fighters, a number of developments in the years immediately after the war paved the way for carrier air power to assume an even more important role. Chief among these were the angled carrier deck, providing more room for aircraft operations and making landings less hazardous; the mirror landing aid to further improve safety margins during landing; and the steam-powered catapult, to launch aircraft at greater weights. Before long, developments in atomic propulsion would see the first nuclear-powered carriers, offering almost unlimited range and increased capacity for even larger and more versatile air wings to be embarked.

## Cold War carriers

The Cold War saw US Navy carrier air wings briefly assume a strategic nuclear role, although it was in a conventional role that carrier aircraft saw combat service in the years after 1945, taking active part in a variety of conflicts and peacekeeping missions around the globe. At the same time, the increasing threat posed by submarines saw carrier aircraft adopt the anti-submarine warfare role, a mission that was increasingly undertaken by carrier-based helicopters.

As navies saw the manifold applications offered by rotary-wing aircraft, helicopter carriers began to be fielded for the amphibious assault role. Vertical take-off was not just limited to helicopters, however, and the emergence of the first generation of

vertical/short take-off and landing (V/STOL) jets permitted smaller ships to embark combat aircraft. A more recent development of the V/STOL carrier concept has been the short take-off but assisted recovery (STOBAR) carrier, in which fixed-wing aircraft are launched via a 'ski jump' ramp and recovered with arrester wires, obviating the need for heavy and expensive steam catapults.

Following the end of the Cold War, the uncertain security environment was one in which the carrier and its aircraft came to play a highly important role. With multi-role air wings offering a range of different capabilities, carriers came to be used increasingly in rapid-reaction and power protection missions, sailing to trouble spots to intervene in conflicts or to support humanitarian missions.

In the new millennium, carriers are now becoming available as an entirely new capability to developing navies that can afford to operate them. With aircraft carriers so often the most visible and mobile expression of a nation's air power, these assets are set to retain their prestige and importance well into the twenty-first century, and a number of advanced new aircraft types are being developed to arm them.

▶ **Lockheed S-3A Viking**

Vikings from VS-29 were shore-based at NAS North Island, California, and for most of the 1980s were assigned to CVW 15, embarked in USS *Carl Vinson* (CVN-70). The squadron was the first to make an operational deployment with the Viking, in late 1975. A total of 187 Vikings had been built by the time production concluded in August 1978. Of these, 119 were later converted to S-3B standard.

# Chapter 1

# The Early Years (1917–39)

World War I saw the emergence of airpower at sea, with early developments in the field led by the British. After launching scouts from platforms built on the turrets of capital ships, and from towed lighters, the British introduced the first true aircraft carrier in the form of HMS *Furious* before the end of the conflict. Between the wars, three countries led the way in the introduction of aircraft carriers and their related aircraft components, and although Japan, the United Kingdom and the United States all adopted different approaches, all had introduced successive generations of carrier-borne fighters, reconnaissance aircraft, torpedo-bombers and dive-bombers before the outbreak of World War II.

◀ **Flight deck**
A British Sopwith Pup is brought up from a hangar on board HMS *Furious*, 1917.

# Pioneers
## 1917–22

**After the groundwork for naval air operations at sea had been laid by seaplanes and their dedicated carriers, the next step was to introduce catapult-launched and deck-landing aircraft.**

ON 1 OCTOBER 1917, Squadron Commander F.J. Rutland took off in his Sopwith Pup from a short platform installed over the gun turret of the battlecruiser HMS *Repulse*. Similar platforms were installed on a number of battlecruisers and larger cruisers, before the arrival of the aircraft carrier proper. Built as a light battlecruiser, HMS *Furious* was converted as the world's first aircraft carrier in 1917, with a flight deck on the foredeck. Senior Flying Officer aboard *Furious* was Squadron Commander E.H. Dunning, and on 2 August 1917 he attempted a first landing on a ship under way. Taking off in his Pup from the deck of the *Furious*, Dunning then put the aircraft down safely, deck crew bringing the Pup to a stop with the aid of rope toggles attached to the aircraft's fuselage and wings. Another successful landing was followed by a third attempt on 7 August, in which the Pup bounced on the deck and went over the side of the ship. Dunning was drowned in the mishap, but he had successfully proven the aircraft carrier concept.

Completed in July 1917, HMS *Furious* was the first true aircraft carrier, as opposed to a seaplane carrier, tender or part-converted naval vessel.

However, operations from *Furious* were hazardous, and the carrier was mainly limited to launching aircraft, rather than recovering them on deck. However, *Furious* was credited with the first successful carrier-based air strike, when seven Sopwith Camels were launched against the Zeppelin airship sheds at Tondern on 19 July 1918. Next in line for service with the Royal Navy were HMS *Argus* and *Eagle*, both arriving too late for World War I but introducing the 'straight-through' or flush-deck carrier to British service.

The first aircraft embarked aboard Royal Navy carriers included navalized adaptations of the Pup and 2F.1 Camel that served with the Royal Naval Air Service, and the Beardmore W.B.III, purpose-built for carrier operations, albeit based on the earlier Pup. Commissioned just weeks before the Armistice of

### Specifications

| | |
|---|---|
| Crew: 2 | Service ceiling: 2500m (8200ft) |
| Powerplant: 1 x 75kN (16,868lbf) Curtiss OXX-6 Vee piston engine | Dimensions: span 14.32m (47ft 0in); length 9.25m (30ft 4in); height 4.01m (13ft 2in) |
| Maximum speed: 117km/h (73mph) | Weight: 931kg (2050lb) loaded |
| Range: 439km (273 miles) | Armament: N/a |

▲ **Aeromarine 39-A**

*US Navy*

New Jersey-based Aeromarine's Model 39 provided the first generation of US Navy aviators with their initial experience of carrier operations. This Model 39-A was one of 50 examples ordered by the US Navy in 1917 as trainers.

### ▼ Beardmore W.B.III

#### Royal Naval Air Service

N-6101, an example of the W.B.III, a shipboard fighter developed by William Beardmore and Co. Ltd on the basis of the successful Sopwith Pup. The Royal Naval Air Service took the W.B.III aboard HMS *Furious*, *Nairana* and *Pegasus*. The aircraft differed from the land-based Pup in its use of non-staggered folding wings, for ease of stowage on carriers. The lengthened fuselage carried emergency flotation gear.

**Specifications**

| | |
|---|---|
| Crew: 1 | Dimensions: span 7.62m (25ft 0in); length |
| Powerplant: 1 x 60kN (13,494lbf) | 6.16m (20ft 0in); height 2.47m (8ft 1in) |
| Maximum speed: 166km/h (103mph) | Weight: 585kg (1289lb) loaded |
| Range: 275km (171 miles) | Armament: One 7.7mm (.303in) Lewis machine |
| Service ceiling: 3780m (12,400ft) | gun |

November 1918, HMS *Argus* introduced a flight group of Sopwith Cuckoo torpedo-bombers.

### American developments

The United States was an early pioneer of aircraft at sea, and as early as 14 November 1910, Eugene Ely had launched a Curtiss pusher biplane from a platform on board the scout cruiser USS *Birmingham*, at anchor in Hampton Roads, Virginia. Ely subsequently became the first man to land an aircraft on a warship, his Curtiss Model D touching down on the armoured cruiser USS *Pennsylvania* on 18 January 1911. The US Navy followed up with its first true carrier, USS *Langley*, a converted fleet collier that began trials in July 1922 after its commissioning in March. *Langley* boasted an impressive aircraft capacity, with hangar space for up to 33 aircraft.

Among the first aircraft embarked in the *Langley* was the Naval Aircraft Factory TS, the first US Navy aircraft designed specifically for carrier operations, which entered service aboard the carrier in December 1922. Meanwhile, the honour of recording the first deck landing on the *Langley* fell to an Aeromarine 39, Lieutenant Commander Geoffrey DeChevalier landing a Model 39-B on 26 October 1922. Aircraft of this type were also used for training prospective carrier aircrew from a simulated carrier deck located at Langley Field, Virginia.

Japan had observed developments in the UK with interest, and laid down its first true aircraft carrier, *Hosho*, in late 1919, this being another example of a converted vessel, having begun life as a naval oiler. The carrier was commissioned in 1922 and although originally operating with an air group of 22 aircraft, this was latterly reduced to just 12. Despite its limited capacity, the *Hosho* played a vital role in providing the Imperial Japanese Navy with experience of carrier operations.

Early aircraft embarked in the *Hosho* included the Mitsubishi 1MF, a fighter biplane designed by Herbert Smith of the British Sopwith company specifically for use aboard the carrier. The 1MF entered production in 1921 as the Navy Type 10-1 Carrier Fighter. It was a 1MF, flown by British pilot Captain Jordan, that performed the first take-off and landing on the *Hosho* in February 1923. Herbert Smith was also responsible for the Mitsubishi B1M, a two-seat torpedo-bomber adopted by the IJN as the Type 13 Carrier Attacker. First flown in 1923, the successful B1M survived to see active service during the Shanghai Incident a decade later. Smith's other notable contribution to the early IJN carrier air groups was the Mitsubishi 2MR or Type 10 Carrier Reconnaissance Aircraft, a two-seat biplane first flown in 1922 and essentially a scaled-up version of the same company's 1MF.

# Japan
## 1929–39

**Japan was the first nation to take the aircraft carrier into battle, during its interwar conflict with China, and development of air groups was spurred by an advanced carrier-building programme.**

THE EARLY AIR groups of the IJN's carrier arm were based around the first-generation 1MF fighter, 2MR reconnaissance and B1M torpedo-bomber types. The latter was the most successful of Herbert Smith's designs for the IJN. At the outbreak of the Shanghai Incident in January 1932, the carriers *Kaga* and *Hosho* were in Chinese waters, and the 1st Air Wing launched 32 B1Ms to attack targets around the city. The B1Ms were escorted by Nakajima A1N Type 3 Carrier Fighters, which clashed in combat with Chinese and American-flown fighters.

The A1N biplane fighter was a licence-built version of the British Gloster Gambet, built for the IJN during 1929–30. The Nakajima A2N was intended to supersede the A1N, and was a single-seat biplane fighter with fixed landing gear that was accepted for service in late 1930 as the Navy Type 90 Carrier Fighter. Nakajima's next carrier fighter was the A4N or Navy Type 95 Carrier Fighter, a conventional single-seat biplane built between 1935–37 and used in combat against China in 1937. The A4N's service tenure was brief, however, thanks to the arrival of the superb Mitsubishi A5M single-seat fighter, one of the most agile aircraft of the period. Designed to a 1934 specification, the A5M was accepted into service as the Navy Type 96 Carrier Fighter and the type was the mainstay of the IJN carrier fighter arm during the Sino-Japanese War.

In terms of offensive carrier assets, the interwar IJN relied on the Aichi D1A dive-bomber and the Mitsubishi B2M, a successor to the B1M in the torpedo-bomber role. Designed in the UK, the B2M entered service in March 1932 as the Type 89 Carrier Attack Aircraft and was also equipped with external bomb racks for level-bombing. The Yokosuka B3Y, meanwhile, was intended to serve in the torpedo-bomber role as the Type 92 Carrier Attack Bomber, but its limited success ensured that the B2M remained in service into the mid-1930s.

## Specifications

Crew: 1

Powerplant: 1 x 585kN (131,574lbf) Nakajima Kotobuki 41 or Kotobuki 41 Kai nine-cylinder single-row radial piston engine

Maximum speed: 435km/h (270mph)

Service ceiling: 9800m (32,150ft)

Dimensions: span 11.00m (36ft 1.13in); length 7.57m (4ft 9.88in); height 3.27m (10ft 8.75in)

Weight: 1822kg (4017lb) loaded

Armament: Two 7.7mm (.303in) fixed forward firing machine guns, one 60kg (132lb) bomb

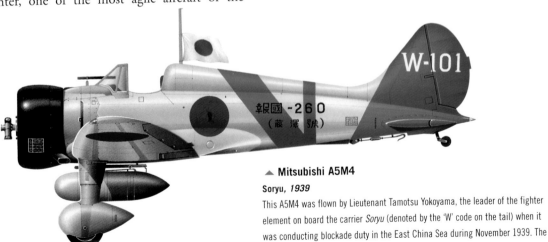

▲ **Mitsubishi A5M4**

**Soryu, *1939***

This A5M4 was flown by Lieutenant Tamotsu Yokoyama, the leader of the fighter element on board the carrier *Soryu* (denoted by the 'W' code on the tail) when it was conducting blockade duty in the East China Sea during November 1939. The A5M received the Allied codename 'Claude'. Natural metal finish was typical for most examples of the type after 1938.

## JAPANESE INTERWAR CARRIER AIR GROUP DEVELOPMENT — SELECTED AIR GROUPS

| 1924 | | *Hosho* |
|---|---|---|
| *Hosho* Carrier Fighter Unit | 1MF1 | Mitsubishi Type 10 Carrier Fighter |
| *Hosho* Carrier Fighter Unit | 1MF3 | Mitsubishi Type 10 Carrier Fighter |
| *Hosho* Carrier Reconnaissance Unit | 2MR2 | Mitsubishi Type 10 Carrier Reconnaissance Aircraft |
| **1927** | | *Akagi* |
| *Akagi* Carrier Fighter Unit | A1N1 | Nakajima Type 3 Carrier Fighter |
| *Akagi* Carrier Dive-Bomber Unit | 1MF3A | Mitsubishi Type 10 Carrier Fighter |
| *Akagi* Carrier Level-Bomber Unit | 1MF3A | Mitsubishi Type 10 Carrier Fighter |
| **1932** | | *Kaga* |
| *Kaga* Carrier Fighter Unit | A1N1 | Nakajima Type 3 Carrier Fighter |
| *Kaga* Carrier Dive-Bomber Unit | A1N2 | Nakajima Type 3 Carrier Fighter |
| *Kaga* Carrier Level-Bomber Unit | B2M2 | Mitsubishi Type 89 Carrier Attack Aircraft |
| **1932** | | *Akagi* |
| *Akagi* Carrier Fighter Unit | A4N1 | Nakajima Type 95 Carrier Fighter |
| *Akagi* Carrier Dive-Bomber Unit | A2N1 | Nakajima Type 90 Carrier Fighter |
| *Akagi* Carrier Level-Bomber Unit | 1MF4 | Mitsubishi Type 10 Carrier Fighter |
| **1937** | | *Hosho* |
| *Hosho* Carrier Fighter Unit | A4N1 | Nakajima Type 95 Carrier Fighter |
| *Hosho* Carrier Level-Bomber Unit | B3Y1 | Yokosuka Type 92 Carrier Attack Bomber |
| **1940** | | *Kaga* |
| *Kaga* Carrier Fighter Unit | A5M4 | Mitsubishi Type 96 Carrier Fighter |
| *Kaga* Carrier Dive-Bomber Unit | D3A1 | Aichi Type 99 Carrier Bomber |
| *Kaga* Carrier Level-Bomber Unit | B5N2 | Nakajima Type 97 Carrier Attack Bomber |

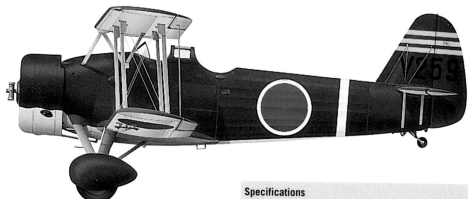

▲ **Aichi D1A2**

**Kaga, *1939***

An example of the D1A2, codenamed 'Susie' by the Allies. The D1A proved its worth during the Sino-Japanese War, in which both D1A1 and D1A2 versions were involved. Respectively designated as the Navy Type 94 and Type 96 Special Bombers, these aircraft comprised the standard dive-bomber equipment of the IJN's carrier arm in the mid-1930s.

**Specifications**

Crew: 2

Powerplant: 1 x 544kN (122,353lbf) Nakajima Hikari 1 radial piston engine

Maximum speed: 310km/h (193mph)

Range: 930km (578 miles)

Service ceiling: 7000m (22,965ft)

Dimensions: span 11.4m (37ft 4in); length 9.3m (30ft 6in); height 3.41m (11ft 2in)

Weight: 2610kg (5754lb) loaded

Armament: Two 7.7mm (.303in) fixed forward firing Type 97 machine guns and one 7.7mm (.303in) Type 92 machine gun in rear cockpit; one 250kg (551lb) and two 30kg (66lb) bombs

# United Kingdom
## 1922–36

**The hastily adapted Pups and Camels that first served aboard Royal Navy carriers were followed by more suitable equipment, as the Fleet Air Arm increased its strength between the wars.**

ALTHOUGH OPTIMIZED FOR operations from ships, the W.B.III and the Gloster Nightjar were both adaptations of land-based fighters, the latter being based on the French Nieuport Nighthawk. A purpose-designed deck-landing fighter was designed to a 1922 specification, this emerging as the Fairey Flycatcher, which equipped eight Fleet Air Arm Fighter Flights by 1930, and which served as the FAA's only carrier fighter between the years 1924 and 1932. An angular single-seater, the Flycatcher used a camber-changing mechanism on the wing to reduce its take-off run, also allowing it to recover on a carrier without the need for arrester wires.

Successor to the Flycatcher was the Hawker Nimrod, a development of the RAF's Kestrel-engined Fury fighter that entered service with three Fleet Air Arm Flights beginning in 1932; the following year these units were re-designated as composite naval fighter squadrons. Contemporary with the Nimrod was the Hawker Osprey, another navalized member of the superlative Hawker Fury family. Designed as a two-seat fleet spotter reconnaissance type, the Osprey was a navalized version of the RAF's Hart bomber, with folding wings and strengthened fuselage. The Osprey entered service in 1932 and proved to be notably versatile, fulfiling both the fleet spotter reconnaissance and carrier fighter roles, and remaining in front-line Fleet service until 1939.

### Birth of the torpedo-bomber

The Short Type 184 was a prolific two-seat torpedo-carrying floatplane that saw much service from seaplane carriers during World War I. Operating with wheeled landing gear from the seaplane carrier HMS *Campania* in 1916, the Type 184 was also used for trials from the foredeck of HMS *Furious* in 1917, before a handful embarked in the aircraft carrier HMS *Pegasus* in 1919. Another seaplane bomber to see use from early carriers was the Fairey Campania, which served aboard the light carriers HMS *Nairana* and *Pegasus* and saw action with the British North Russian Expeditionary Force in 1919. The Campania

▲ **Fairey Flycatcher**

*Fleet Air Arm, 1932*

Flycatchers saw service with Nos 401, 402, 403, 404, 405, 406, 407 and 408 Flights of the Fleet Air Arm aboard the aircraft carriers HMS *Argus, Courageous, Eagle, Furious, Glorious* and *Hermes*. The diminutive fighter did not require folding wings for carrier stowage, and on occasions was flown out of the below-decks hangar over the bows of an aircraft carrier. By 1924 the Flycatcher had replaced all previous FAA carrier and catapult fighters.

**Specifications**

Crew: 1

Powerplant: 1 x 358kN (80,519lbf) Bristol Mercury IIA 9-cylinder radial piston engine

Maximum speed: 247km/h (153mph)

Range: 500km (311 miles)

Service ceiling: 5791m (19,000ft)

Dimensions: span 10.67m (35ft 0in); length 7.55m (24ft 9in); height 3.28m (10ft 9in)

Weight: 1481kg (3266lb) loaded

Armament: Two 7.7mm (.303in) Vickers Mk II machine guns; four 9kg (20lb) bombs

# BRITISH INTERWAR CARRIER AIR GROUP DEVELOPMENT

## Royal Air Force Fleet Air Arm, 1927

### Coastal Area

| | | |
|---|---|---|
| No. 442 Fleet Reconnaissance Flight | Fairey IIID | Leuchars |
| No. 404 Fleet Fighter Flight | Flycatcher | Donibristle |
| No. 406 Fleet Fighter Flight | Flycatcher | Donibristle |
| No. 422 Fleet Spotter Flight | Blackburn | Gosport |

### Mediterranean Command

| | | |
|---|---|---|
| No. 481 Coastal Reconnaissance Flight | Fairey IIID | Malta |
| **HMS Furious** | | |
| No. 405 Fleet Fighter Flight | Flycatcher | |
| No. 420 Fleet Spotter Flight | Blackburn | |
| No. 421 Fleet Spotter Flight | Bison | |
| No. 443 Fleet Reconnaissance Flight | Fairey IIID | |
| No. 461 Fleet Torpedo Flight | Dart | |
| No. 462 Fleet Torpedo Flight | Dart | |
| **HMS Hermes** | | Mediterranean |
| No. 403 Fleet Fighter Flight | Flycatcher | |
| No. 440 Fleet Reconnaissance Flight | Fairey IIID | |
| **HMS Eagle** | | Mediterranean |
| No. 402 Fleet Fighter Flight | Flycatcher | |
| No. 423 Fleet Spotter Flight | Bison | |
| No. 441 Fleet Reconnaissance Flight | Fairey IIID | |
| No. 460 Fleet Torpedo Flight | Dart | |
| **HMS Vindictive** | | China Station |
| No. 401 Fleet Fighter Flight | Flycatcher | |
| No. 444 Fleet Reconnaissance Flight | Fairey IIID | |
| No. 460 Fleet Torpedo Flight | Dart | |

| | | |
|---|---|---|
| **HMS Argus** | | China Station |
| No. 404 Fleet Fighter Flight (Det) | Flycatcher | |
| No. 406 Fleet Fighter Flight | Flycatcher | |
| No. 442 Fleet Reconnaissance Flight | Fairey IIID | |
| No. 443 Fleet Reconnaissance Flight (Det) | Fairey IIID | |

## Royal Air Force Fleet Air Arm, 1934

### Coastal Area

| | | |
|---|---|---|
| 802 Fleet Fighter Squadron | Nimrod Osprey | 9 3 |
| 803 Fleet Fighter Squadron | Osprey | 9 |
| 812 Fleet Torpedo-Bomber Squadron | Baffin | 12 |
| 823 Fleet Spotter-Reconnaissance Squadron | Fairey IIIF | 12 |
| 824 Fleet Spotter-Reconnaissance Squadron | Fairey IIIF | 12 |
| No. 403 Fleet Fighter Flight | Osprey | 5 |
| No. 406 Fleet Fighter Flight | Osprey | 2 |
| No. 407 Fleet Fighter Flight | Osprey | 5 |
| No. 443 Fleet Spotter-Reconnaissance Flight | Fairey IIID | 5 |
| No. 444 Fleet Spotter-Reconnaissance Flight | Fairey IIID | 4 |
| No. 447 Fleet Spotter-Reconnaissance Flight | Fairey IIID | 6 |
| **HMS Courageous** | | |
| 800 Fleet Fighter Squadron | Nimrod Osprey | 9 3 |
| 810 Fleet Torpedo-Bomber Squadron | Dart Ripon | 6 6 |
| 820 Fleet Spotter-Reconnaissance Squadron | Fairey IIIF Seal | 6 3 |
| 821 Fleet Spotter-Reconnaissance Squadron | Seal | 9 |
| **HMS Furious** | | |
| 801 Fleet Fighter Squadron | Nimrod Osprey | 6 3 |
| 811 Fleet Torpedo-Bomber Squadron | Ripon | 12 |
| 822 Fleet Spotter-Reconnaissance Squadron | Fairey IIIF | 12 |

◀ **Blackburn Dart**

Deck crew manhandle a Dart on a Royal Navy carrier in 1932. The Dart torpedo-bomber entered service with two Fleet Torpedo Flights aboard HMS *Eagle* and *Furious* in 1924, and in 1926 an example of the type completed the first night landing on a carrier at sea, when it recovered on *Furious*.

had been designed to serve aboard HMS *Campania* and was appropriately equipped with a wheeled take-off trolley, the aircraft landing on floats and being recovered by crane after its sortie. A purpose-built Fleet torpedo-carrier appeared in the form of the Sopwith Cuckoo, which arrived just too late for wartime service, going aboard HMS *Argus* in October 1919, and embarking in *Furious* the following year. It

▲ **Hawker Nimrod Mk I**

*No. 800 NAS, HMS* **Courageous,** *1935*

The Fleet Air Arm eventually boasted seven squadrons of Hawker Nimrods, a navalized version of the RAF's Fury fighter. No. 800 NAS was typically embarked in HMS *Courageous* and served primarily in home waters. The Nimrod served with four front-line Flights, which later became front-line Squadrons.

**Specifications**

Crew: 1

Powerplant: 1 x 391kN (87,941lbf) Rolls-Royce Kestrel VFP inline piston engine

Maximum speed: 311km/h (194mph)

Range: 488km (305 miles)

Service ceiling: 8535m (28,000ft)

Dimensions: span 10.23m (33ft 7in); length 8.09m (26ft 6in); height 3.0m (9ft 10in)

Weight: 1841kg (4050lb) loaded

Armament: Two 7.7mm (.303in) Vickers machine guns; four 9kg (20lb) bombs

▲ **Blackburn Baffin**

*No. 810 NAS, 1935*

Blackburn's B-5 Baffin was the successor to the company's Ripon, and paved the way to the more advanced Shark. The key change was the introduction of an air-cooled engine on the Baffin, inspired by Finland's radial-engined Ripons. The initial operator was No. 812 NAS aboard HMS *Glorious* in January 1934, followed by Nos 810 and 811 NAS (in HMS *Courageous* and *Furious*, respectively).

**Specifications**

Crew: 2

Powerplant: 1 x 421kN (94,688lbf) Bristol Pegasus I.M3 9-cylinder radial piston engine

Maximum speed: 219km/h (136mph)

Range: 789km (490 miles)

Service ceiling: 4570m (15,000ft)

Dimensions: span 13.67m (44ft 10in); length 11.68m (38ft 4in); height 3.91m (12ft 10in)

Weight: 3459kg (7610lb) loaded

Armament: One 7.7mm (.303in) Vickers mahine gun and one 7.7mm (.303in) Lewis machine gun; one 816kg (1800lb) torpedo or up to 726kg (1600lb) bombs was replaced by the Blackburn Dart, a contemporary of the Flycatcher and Fairey IIID that appeared in 1920 and which entered service with two Fleet Torpedo Flights in 1924, going aboard the carriers HMS *Eagle* and *Furious* in 1924. Another Blackburn type replaced the Dart, with the Ripon torpedo-bomber entering service in 1929. Blackburn's Baffin was in turn developed as a replacement for the Ripon, the first of three squadrons equipping with the new type in 1934.

## Reconnaissance types

The versatile Fairey III saw carrier use, a number of IIIC bomber-reconnaissance seaplanes embarking in *Pegasus* in 1919 as part of the British North Russian Expeditionary Force. A development of the IIIC, the Fairey IIID went on to make the role of Fleet bomber/reconnaissance aircraft its own. In 1927, units serving in this role were renamed as Fleet Spotter Flights. Seven of the latter equipped with the Fairey IIIF, which remained in front-line FAA use until 1936. Fairey followed its III series with the Seal fleet spotter/reconnaissance bomber. Blackburn's entry in the fleet spotter/reconnaissance role was the Shark, a contemporary of the company's Baffin torpedo-bomber, and structurally very similar. The Shark was not a great success in the Fleet 'general purpose' role, and gave way to the Fairey Swordfish.

▲ **Blackburn Shark Mk II**

*No. 820 NAS, HMS Courageous, 1937*

After deck-landing trials on HMS *Courageous*, the B-6 Shark entered service with No. 820 NAS in early 1935, replacing that unit's Fairey Seals aboard the same carrier. The Shark's career as a front-line torpedo-bomber was cut short by the appearance of the superlative Fairey Swordfish.

**Specifications**

Crew: 3

Powerplant: 1 x 567kW (760hp) x Armstrong Siddeley Tiger VI 14 cylinder radial

Maximum speed: 242km/h (150mph)

Range: 1006km (625 miles)

Service ceiling: 4760m (15,600ft)

Dimensions: span 14.02m (46ft); length 10.75m (35ft 3in);

height 3.68m (12ft 1in)

Weight: 3687kg (8111lb) loaded

Armament: 1 x fixed forward firing 7.7mm (.303in) Vickers machine gun and 1 x flexible 7.7mm (.303in) Vickers K or Lewis machine gun; 1 x 820kg (1800lb) 460mm (18in) torpedo or 730kg (1600lb) bomb

▲ **Fairey Swordfish Mk I**

*No. 823 NAS, HMS Glorious, 1936*

K5972 was part of the initial production batch of 86 Swordfish aircraft, built by Fairey. The aircraft wears fin stripes to denote its particular Flight. Other Swordfish from the initial production batch went to Nos 822 and 825 NAS.

**Specifications**

Crew: 2–3

Powerplant: 1 x 578kN (130,000lbf) Bristol Pegasus IIIM.3 radial piston engine

Maximum speed: 224km/h (139mph)

Range: 1658km (1030 miles)

Service ceiling: 3780m (12,400ft)

Dimensions: span 13.87m (45ft 6in); length 11.07m (36ft 1in); height 3.92m (12ft)

Weight: 3964kg (8700lb) loaded

Armament: Two 7.7mm (.303in) machine guns; one 726kg (1600lb) torpedo load or up to 680kg (1500lb) bombs

# United States
## 1923–39

**Although trailing Japan and the UK in the introduction of the carrier, the US followed suit in 1920, and had introduced the first powerful fleet carriers before the end of the decade.**

PRODUCTS FROM THE prolific Boeing, Curtiss and Grumman companies dominated the various fighter squadrons that served on board US Navy carriers in the years between the wars.

Boeing's first naval fighter was the FB, or Model 15, a single-seat biplane flown in 1923. Although ordered in small numbers for US Navy service, where two examples served aboard the carrier USS *Langley*, others were diverted to the US Marine Corps for land-based service. More prolific was the Model 69, or F2B, 32 of which began to enter service with US Navy Squadrons VF-1B (fighter) and VB-2B (bomber) aboard the USS *Saratoga* in January 1928.

A further development, Boeing's F3B (Model 77) underwent a rigorous redesign and won orders for 74 aircraft from the Navy, these first entering service with VF-2B aboard *Langley* in August 1928. The F4B was intended to replace both the F2B and F3B, retaining the same Pratt & Whitney Wasp engine, but with design changes to enhance performance. As a carrier-based fighter, the first F4Bs were inducted to service in 1929 and four sub-variants were eventually produced for carrier operations.

## Curtiss Hawks for the Navy

From the Curtiss stable, the F4C was, despite its designation, the company's first fighter for the Navy, the two aircraft essentially being aluminium-structure versions of the previous Model TS wooden fighter. Part of the successful Hawk family of biplane fighters, the Curtiss Model 34 was adopted for Navy service as the F6C. In both Navy and Marine hands, the F6C served from carrier decks, going to sea aboard USS *Langley* and *Lexington* from 1928 with VF-9M (Marine), VF-2, VF-5S (later VB-1B) and VF-2B. Experience with the F6C demonstrated the Navy's preference for radial-engined fighters for carrier operations, and the Wasp-engined F6C-4 was therefore followed by the F7C, with an air-cooled engine from the outset. Seventeen production F7C Seahawks were delivered from 1927, although these served with land-based Marine units.

A further refinement of the F7C, the F11C marked a return to deck operations, and was ordered in 1932 as a fighter-bomber, initially to equip VF-1B aboard the *Saratoga* from the following year. Redesignated BFC-2 to properly reflect its role, the

▲ **Martin T3M-2**

*VT-2B, USS* Saratoga, *late 1920s*

The T3M was developed by Martin as an improvement of the T2M (SC-2), with a fuselage construction based on steel tube and with the pilot and torpedoman located farther forward. A total of 100 Packard-engined T3M-2s were ordered.

**Specifications**

Crew: 3

Powerplant: 1 x 574kW (770hp) Packard 3A-
 2500 liquid cooled V-12 engine

Maximum speed: 175km/h (109mph)

Range: 1020km (634 miles)

Service ceiling: 2400m (7900ft)

Dimensions: span 17.25m (56ft 7in); length
 12.60m (41ft 4in); height 4.60m (15ft 1in)

Weight: 4320kg (9503lb) loaded

Armament: 1 x flexibly mounted 7.62mm (.3in)
 machine gun in rear cockpit; 1 x torpedo or
 bombs under fuselage

## ▲ Boeing F4B-4

### VF-6B, USS Saratoga, 1930

One of 92 examples of this variant delivered to the US Navy from July 1932, this F4B-4 wears the markings of Fighter Squadron SIX B (VF-6B), among the first units to receive the fighter. Developed from the F4B-3 (itself essentially a navalized version of the US Army's P-12E), to which it added an increased-area fin, the F4B-4 remained in front-line service aboard US Navy carriers until 1937.

### Specifications

Crew: 1

Powerplant: 1 x 373kN (82,892lbf) Pratt & Whitney R-1340-D Wasp air-cooled nine-cylinder radial piston engine

Maximum speed: 303km/h (188mph)

Range: 595km (370 miles)

Service ceiling: 8200m (26,903ft)

Dimensions: span 9.14m (30ft 0in); length 6.12m (20ft 8in); height 2.84m (9.32ft)

Weight: 1638kg (3611lb) loaded

Armament: Two 7.7mm (.303in) machine guns, 111kg (244lb) external bomb load

## ▲ Martin T4M-1

### VT-2B, USS Saratoga, 1930

This T4M-1 served with Torpedo and Bombing Squadron TWO B (VT-2B), and wears green fin trim to signify allocation to USS Saratoga. A total of 102 T4Ms were delivered during 1927–28 before Great Lakes assumed production as the TG-1/2.

### Specifications

Crew: 3

Powerplant: 1 x 292kW (525hp) Pratt & Whitney R-1690 Hornet 9 cylinder air-cooled radial engine

Maximum speed: 184km/h (114mph)

Range: 584km (364 miles)

Service ceiling: 3095m (10,150ft)

Dimensions: span 16.60m (53ft); length 10.85m (35ft 7in); height 4.50m (14ft 9in)

Weight: 4320kg (9503lb) loaded

Armament: 1 x flexibly mounted 7.62mm (.3in) machine gun in rear cockpit; 1 x torpedo or bombs under fuselage

aircraft flew with VF-1B (later renumbered as VB-2B and then as VB-3B) until 1938. The BFC-2 was joined by the BF2C, originally designated F11C-3, this featuring retractable undercarriage and entering service with VB-5B aboard USS *Ranger* in 1934.

Grumman's long tradition of building fighters for the Navy began with the FF, the response to a 1931 contract resulting in a two-seat, all-metal biplane fighter with retractable landing gear. Faster than the single-seat Boeing F4B-4, the FF was delivered in 1933, 27 examples serving with VF-5B aboard USS

*Lexington*. Grumman then embarked on a project to refine the already impressive performance of its naval fighter, with the F2F first flown in 1933. A single-seater, the compact F2F was ordered into production in 1934, replacing the F4B-2s assigned to VF-2B aboard *Lexington* from 1935. The F2F suffered from some directional instability and poor handling, rectified on the F3F that entered service in 1936, initially with VF-5B aboard *Ranger*. As the apogee of the series, the biplane F3F remained in front-line service with the Marine Corps until October 1941.

### ▲ Curtiss BF2C-1

*VB-5B, USS* Ranger, *1934–35*

Operated by Bombing Squadron Five B (VB-5B), this is an example of the BF2C-1, or Curtiss Model 67A, which had originated as a fighter prototype, the XF11C-3. The new aircraft introduced retractable landing gear, although this was plagued by problems in service, and the 27 aircraft that were delivered from October 1934 had been disposed of within a year. Further difficulties related to the wing structure, which was found to suffer from vibration.

### Specifications

| | |
|---|---|
| Crew: 1 | Dimensions: span 9.6m (31ft 6in); length |
| Powerplant: 1 x 448kN (100,761lbf) Wright SR- | 6.88m (22ft 7in); height 2.96m (9ft 8in) |
| 1820F2 Cyclone radial piston engine | Weight: 1874kg (4132lb) loaded |
| Maximum speed: 325km/h (202mph) | Armament: Two 7.62 x 51mm (.30in) forward |
| Range: 840km (522 miles) | firing machine guns; four 227kg (500lb), or |
| Service ceiling: 7650m (25,100ft) | four 51kg (112lb) bombs |

### ▲ Grumman SF-1

*VS-3B, USS* Lexington, *mid-1930s*

Known to the Grumman 'Ironworks' factory as the G-6, the SF-1 was ordered in prototype form in June 1931, as a scout version of the FF-1 fighter, with additional fuel capacity and reduced armament. First flown in 1932, 33 examples were ordered in August that year, with deliveries between February and July 1934. The first unit was VS-3B, which received its initial SF-1s in March 1934.

### Specifications

| | |
|---|---|
| Crew: 2 | Dimensions: span 10.52m (34ft 6in); length |
| Powerplant: 1 x 522kN (117,404lbf) Wright R- | 7.47m (24ft 6in); height 3.38m (11ft 1in) |
| 1820- 78 9-cylinder radial piston engine | Weight: 2190kg (4828lb) loaded |
| Maximum speed: 333km/h (207mph) | Armament: One 7.62 x 51mm (.30in) Browning |
| Range: 1428km (921 miles) | machine gun on a gimballed mounting |
| Service ceiling: 6400m (21,000ft) | attached to observer's seat |

It was the Brewster company, meanwhile, which provided the Navy with its first monoplane fighter, the F2A Buffalo, built to a 1936 requirement and entering service from mid-1939 aboard *Saratoga*.

Developed as a Scout version of the company's FF, the Grumman SF was ordered in 1931, with 33 examples being delivered to the Navy in 1934. The initial operating unit was VS-3B, which began to re-equip with the type in 1934, taking its aircraft aboard the *Lexington*.

In the Scout-Bomber category, the Brewster SBA was a two-seat monoplane intended for service aboard the new carriers USS *Enterprise* and *Yorktown*, which were expected to enter service in 1936. Built in series by the Naval Aircraft Factory as the SBN-1, the aircraft was primarily used for training, including with VT-8 aboard USS *Hornet*. Brewster's improved version of its SBA was the SB2A, procured in small numbers by the Navy. The Curtiss Helldiver was first flown in 1933, as the XF12C-1, a parasol-wing, two-seat fighter, before adopting the SBC designation when its role was changed to scout-bomber, together with the adoption of a biplane configuration better suited to dive bombing. The initial-production

SBC-3 was issued to VS-5 from July 1937, and was followed by the SBC-4, delivered from March 1939. The outbreak of World War II saw a number of SBC-4s diverted to France. When the US entered that conflict, the SBC-4 remained in use with VB-8 and VS-8 aboard USS *Hornet*.

Vought's final biplane to be designed and built for the Navy, the SBU Corsair, originated as a two-seat fighter biplane prototype before being completed as a scout-bomber, with provision for below-fuselage bomb carriage. Vought followed up its SBU with the SB2U Vindicator, prototypes of which were ordered in 1934–35. The monoplane SB2U was powered by a Twin Wasp engine, remaining in service into 1942.

The most successful US Navy dive-bomber was undoubtedly the Douglas SBD Dauntless, a continuation of the concept established by the

### ▲ Grumman F2F-1

**VF-2B, USS Lexington, *1935***

'Fighting Two' introduced the F2F-1 to service and was also the final front-line operator of the type. VF-2B accepted its first F2F-1 in February 1935 and did not give up the fighter until September 1940, after which the aircraft were relegated to a training role. The F2F-1 replaced the Boeing F4B-2 in service with 'Fighting Two'. The example illustrated was the second production machine.

## Specifications

Crew: 1

Powerplant: 1 x 522kN (117,404lbf) Pratt & Whitney R-1535-72 Twin Wasp radial piston engine

Maximum speed: 383km/h (238mph)

Range: 1585km (985 miles)

Service ceiling: 8380m (27,500ft)

Dimensions: span 8.69m (28ft 6in); length 6.53m (21ft 5in); height 2.77m (9ft 1in)

Weight: 1745kg (3847lb) loaded

Armament: Two 7.62 x 51mm (.30in) forward firing Browning machine guns; underwing racks for two 53kg (116lb) bombs

## ▲ Grumman F3F-1

**VF-7, *1935***

The final US Navy operator of the F3F-1 was VF-7, later redesignated as VF-72, which retired its last examples in February 1941. A total of 54 production F3F-1 fighters were completed, and these began to be delivered in January 1936, entering service with VF-5B aboard USS *Ranger* in April that year, followed by VF-6B in USS *Saratoga* that June. In comparison with the F2F, in the F3F Grumman improved upon its predecessor's directional stability, spinning characteristics and overall manoeuvrability.

## Specifications

Crew: 1

Powerplant: 1 x 522kN (117,404lbf) Pratt & Whitney R-1535-84 Twin Wasp Junior 14-cylinder radial piston engine

Maximum speed: 372km/h (231mph)

Range: 1609km (1000 miles)

Service ceiling: 8685m (28,500ft)

Dimensions: span 9.75m (32ft 0in); length 7.09m (23ft 3in); height 2.77m (9ft 1in)

Weight: 1997kg (4403lb) loaded

Armament: One 12.7 x 99mm (.50in) forward firing machine gun; one 7.62 x 51mm (.30in) forward firing machine gun; plus external bomb load of 105kg (232lb)

## US INTERWAR CARRIER AIR GROUP DEVELOPMENT

USS *Lexington* (CV-2) air groups     'Lexington' class

**1928**

| VB-2 | SB2U-1 Vindicator | 18 |
|---|---|---|
| VF-2 | F3F-3 | 18 |
| VS-2 | SBU-1 Corsair | 18 |
| VT-2 | TBD-1 Devastator | 18 |

**1934**

| VB-2 | F4B-4 | 18 |
|---|---|---|
| VF-2 | F4B-4 | 18 |
| VS-2 | SBU-1 Corsair | 18 |
| VT-2 | TBD-1 Devastator | 18 |

**1938**

| VB-2 | SB2U-1 Vindicator | 18 |
|---|---|---|
| VF-2 | F2A-1 Buffalo | 18 |
| VS-2 | SBC-4 Helldiver | 18 |
| VT-2 | TBD-1 Devastator | 18 |

**1939**

| VB-3 | F4B-4 | 18 |
|---|---|---|
| VF-3 | F2A-2 Buffalo | 18 |
| VS-3 | SBC-3 Helldiver | 18 |
| VT-3 | TBD-1 Devastator | 18 |

### Specifications

Crew: 2

Powerplant: 1 x 522kN (117,404lbf) Pratt & Whitney R-1535-82 Twin Wasp radial engine

Maximum speed: 377km/h (234mph)

Range: 625km (405 miles)

Service ceiling: 7315m (24,000ft)

Dimensions: span 10.36m (34ft 0in); length 8.57m (28ft 1in); height 3.17m (10ft 5in)

Weight: 3211kg (7080lb) loaded

Armament: One 7.62 x 51 mm (.30in) fixed forward firing machine gun; one 7.62 x 51mm (.30in) machine gun on a flexible mount, under-fuselage rack for one 227kg (500lb) bomb

### ▼ Curtiss SBC-3 Helldiver

*VS-5, USS* Yorktown, *1937*

A scout-bomber developed from a prototype two-seat fighter (the monoplane XF12C-1), the Curtiss Model 77 was accepted for service as the biplane SBC, the production models being the SBC-3 and SBC-4. VS-5 was the initial operator of the Helldiver, receiving the first of 83 examples ordered in July 1937.

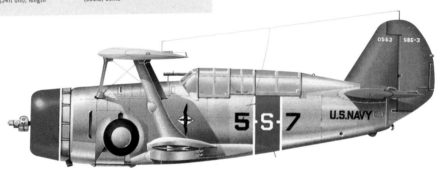

Northrop BT-1, a tandem two-seat low-wing monoplane that had begun to enter service in 1938. The Dauntless was ordered in April 1939, in both SBD-1 and SBD-2 versions, the SBD-2s entering service in late 1941 with VB-6 and VS-6 on USS *Enterprise* and VB-2 on *Lexington*.

### Douglas dynasty

Interwar torpedo-bombers for the US Navy included the Douglas DT, derived from the Cloudster that had been designed for a US coast-to-coast flight. The DT was a two-seat biplane with provision for a single torpedo and was ordered in 1921. While most were completed as floatplanes, one example conducted catapult launch trials on *Langley* in 1925. The Douglas T2D ordered in 1925 was unusual in that it was a twin-engine biplane. First operated on a trials basis by VT-2 in 1927, the T2D was the first twin-engined type to go aboard carriers, although its size meant it was better suited to land-based patrol work, to which it was soon reassigned.

Alongside Douglas, Martin was the major source of interwar torpedo-bombers for the US Navy. Martin's involvement in the field began with the Curtiss CS-1 and CS-2, three-seat biplanes with float or wheel landing gear that differed in their type of Wright engine. Martin was selected as subcontractor to build additional examples, under the new

## Specifications

Crew: 2 (pilot and gunner)

Powerplant: 1 x 615 kW (825hp) Pratt & Whitney R-1535-94 Twin Wasp Jr. double row radial air-cooled engine

Maximum speed: 357km/h (222mph)

Range: 852km (529 miles)

Service ceiling: 7710m (25,300ft)

Dimensions: span 12.65m (41ft 6in); length 9.65m (31ft 8in); height 3.02m (9ft 11in)

Weight: 2094kg (4606lb) empty

Armament: 1 x 12.7mm (.50in) machine gun, 1 x 7.62 mm (.30in) machine gun; 1 x 454kg (1000lb) bomb under fuselage

### ▼ Northrop BT-1

#### VB-5, 1938

Best known as the precursor to the legendary SBD Dauntless, the Northrop BT originated as the XFT-1 all-metal fighter prototype for the US Navy. The design later found favour as the BT-1, a torpedo-bomber with semi-retractable undercarriage that was a naval parallel to the Northrop 3-A intended for the US Army. The first production BT-1s were delivered to VB-5 in April 1938.

### ▼ Douglas TBD-1 Devastator

#### VT-6, USS Enterprise, 1938

This TBD-1 was aircraft number 1, assigned to the commander of VT-6, and is seen in pre-war markings, camouflage later being adopted for combat duties. Having equipped with the TBD in 1938, VT-6 was still flying the Devastator at the Battle of Midway in June 1942, still aboard USS *Enterprise*. This particular aircraft was lost in an accident at sea in March 1939.

## Specifications

Crew: 3

Powerplant: 1 x 671kW (900hp) Pratt & Whitney Twin Wasp radial piston engine

Maximum speed: 331km/h (206mph)

Range: 1152km (716 miles)

Service ceiling: 6000m (19,700ft)

Dimensions: span 15.24m (50ft 0in); length 10.67m (35ft 0in); height 4.60m (15ft 1in)

Weight: 4623kg (10,194lb) loaded

Armament: Two or three 7.62 x 51mm (.30in) machine guns; one 453kg (1000lb) bomb or one 544kg (1200lb) torpedo

designations SC-1 and SC-2, respectively. In US Navy service, the SC-2 was known as the T2M. An improved version was the T3M, with a structure primarily of steel tube, and which was delivered from 1926. The final model was the T4M with a Pratt & Whitney Hornet radial engine that was in production from 1927–28 before manufacture was assumed by Great Lakes, which built the aircraft as the TG-1 and TG-2. Equipped with wheeled undercarriage, the T3M-2 and T4M-1 served aboard the *Lexington* and *Saratoga*. The US Navy's interwar torpedo-bomber series also included the Martin BM (otherwise designated T5M), a two-seat biplane torpedo-bomber delivered from 1931 for service with VT-1S embarked in the *Lexington*. BM-1s and BM-2s later also flew from the *Langley*.

In 1935 the new Torpedo-Bomber designation was introduced, beginning with the three-seat Douglas TBD Devastator monoplane that survived to see action in the first months of the US Navy's war in the Pacific. An initial contract for the Devastator was issued in 1936, and the type began to enter service with VT-3 in October 1937, followed in 1938 by VT-2, VT-5 and VT-6.

# Chapter 2

# World War II (1939–45)

**World War II saw the emergence of the aircraft carrier as a decisive arbiter in naval battles, as it overtook the battleship to become the pre-eminent weapon in the war at sea. Once again, only Japan, the United Kingdom and the United States managed to field operational carriers during the conflict, while Germany's efforts to commission an aircraft carrier were ultimately fruitless. While the Pacific theatre saw the most extensive use of carrier airpower, carrier-based aircraft were pivotal in numerous and varied campaigns, protecting convoys, waging war on submarines and providing cover for amphibious assaults.**

◀ **USS *Belleau Wood***

As carrier-borne airpower reached its zenith during World War II, several Pacific battles were waged – and decided – using carrier aircraft alone. Here, the US Navy's light carrier *Belleau Wood* (CVL-24) burns after being hit by a kamikaze in the Philippines on 30 October 1944. Arranged on deck are Avengers and Hellcats. In the background is the burning USS *Franklin*, an 'Essex'-class carrier, also hit by the Japanese. Both carriers were returned to active service.

# Germany
## 1936–42

**Although Nazi Germany's efforts to field an aircraft carrier came to naught, its aircraft industries developed the equipment required to provide an air wing for the stillborn *Graf Zeppelin*.**

DEVELOPMENT OF A carrier-based fighter with which to arm what was then codenamed 'Carrier A' began in Germany in 1936. The first effort was the Arado Ar 197, a conventional biplane that was schemed at a time when other carrier nations were turning to monoplanes. Germany's last biplane fighter, the single-seat, all-metal Ar 197 was first flown in 1937 and was tested with both inline and radial powerplants. Three prototypes were built, but the Luftwaffe considered the programme to be premature, and development was not a priority. By the end of 1937 it was clear that by the time the carrier itself was ready – expected to take at least another two years – the biplane concept would be obsolete, and the Ar 197 was abandoned.

In 1937, Arado and Fieseler entered proposals for a two-seat multi-purpose shipboard aircraft, with prototypes of the Ar 195 and Fi 167 ordered. When the Arado prototype, completed in 1938, proved unable to meet the requirements, the focus turned to the Fi 167, and a pre-production batch of 12 of the biplanes was ordered. In December 1938 'Carrier A' was launched as the *Graf Zeppelin*, but with commissioning not expected until summer 1940, the Fi 167 project moved slowly. In 1938 a decision was made to include the Junkers Ju 87C in the air wing.

This was a shipboard version of the famous dive-bomber, and relegated the Fi 167 to torpedo and reconnaissance work. A batch of pre-production Ju 87C-0s was completed in summer 1939, these navalized Ju 87Bs being delivered to Trägergruppe 186 at Kiel. By September 1939, the unit included Ju 87Bs and Cs, and these were employed in the campaign in Poland. With work on the carrier suspended in October 1939, the production-standard Ju 87C-1 was abandoned.

Flight testing of the pre-production Fi 167A began in early 1940, and although carrier construction was halted in May of that year, the 12 Fi 167s were completed anyway, and after operational suitability trials they served in a variety of test roles.

The revised fighter component comprised the Messerschmitt Bf 109T, a specialized shipboard

### Specifications

| | |
|---|---|
| Crew: 2 | 11.4m (37ft 4in); height 4.7m (15ft 9in) |
| Powerplant: 1 x 809kW (1200hp) Daimler-Benz | Weight: 4850kg (9920lb) loaded |
| DB 601B liquid cooled inverted V12 | Armament: Two 7.92 (.318in) MG 17 machine |
| Maximum speed: 325km/h (203mph) | guns. One MG15 machine gun in rear cabin, |
| Range: 1500km (808 miles) | or one 1000kg (2200lb), one 765kg (1685lb) |
| Service ceiling: 8200m (24,606ft) | torpedo |
| Dimensions: span 15.5m (44ft 4in); length | |

▲ **Fieseler Fi 167A-0**

*Erprobungsstaffel 167, 1940–42*

This Fi 167 was one of nine that was operated in Dutch coastal areas on 'advanced service trials'. The Fi 167s remained in the Netherlands until early 1943, latterly undertaking a range of experimental programmes.

▲ **Messerschmitt Bf 109T**

Fitted with long-span wings, the Bf 109T-2 was built under contract by Fieseler. The Bf 109T-2s had begun life as Bf 109T-1 carrier fighters, but were ultimately completed for land-based duty, and with carrier equipment deleted they served with I./JG 77 in Norway. The long-span wings of the Bf 109T endowed it with improved short-field performance, and during its land-based career, the variants mainly operated from smaller, exposed airfields.

development of the Bf 109E, design of which was finalized in early 1939. The Bf 109T featured increased wing area, plus catapult and arrester gear. A pre-production batch of Bf 109T-0s was tested in 1939–40 but work on the 60 Bf 109T-1s was halted in May 1940. The fighters were eventually completed as Bf 109T-2s, with adaptations for land-based use and they thus saw out their service with the Luftwaffe.

## Carrier reconsidered

Priorities had changed by spring 1942 such that the Grand Admiral of the German Navy was demanding completion of the *Graf Zeppelin* for use in the escort of commerce raiders. In May 1942 an order was issued to resume work on the ship, which would carry a revised air group of 28 bombers and 12 fighters. The Fi 167 and Ju 87C-0 were planned to make way for the Ju 87E, a torpedo-bomber version of the Ju 87D. With the Bf 109T now obsolescent, Messerschmitt was instructed to develop a new carrier fighter, the Me 155, using many Bf 109 components. Design was complete by September 1942, the fighter allying the Bf 109G fuselage and tail with a new wing and a DB 605 inline engine. By now, it was clear that it would be another two years before *Graf Zeppelin* became operational. The Me 155 was shelved (although it would re-emerge as a high-altitude fighter). Construction of the carrier, towed to Kiel for work in December 1942, was terminated for good the following February.

| *GRAF ZEPPELIN* AIR GROUP (PLANNED) | |
|---|---|
| **Initial planned air group, circa 1940** | |
| Bf 109T | 8–10 |
| Fi 167A | 16–20 |
| Ju 87C | 13–16 |
| | |
| **Planned air group, revised** | |
| Bf 109T | 16 |
| Ju 87C | 24 |
| or | |
| Bf 109T | 30 |
| Ju 87C | 12 |
| | |
| **Trägergruppe 186** | Kiel-Holtenau |
| 1938–39 | |
| 4. Trägersturzkampfstaffel/186 | Ju 87A/B/C |
| 5. Trägerjagdstaffel/186 | Bf 109B |
| 6. Trägerjagdstaffel/186 | Bf 109B |

# Japan
## 1940–45

**With an emphasis on large-scale operations, the carrier air groups of the IJN were devastatingly effective early in the Pacific War, although the tables would be turned after Midway in 1942.**

IN COMMON WITH the US Navy, the Imperial Japanese Navy was aware of the value of larger air groups when operating in the Pacific. For the attack on Pearl Harbor on 7 December 1941, the IJN assembled the First Air Fleet, with six carriers led by the flagship *Akagi* and embarking an expanded air group of some 430 aircraft. For offensive operations such as Peal Harbor, the IJN emphasized attack aircraft, in this case Nakajima B5N level bombers also capable of carrying torpedoes, Aichi D3A dive-bombers, and support by Mitsubishi A6M fighters.

At the time of its appearance, the A6M was capable of out-performing any contemporary land-based fighter in theatre. At the beginning of the Pacific War, however, the IJN continued to operate the Mitsubishi A5M from its carriers, although it suffered when faced by more modern opposition and had been withdrawn front front-line use by summer 1942. The A6M that was schemed as a replacement for the A5M went on to become the most famous Japanese single-seat fighter in history. A low-wing monoplane with radial engine, the initial production A6M2 model was ordered into production in July 1940 as the Navy Type 0 Carrier Fighter. The Zero was fielded with both clipped wings and folding wingtips, while the A6M3 version had a new Sakae 21 engine. The major production version was the A6M5 of 1943, produced in a range of sub-variants for carrier-borne and land-based use and rushed into service as a counter to the new US fighters then appearing in the Pacific. The final versions included the re-engined A6M6 of late 1944 and the A6M7 fighter/dive-bomber from mid-1945.

### Zero in action

The Zero excelled in combat when introduced on a trial basis during the Sino-Japanese War, and in 1941 and early 1942 was dominant over the Pacific, gaining supremacy over the East Indies and Southeast Asia. The A6M2 escorted the IJN carrier strike

### Specifications

| | |
|---|---|
| Displacement: standard: 17,300 tons. Fully loaded: 20,165 tons | Range: 14,204km (7670nm) |
| Length: 222.0m (728ft 5in, waterline) | Aircraft: 18 Zeros, 18 Vals, 18 Kates |
| Beam: 22.3m (73ft 2in) | Armament: 12 x 127mm (5in) guns, 31 x 25mm (1in) anti-aircraft guns |
| Draught: 7.74m (25ft 5in) | Complement: 1103 + 23 officers for Carrier Division 2 headquarters |
| Speed: 63.9km/h (34.5 knots) | |

▼ *Akagi*

*Akagi* as she appeared in December 1941, with A6M fighters ranged on the deck aft. Completed in March 1927, *Akagi* was the 'half-sister' to *Kaga*, and similarly served with the First Carrier Division. For the Pearl Harbor raid, the carrier served as Vice Admiral Nagumo's flagship, and led the attacks. *Akagi* then led a series of stunning raids through the East Indies and Indian Ocean, before being finally crippled by aircraft from USS *Enterprise* at Midway.

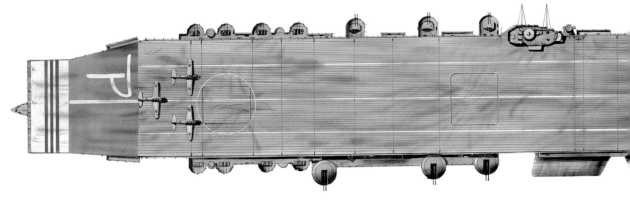

## Specifications

Crew: 2

Powerplant: 1 x 969kW (1070hp) Mitsubishi
    Kinsei 54 radial piston engine

Maximum speed: 430km/h (267mph)

Range: 1352km (840 miles)

Service ceiling: 10500m (34,450ft)

Dimensions: span 14.37m (47ft 2in); length
    10.2m (33ft 5in); height 3.8m (12ft 8in)

Weight: 4122kg (9100lb) loaded

Armament: Two 7.7mm (.303in) Type 97
    machine guns and one 7.7mm (.303in) Type
    92 machine gun; 2 x 60kg (132lb)
    bomb load

### ▼ Aichi D3A1 Model 11

*Yokosuka Kokutai, 1940*

The standard dive-bomber among IJN carrier air groups during the early years of
the Pacific War, the D3A – identified by the Allies using the codename 'Val' –
scored notable successes during the raid on Pearl Harbor and in the sinking of
the British carrier HMS *Hermes*. Typical armament was one 250-kg (551-lb) bomb
on the centreline and a pair of 60-kg
(132-lb) bombs underwing.

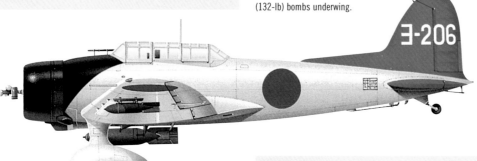

### ▼ Aichi D3A2 Model 22

*Meikoya Kokutai, 1942*

Introduced in 1942, the D3A2 version introduced increased fuel capacity and a
more powerful Mitsubishi Kinsei 54 radial engine. The D3A2 became the major
production version, with 1016 completed compared to 476 D3A1s. This is a late-
model D3A2, designated as the Model 22 by the IJN, and was licence-built by
Showa Hikoki Kogyo. By 1945 the type was thoroughly outclassed by Allied
fighters, and it was relegated to smaller carriers and land bases.

## Specifications

Crew: 2

Powerplant: 1 x 969kW (1300hp) Mitsubishi
    Kinsei 54 radial piston engine

Maximum speed: 430km/h (267mph)

Range: 1352km (840 miles)

Service ceiling: 10,500m (34,450ft)

Dimensions: span 14.37m (47ft 2in); length
    10.2m (33ft 5.4in); height 3.8m (12ft 7.5in)

Weight: 4122kg (9100lb) loaded

Armament: Two fixed 7.62 x 58mm (.303in)
    Type 97 machine guns, 1 flexible rearward-
    firing 7.62 x .58mm Type 92 machine gun,
    one 250kg (551lb) or two 60kg (132lb) bombs

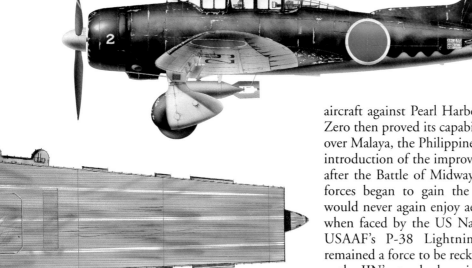

aircraft against Pearl Harbor and this version of the
Zero then proved its capabilities in the air campaigns
over Malaya, the Philippines and Burma. Despite the
introduction of the improved A6M3 in spring 1942,
after the Battle of Midway in June 1942 the Allied
forces began to gain the initiative, and the Zero
would never again enjoy aerial supremacy, especially
when faced by the US Navy's F6F Hellcat and the
USAAF's P-38 Lightning. However, the Zero
remained a force to be reckoned with, and continued
as the IJN's standard carrier fighter until the end of
the war, by which time over 10,000 examples had
been completed. Even when 'demoted' to kamikaze

## IMPERIAL JAPANESE NAVY CARRIER AIR GROUPS – PEARL HARBOR 1940

### First Carrier Division

*Akagi*

Cdr Fuchida Mitsuo

| | | |
|---|---|---|
| 1st Squadron | B5N2 | 5 |
| 2nd Squadron | B5N2 | 5 |
| 3rd Squadron | B5N2 | 5 |

Lt Cdr Murata Shigeharu

| | | |
|---|---|---|
| 1st Squadron | B5N2 | 3 |
| 2nd Squadron | B5N2 | 3 |
| 3rd Squadron | B5N2 | 3 |
| 4th Squadron | B5N2 | 3 |

Lt Chihaya

| | | |
|---|---|---|
| 21st Squadron | D3A1 | 3 |
| 22nd Squadron | D3A1 | 3 |
| 23rd Squadron | D3A1 | 3 |
| | | |
| 25th Squadron | D3A1 | 3 |
| 26th Squadron | D3A1 | 3 |
| 27th Squadron | D3A1 | 3 |

Lt Cdr Itaya Shigeru

| | | |
|---|---|---|
| 1st FCU Wave 1 | A6M2 | 9 |
| 1st FCU Wave 2 | A6M2 | 9 |
| CAP | A6M2 | 9 |

### Third Carrier Division

*Kaga*

Lt Cdr Hashiguchi

| | | |
|---|---|---|
| 1st Squadron | B5N2 | 5 |
| 2nd Squadron | B5N2 | 5 |
| 3rd Squadron | B5N2 | 5 |

Lt Kitajima

| | | |
|---|---|---|
| 1st Squadron | B5N2 | 3 |
| 2nd Squadron | B5N2 | 3 |
| 3rd Squadron | B5N2 | 3 |
| 4th Squadron | B5N2 | 3 |

Lt Makino

| | | |
|---|---|---|
| 21st Squadron | D3A1 | 3 |
| 22nd Squadron | D3A1 | 3 |
| 23rd Squadron | D3A1 | 3 |
| 24th Squadron | D3A1 | 3 |
| 25th Squadron | D3A1 | 3 |
| 26th Squadron | D3A1 | 3 |
| 27th Squadron | D3A1 | 3 |
| 28th Squadron | D3A1 | 3 |
| 29th Squadron | D3A1 | 3 |

Lt Shiga

| | | |
|---|---|---|
| 2nd FCU Wave 1 | A6M2 | 9 |
| 2nd FCU Wave 2 | A6M2 | 9 |
| CAP | A6M2 | 9 |

### Second Carrier Division

*Soryu*

Lt Abe

| | | |
|---|---|---|
| 1st Squadron | B5N2 | 5 |
| 2nd Squadron | B5N2 | 5 |

Lt Nagai

| | | |
|---|---|---|
| 1st Squadron | B5N2 | 2 |
| 2nd Squadron | B5N2 | 2 |
| 3rd Squadron | B5N2 | 2 |
| 4th Squadron | B5N2 | 2 |

Lt Cdr Egusa Takeshige

| | | |
|---|---|---|
| 21st Squadron | D3A1 | 3 |
| 22nd Squadron | D3A1 | 3 |
| 23rd Squadron | D3A1 | 3 |
| 24th Squadron | D3A1 | 3 |
| 25th Squadron | D3A1 | 3 |
| 26th Squadron | D3A1 | 3 |

Lt Suganami

| | | |
|---|---|---|
| 3rd FCU Wave 1 | A6M2 | 9 |
| 3rd FCU Wave 2 | A6M2 | 9 |
| CAP | A6M2 | 9 |

### Fourth Carrier Division

*Hiryu*

Lt Cdr Kosumi

| | | |
|---|---|---|
| 1st Squadron | B5N2 | 5 |
| 2nd Squadron | B5N2 | 5 |

Lt Matsumura

| | | |
|---|---|---|
| 1st Squadron | B5N2 | 2 |
| 2nd Squadron | B5N2 | 2 |
| 3rd Squadron | B5N2 | 2 |
| 4th Squadron | B5N2 | 2 |

Lt Kobayashi

| | | |
|---|---|---|
| 21st Squadron | D3A1 | 3 |
| 22nd Squadron | D3A1 | 3 |
| 23rd Squadron | D3A1 | 3 |
| 24th Squadron | D3A1 | 3 |
| 25th Squadron | D3A1 | 3 |
| 26th Squadron | D3A1 | 3 |

Lt Okajima

| | | |
|---|---|---|
| 4th FCU Wave 1 | A6M2 | 6 |
| 4th FCU Wave 2 | A6M2 | 9 |
| CAP | A6M2 | 9 |

## IMPERIAL JAPANESE NAVY CARRIER AIR GROUPS – PEARL HARBOR 1940

| Fifth Carrier Division | | | Sixth Carrier Division | | |
|---|---|---|---|---|---|
| *Shokaku* | | | *Zuikaku* | | |
| Lt Cdr Shimazaki Shigekazu | | | Lt Ichihara | | |
| 1st Squadron | B5N2 | 9 | 1st Squadron | B5N2 | 9 |
| 2nd Squadron | B5N2 | 9 | 2nd Squadron | B5N2 | 9 |
| 3rd Squadron | B5N2 | 9 | 3rd Squadron | B5N2 | 9 |
| Lt Cdr Takahashi Kakuichi | | | Lt Cdr Sakamoto Akira | | |
| 1st Squadron | D3A1 | 9 | 1st Squadron | D3A1 | 9 |
| 2nd Squadron | D3A1 | 9 | 2nd Squadron | D3A1 | 9 |
| 3rd Squadron | D3A1 | 9 | 3rd Squadron | D3A1 | 9 |
| Lt Kaneko | | | Lt Sato | | |
| 5th FCU Wave 1 | A6M2 | 6 | 6th FCU Wave 1 | A6M2 | 6 |
| CAP | A6M2 | 9 | CAP | A6M2 | 9 |

use, the Zero made its mark on the Pacific War, A6Ms of the Shikishima Kamikaze sinking the carrier USS *St Lo* and damaging three others in a raid on 25 October 1944.

Prior to the appearance of the B5N, the level bomber/torpedo-bomber role was entrusted to the biplane Yokosuka B4Y1. As the Navy Type 96 Carrier Attack Aircraft, the B4Y had replaced the Mitsubishi B2M and saw service from 1936 to 1943, making it the final biplane bomber to see operational use with the Japanese Navy. After service in the Sino-Japanese War the B4Y1 had mainly been replaced by 1940, but a handful survived to see action in the Battle of Midway, operating from the carrier *Hosho*. The B5N emerged from a 1935 requirement to replace the

B4Y1, and Nakajima's offering was a low-wing monoplane with a crew of three, retractable landing gear and radial engine. The initial B5N1 was approved for production as the Type 97 Carrier Attack Bomber and went aboard IJN carriers in 1938. Like the A6M, it was blooded during the Sino-Japanese War, during which it served with shore-based units. The type's shortcomings in modern aerial warfare ensured that an improved B5N2 was introduced in 1939, this featuring a more powerful Sakae engine beneath a re-profiled cowling. By the time Japan entered World War II the B5N2 had wholly supplanted the B5N1, and it was in this form that the type spearheaded the attack on Pearl Harbor, 144 examples being involved in the raid, and the

### Specifications

Crew: 1

Powerplant: 1 x 709kW (950hp) Nakajima
Sakae 12 radial piston engine

Maximum speed: 533km/h (331mph)

Range: 3105km (1929 miles)

Service ceiling: 10,000m (33,000ft)

Dimensions: span 12.0m (39ft 4in); length
9.06m (29ft 9in); height 3.05m (10ft 0in)

Weight: 2410kg (5313lb) loaded

Armament: Two 7.7mm (.303in) Type 97
machine guns; two 20mm (0.78in) Type
99 cannon

### ▼ Mitsubishi A6M2 Reisen

*2nd Sentai, 1st Koku Kantai*, Hiryu, *1942*

This Zero was one of those that took part in the Battle of Midway in June 1942. This aircraft, which received the Allied reporting name 'Zeke', was operated by the 2nd Sentai (as indicated by the twin blue bands) of the 1st Koku Kantai (air fleet). Midway saw the loss of *Hiryu* and three other Japanese carriers.

## Specifications

**Crew:** 3

**Powerplant:** 1 x 750kW (1005hp) Nakajima Sakae 11 radial piston engine

**Maximum speed:** 378km/h (235mph)

**Range:** 1992km (1237 miles)

**Service ceiling:** 8260m (27,100ft)

**Dimensions:** span 15.52m (50ft 11in); length 10.30m (33ft 10in); height 3.70m (12ft 2in)

**Weight:** 3800kg (8380lb) loaded

**Armament:** One 7.7mm (.303in) Type 92 machine gun; one 800kg (1760lb) Type 91 torpedo or up to 250kg (550lb) bomb load

### ▼ Nakajima B5N2

#### Akagi, 1941–42

At the outbreak of the Pacific War, the aircraft dubbed 'Kate' by the Allies was the world's most advanced in-service torpedo-bomber. The B5N2 was introduced in 1939 and featured a more powerful engine, the Nakajima Hikari 3 of the B5N1 giving way to a Nakajima NK1B Sakae. The B5N was hampered by its limited defensive armament, typically comprising just a single rear-firing machine gun. Another drawback was the limited armour protection.

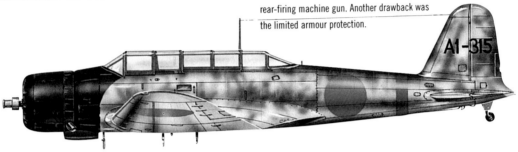

## Specifications

**Crew:** 3

**Powerplant:** 1 x 1379kW (1848hp) Mitsubishi MK4T Kasei 25 14-cylinder two-row radial engine

**Maximum speed:** 481km/h (299mph)

**Range:** 3045km (1892 miles)

**Service ceiling:** 9040m (29,660ft)

**Dimensions:** span 14.89m (48ft 11in); length

10.87m (35ft 8in); height 3.8m (12ft 6in)

**Weight:** 5650kg (12,456lb) loaded

**Armament:** One 7.7mm (.303in) Type 92 machine gun in the rear cockpit and one 7.7mm (.303in) Type 92 machine gun firing through ventral tunnel; one torpedo or 800kg (1760lb) bomb load

### ▼ Nakajima B6N2 Tenzan

#### Taiho, 1944

Designed to supersede the B5N, the 'Jill' was widely employed during the second half of the war, but suffered heavily in the Battle of the Philippine Sea in June 1943, when large numbers of B6N1s were lost with the destruction of the carriers *Shokaku, Taiho* and *Hiyo*. Others were embarked in the *Junyo* and *Zuikaku* for the same action. Concurrently, production of the improved B6N2 began, although many were restricted to land bases after the Battle of Leyte Gulf.

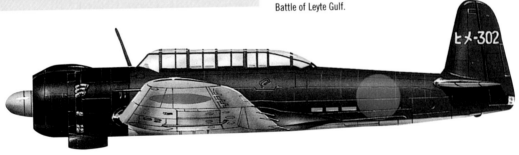

aircraft continued to play a major role in the Pacific War thereafter, being responsible for sinking the carriers USS *Hornet, Lexington* and *Yorktown*. At the outbreak of the war in the Pacific, the B5N represented the most capable carrier-based torpedo-bomber in service anywhere in the world. However, by 1944 the B5N was showing its age, and it was withdrawn from front-line service after the battles in the Philippine Sea in that year.

### Venerable dive-bomber

Having originally been designed to a 1936 requirement to replace the Aichi D1A biplane, the D3A was the key IJN dive-bomber for the early part

of the war, although in many ways the design was obsolescent by the time Japan entered the fighting. The D3A was a low-wing monoplane with non-retractable spatted undercarriage, all-metal construction and a Kinsei radial engine. The D3A was ordered into production in favour of a rival Nakajima design, and was accepted as the Navy Type 99 Carrier Bomber. The D3A1 was available for service in time to take part in the campaigns in China and Indo-China, during which it was land-based, and a total of 129 of these aircraft were launched in the Pearl Harbor raid, becoming the first Japanese aircraft to drop bombs on American targets. D3A1s were also responsible for sinking the British carrier

## IMPERIAL JAPANESE NAVY CARRIER AIR GROUPS – BATTLE OF MIDWAY AND ALEUTIANS

3–7 June 1942

**Carrier Group: Main Force**

*Hosho*

| Kanko Buntai | B4Y1 | 8 | Lt Irikiin | | | | |
|---|---|---|---|---|---|---|---|

**First Carrier Division**

| *Akagi* | | | | *Kaga* | | | |
|---|---|---|---|---|---|---|---|
| *Akagi* Air Unit | B5N2 | 1 | Cdr Fuchida | *Kaga* Air Unit | B5N2 | 1 | Lt Cdr Kusumi |
| Kansen Buntai | A6M2 | 18 | Lt Itaya Shigeru | Kansen Buntai | A6M2 | 18 | Lt Sato Masao |
| Kanbaku Buntai | D3A1 | 18 | Lt Chihaya Takehiro | Kanbaku Buntai | D3A1 | 18 | Lt Ogawa Shoichi |
| Kanko Buntai | B5N2 | 17 | Lt Cdr Murata Shigeharu | Kanko Buntai | B5N2 | 26 | Lt Kazuraki Masuhiko |
| 6th Kokutai | A6M2 | 6 | Lt Cdr Kaneko Tadashi | 6th Kokutai | A6M2 | 9 | Lt Cdr Kaneko Tadashi |
| | | | | *Soryu* Kanbaku Buntai | D3A1 | 2 (spares) | |

**Second Carrier Division**

| *Hiryu* | | | | *Soryu* | | | |
|---|---|---|---|---|---|---|---|
| *Hiryu* Air Unit | B5N2 | 1 | Lt Tomanga Joichi | *Soryu* Air Unit | D3A1 | 1 | Lt Cdr Egusa |
| Kansen Buntai | A6M2 | 18 | Lt Mori Shigeru | Kansen Buntai | A6M2 | 18 | Lt Suganami Masaji |
| Kanbaku Buntai | D3A1 | 18 | Lt Kobayashi Michio | Kanbaku Buntai | D3A1 | 15 | Lt Ikeda Masatake |
| Kanko Buntai | B5N2 | 17 | Lt Kikuchi Rokuro | Kanko Buntai | B5N2 | 18 | Lt Abe Heijiro |
| 6th Kokutai | A6M2 | 3 | | 6th Kokutai | A6M2 | 3 | |
| | | | | | D4Y1C | 2 | |

**Carrier Group: Midway Invasion Force**

*Zuiho* ('Zuiho' class)

| Kansen Buntai | A5M4 | 12 | Lt Hidaka Moriyasu | | | | |
|---|---|---|---|---|---|---|---|
| Kanko Buntai | B5N1 | 12 | Lt Matsuo Kaji | | | | |

**2nd Carrier Striking Force**

| *Ryujo* ('Ryujo' class) | | | | *Junyo* ('Hiyo' class) | | | |
|---|---|---|---|---|---|---|---|
| Kansen Buntai | A6M2 | 16 | Lt Kobayashi | Kansen Buntai | A6M2 | 8 | Lt Shiga |
| Kanko Buntai | B5N1 | 20 | Lt Yamagami Masayuki | Kanbaku Buntai | D3A1 | 19 | Lt Abe Zenji |
| | | | | 6th Kokutai | A6M2 | 12 | |

HMS *Hermes* (the first ship of its type to fall victim to carrier aircraft) and the cruisers HMS *Cornwall* and *Devonshire* in April 1942. During the first 10 months of the war in the Pacific, the D3A took part in all major carrier actions, and was responsible for sinking more Allied vessels than any other Axis type. The D3A suffered its own losses during the Battle of the Coral Sea, and despite the introduction of the improved D3A2 in 1942, by the second half of the Pacific campaign the aircraft was clearly obsolete and was relegated to second-line duties.

A second generation of IJN carrier aircraft included direct replacements in the level bomber/torpedo-bomber and dive-bomber

## ▾ Yokosuka D4Y3 Suisei Model 33

### 501st Kokutai, 1945

This 'Judy' is an example of the D4Y3 version of the Suisei (Comet), which improved overall reliability through the introduction of the Mitsubishi MK8P Kinsei 62 radial in place of the problematic Aichi Atsuta engine fitted previously. In order to permit operations from smaller Japanese carriers towards the end of the war, later D4Ys were equipped with three solid-fuel rocket-assisted take-off units under the rear fuselage.

### Specifications

Crew: 2

Powerplant: 1 x 1163kW (1560hp) Mitsubishi Kinsei 62 radial engine

Maximum speed: 550km/h (342mph)

Range: 1465km (910 miles)

Service ceiling: 10,700m (35,105ft)

Dimensions: span 11.50m (37ft 9in); length 10.22m (33ft 6in); height 3.74m (12ft 3in)

Weight: 4250kg (9370lb) loaded

Armament: Two 7.62mm (.303in) forward firing machine gun; one rearward-firing 7.92mm (0.31in) machine gun; 500kg (1102lb) bomb load, 800kg (1764lb) bomb load (Kamikaze)

### Specifications

Crew: 2

Powerplant: 1 x 1360kW (1825hp) Nakajima NK9C Homare 18-cylinder radial engine

Maximum speed: 566km/h (351mph)

Range: 1850km (1149 miles)

Service ceiling: 8950m (29,363ft)

Dimensions: span 11.40m (37ft 40in); length 11.49m (37ft 8in); height 4.07m (13ft 4in)

Weight: 3614kg (7967lb) loaded

Armament: One 13mm (0.51in) Type 2 tailgun, two 20mm (0.78in) Type 99 cannons in the wings, up to 800kg (1763lb) torpedo

## ▾ Aichi B7A2 Ryusei

### Yokosuka Kokutai, 1944

Codenamed 'Grace' by the Allies, the B7A Ryusei (Shooting Star) arrived too late to see service in its intended capacity, with the Japanese no longer having the requisite carriers. Indeed, *Taiho*, the only carrier considered large enough to operate the B7A, was sunk during the Battle of the Philippine Sea in June 1944. *Shinano*, another suitable carrier, was sunk only 10 days after commission, in November 1944.

categories. The Nakajima B6N was drawn up to a 1939 specification for a new torpedo-bomber to replace the B5N, and was based on a similar airframe allied to a new engine and revised tail surfaces. The B6N entered production in 1943 as the Navy Carrier Attack Bomber Tenzan (Heavenly Mountain), with the first 135 aircraft powered by a Nakajima radial. Subsequent aircraft used a Mitsubishi engine, as the B6N2. Both versions saw extensive use in the final two years of the air, including kamikaze missions.

## German influence

The Yokosuka D4Y was a fast carrier-based attack bomber, design of which was influenced by the German Heinkel He 118. Originally flown with a Daimler-Benz DB 600 engine, the D4Y1 took to the air in December 1941, with the first production aircraft being completed in late spring 1942, these being outfitted for the reconnaissance role. Soon after delivery the aircraft was embroiled in the Battle of Midway, with early losses including the aircraft sunk along with the carrier *Soryu*. In the dive-bomber role, the D4Y1 Suisei required strengthened wings and improved dive brakes and saw large-scale service in the Battle of the Philippine Sea, for which 174 examples were embarked in nine carriers. The D4Y2

## IMPERIAL JAPANESE NAVY CARRIER AIR GROUPS – BATTLE OF THE PHILIPPINE SEA
19–20 June 1944

| 3rd Carrier Squadron | | Air Group 653 | | | |
|---|---|---|---|---|---|
| *Chitose* ('Chitose' class) | | *Chiyoda* ('Chitose' class) | | *Zuiho* ('Zuiho' class) | |
| A6M5b | 21 | A6M5b | 21 | A6M5b | 21 |
| B6N | 3 | B6N | 3 | B6N | 3 |
| B5N | 6 | B5N | 6 | B5N | 6 |
| | | | | | |
| **1st Carrier Squadron** | | Air Group 601 | | | |
| *Taiho* ('Taiho' class) | | *Shokaku* ('Shokaku' class) | | *Zuikaku* ('Shokaku' class) | |
| A6M5 | 26 | A6M5 | 26 | A6M5 | 27 |
| D4Y | 23 | D4Y | 24 | D4Y | 23 |
| B6N | 17 | B6N | 17 | B6N | 17 |
| D3A | 2 | D3A | 2 | D3A | 3 |
| | | | | | |
| **2nd Carrier Squadron** | | Air Group 652 | | | |
| *Junyo* ('Hiyo' class) | | *Hiyo* ('Hiyo' class) | | *Ryuho* ('Ryuho' class) | |
| A6M5 | 27 | A6M5 | 26 | A6M5 | 27 |
| B6N | 6 | B6N | 6 | B6N | 6 |
| D4Y | 9 | D3A | 18 | – | – |
| D3A | 9 | – | – | – | – |

of 1944 was powered by a new Atsuta (DB 601) engine but, with limited defensive armament and armour, it suffered at the hands of US Navy fighters. The D4Y3 introduced a more reliable Kinsei engine, while the final months of the war saw use of the similar D4Y4, a single-seat version intended for the suicide dive-bomber role.

With specifications for new and larger carrier drawn up in 1941, the IJN hoped to introduce a heavy level bomber/torpedo-bomber to replace both the B6N and D4Y. This new aircraft was the Aichi B7A Ryusei, capable of carrying bombs internally, or an external torpedo. Powered by a radial engine, the two-seat B7A offered high speed and long range, and an initial prototype flew in mid-1942. Dogged by poor engine reliability and airframe deficiencies, the Navy Carrier Attack Bomber Ryusei did not enter service until 1945, in revised B7A2 form. Only 80 examples had been completed before the factory responsible for production was destroyed by an earthquake in May 1945. Arriving too late to make

an impact on the course of the Pacific campaigns, the decimation of the IJ carrier arm meant that the B7A would be primarily operated from land bases, with only limited carrier operations in home waters.

### Reconnaissance effort

With its emphasis on offensive missions, one area lacking in the IJN air wings compared to those of the Royal Navy and US Navy was reconnaissance. The IJN high command was made aware of this early in the Pacific War, and efforts were made to introduce a long-range carrier-based reconnaissance aircraft, as the Nakajima C6N, or Navy Carrier Reconnaissance Aircraft Saiun (Painted Cloud). Developed from early 1942, the C6N was similar in concept to the B6N, but was outfitted with camera equipment and observation ports and was powered by a Homare radial engine. First flown in May 1943 and ordered into production in early 1944, the C6N1 entered service in summer 1944, and was sufficiently fast to outrun most Allied fighters it encountered.

# United Kingdom
## 1939–45

**Although well versed in naval air operations, the carrier air groups available to the Royal Navy at the outbreak of World War II were limited in size and capability, with the mainstay of the Naval Air Squadrons provided by obsolete biplane fighters and torpedo-reconnaissance types.**

THE ROYAL NAVY possessed only six carriers in 1939, only two of which had been designed as such from the outset, the others being conversions. Such was the shortage of carriers that the Admiralty turned to the US to provide Merchant Aircraft Carriers (MAC ships) with which to prosecute the Battle of the Atlantic. These comprised merchant vessels with small flight decks and escort carriers – merchant vessels converted with below-decks hangars and fully equipped flight decks. British carriers were also comparatively small, and often operated singly or in small groups, in a colonial-policing capacity.

### Biplane backbone

The aircraft that equipped British carriers at the beginning of the war were also limited, the most important being the Fairey Swordfish biplane torpedo-bomber and the Gloster Sea

▲ **Blackburn Roc**

The Royal Navy pinned its hopes on the Roc turret-armed fighter, but the concept proved flawed, and it saw only limited use in second-line roles.

▲ **Fairey Swordfish Mk I**

*No. 821 NAS, HMS Ark Royal, 1940*

This Swordfish was embarked in the 'Ark' as part of the Home Fleet in 1940. The aircraft carries the 'standard' armament of a single 457mm (18in) torpedo. No. 821 NAS operated the Swordfish from 1937 to 1942, and was responsible for the first Allied U-boat kill of the war, sinking *U-39* on 14 September 1939.

### Specifications

Crew: 2–3

Powerplant: 1 x 578 kW (690hp) Bristol Pegasus IIIM.3 radial piston engine

Maximum speed: 224km/h (139mph)

Range: 1658km (1030 miles)

Service ceiling: 3780m (12,400ft)

Dimensions: span 13.87m (45ft 6in); length 11.07m (36ft 1in); height 3.92m (12ft 11in)

Weight: 3946kg (8700lb) loaded

Armament: 2 x 7.62mm (.303in) machine guns; 1 x 726kg (1600lb) torpedo or up to 680kg (1500lb) bomb load

**▲ Gloster Sea Gladiator Mk I**

*Hal Far Fighter Flight, Hal Far, 1940*

Subsequently named *Faith* in recognition of its actions, N5520 was one of a handful of Sea Gladiators involved in the frantic early defence of Malta in August 1940. Based at the Royal Air Force's Hal Far airfield, the Sea Gladiators, from No. 802 NAS, were brought to Malta by the carrier HMS *Glorious* in early 1940.

### Specifications

Crew: 1

Powerplant: 1 x 619kW (830hp) Bristol Mercury VIIIAS air-cooled 9-cylinder radial engine

Maximum speed: 407km/h (253mph)

Range: 684km (425 miles)

Service ceiling: 9845m (32,300ft)

Dimensions: span 9.83m (32ft 3in); length 8.36m (27ft 5in); height 3.52m (11ft 7in)

Weight: 2272kg (5020lb) loaded

Armament: Four 7.62 x 51mm (.303in) Browning machine guns

Gladiator biplane fighter. More modern monoplane types were being delivered, typified by the Fairey Fulmar fighter and the Blackburn Skua dive-bomber, both of which had serious shortcomings in terms of operational capability.

Anachronistic in appearance, the Swordfish had first flown in 1934 and was intended to fulfil a requirement for a Torpedo Spotter Reconnaissance aircraft, and 689 examples had been delivered or were on order by September 1939. Employing all-metal construction with fabric covering, the Swordfish served on both wheels and floats, equipping carriers as well as battleships, battlecruisers and cruisers. The Swordfish assembled an enviable war record, serving with distinction in the raid on Taranto on 11 November 1940, when aircraft launched from HMS *Illustrious* severely damaged three Italian battleships. Swordfish were also responsible for crippling the *Bismarck* in the Atlantic, and were sent against the *Scharnhorst*, *Gneisenau* and *Prinz Eugen* during the Channel Dash in February 1942. Production of the Swordfish continued until August 1944, by which

### Specifications

Crew: 2

Powerplant: 1 x 890hp (664kW) Bristol Perseus XII radial engine

Maximum speed: 362km/h (225mph)

Range: 1223km (760 miles)

Service ceiling: 6160m (20,200ft)

Dimensions: span 14.07m (46ft 2in); length 10.85m (35ft 7in); height 3.81m (12ft 6in)

Weight: 3732kg (8228lb) loaded

Armament: 4 x 7.62 x 51mm (.303in) machine guns in wings, Lewis machine gun in rear; 1 x 227kg (550lb) bomb beneath fuselage

**▼ Blackburn Skua Mk II**

*No. 806 NAS, HMS* Argus, *1940*

This Skua was lost during the ill-fated Operation White in November 1940, when it was launched from HMS *Argus* as a pathfinder for a group of Hurricanes bound for Malta. The formation became lost, some Hurricanes ending up in the sea, while the Skua made a forced landing in Sicily.

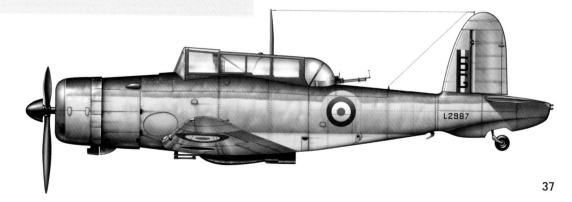

## TYPICAL BRITISH EARLY-WAR CARRIER AIR GROUPS

### Mers-el-Kebir (Operation Catapult)

3 July 1940

HMS *Ark Royal*

| | | |
|---|---|---|
| 800 NAS | Skua | 12 |
| 803 NAS | Skua | 12 |
| 810 NAS | Swordfish | 12 |
| 818 NAS | Swordfish | 9 |
| 820 NAS | Swordfish | 9 |

### Crete

14 May–1 June 1941

HMS *Formidable*

| | | |
|---|---|---|
| 803 NAS | Fulmar | 6 |
| 806 NAS | Fulmar | 6 |
| 826 NAS | Albacore | 6 |
| 829 NAS | Albacore | 4 |

### Operation Harpoon and Battle of Pantelleria

15 June 1942

HMS *Argus*

| | | |
|---|---|---|
| 807 NAS | Fulmar | 4 |
| 824 NAS | Swordfish | 4 |

HMS *Eagle*

| | | |
|---|---|---|
| 813 NAS | Swordfish | 9 |
| | Sea Hurricane | 4 |
| 801 NAS | Sea Hurricane | 12 |

time the aircraft had been equipped with rocket armament (Swordfish Mk II) and ASV radar (Mk III). Even in the final months of the war the Swordfish proved its worth, harassing German shipping in the North Sea to great effect.

Schemed as a replacement for the Hawker Nimrod and Osprey, the original Sea Gladiator was only ever intended to provide interim equipment, with the first 38 examples being converted from Royal Air Force Gladiator Mk IIs, and being transferred to the Fleet Air Arm in December 1938. A fully navalized Sea Gladiator then followed, this having full catapult and arrester gear equipment and stowage for a rescue dinghy. Notable campaigns in which the Sea Gladiator was involved included Norway (No. 804 NAS), while the Hal Far Fighter Flight took part in the defence of Malta between April and June 1940.

### Pioneering dive-bomber

The Blackburn Skua represented several important developments, being the UK's first purpose-designed naval dive-bomber and its first carrier aircraft with

### Specifications

Crew: 3

Powerplant: 1 x 560kW (750hp) Bristol Pegasus 30 9-cylinder radial engine

Maximum speed: 222km/h (138mph)

Range: 885km (550 miles)

Service ceiling: 3260m (10,700ft)

Dimensions: span 13.92m (45ft 6in); length 11.12m (36ft 4in); height 3.93m (12ft 10in)

Weight: 4196kg (9250lb) loaded

Armament: One 7.7mm (.303in) Vickers machine gun; one 7.7mm (.303in) Vickers 'K' machine gun or Browning machine gun on a flexible mount in rear cockpit; underfuselage crutch for one 457mm (18in), 731kg (1610lb) torpedo, or 681kg (1500lb) bomb or mine, or up to eight 76.2mm (3in), 27kg (60lb) rockets or four 113kg (250lb) bombs on rails under the wings

▲ **Fairey Swordfish Mk II**

*No. 811 NAS, HMS Biter, 1944*

Wearing invasion stripes, this Swordfish Mk II is fitted with the underwing rocket projectile launch rails that were introduced on this variant, which appeared in service in 1943. The RP rails were combined with a strengthened and metal-skinned lower wing. As such, these aircraft saw considerable use during the pre- and post-invasion phases of Operations Neptune and Overlord.

## Specifications

Crew: 2

Powerplant: 1 x 969kW (1300hp) Rolls-Royce
   Merlin 30 V-12 pistol engine

Maximum speed: 440km/h (273mph)

Range: 1255km (780 miles)

Service ceiling: 8300m (27,230ft)

Dimensions: span 14.14m (46ft 4in); length
12.24m (40ft 2in); height 3.25m (10ft 8in)

Weight: 4627kg (10,200lb) loaded

Armament: Eight 7.7mm (.303in) Browning
machine guns; two 113kg (350lb) bombs

### ▼ Fairey Fulmar Mk I
#### No. 806 NAS, 1940

This Fulmar is seen shortly before going aboard HMS *Illustrious*, from which it took
part in the Malta campaign in September/October 1940, defending convoys
against the Italian air force. Part of the Mediterranean Fleet, the *Illustrious*
became the first carrier to operate Fulmar fighters when it embarked No. 806 NAS.
The carrier arrived in theatre in August 1940 and in
December took part in Operation Judgement, the
raid on the Italian naval base at Taranto.

flaps, retractable undercarriage and a variable-pitch
propeller. An all-metal monoplane, the Skua first flew
in production form in 1938, with 190 examples
being delivered between October 1938 and March
1940. Entering service with Nos 800 and 803 NAS
in 1938, the Skua replaced Nimrods and Ospreys
aboard HMS *Ark Royal*. Although envisaged as a
dual-role fighter/dive-bomber, the Skua was clearly
outclassed in aerial combat, but as a dive-bomber
enjoyed early success when 16 aircraft flying from the
Orkneys sunk the German cruiser *Königsberg* at

Bergen on 10 April 1940. Less than two weeks later,
however, the type was mauled over Narvik, and after
helping cover the evacuation from Dunkirk, the type
was withdrawn in 1941, to be replaced by the Fulmar
and Sea Hurricane.

Derived from the Skua, the Blackburn Roc marked
an attempt to provide the FAA with its first turret-
armed fighter. Despite the limited utility of this
arrangement, the Roc entered service with No. 806
NAS at Eastleigh in February 1940, serving alongside
the Skua in a mixed squadron. Others went to

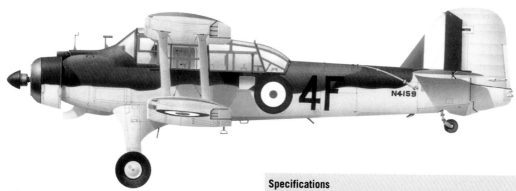

### ▲ Fairey Albacore
#### No. 826 NAS, 1941

Land-based at Ford in March 1940, No. 826 NAS moved to Bircham Newton the
following month, from where it launched night attack, minelaying and anti-
shipping strike missions. Between November 1940 and April 1941 the squadron
was embarked in HMS *Formidable* and thereafter was land-based in the eastern
Mediterranean and the Western Desert.

## Specifications

Crew: 3

Powerplant: 1 x 843kW (1130hp) Bristol Taurus
   XII 14-cylinder radial piston engine

Maximum speed: 259km/h (161mph)

Range: 1497km (930 miles)

Service ceiling: 6310m (20,700ft)

Dimensions: span 15.24m (50ft 0in); length

12.14m (39ft 10in); height 4.32m (14ft 2in)

Weight: 4745kg (10,460lb) loaded

Armament: One 7.7mm (.303in) Vickers
machine gun in starboard wing; two 7.7mm
(.303in) Vickers K machine guns in rear
cockpit; one 730kg (1610lb) torpedo or 227kg
(500lb) bombs

## Specifications

Crew: 1

Powerplant: 1 x 1088kW (1458hp) Rolls-Royce
Merlin XXII V-12 piston engine

Maximum speed: 550km/h (342mph)

Range: 1545km (960 miles)

Service ceiling: 10,851m (35,600ft)

Dimensions: span 12.19m (40ft 0in); length
9.83m (32ft 3in); height 4.04m (13ft 3in)

Weight: 3538kg (7800lb) loaded

Armament: Four 20mm (.79in) cannon

### ▼ Hawker Sea Hurricane Mk XIIA

*126 (F) Sqn, RCAF, Dartmouth, Nova Scotia, 1942*

Clearly displaying its arrester hook and with its original Royal Navy titles over-
painted, this Sea Hurricane was held in reserve for the Merchant Ship Fighter Unit
and flown by the Royal Canadian Air Force. Among Canadian-built Sea Hurricanes
were the Mk Xs and XIIA, armed respectively with eight and 12 machine guns.

No. 801 NAS at Hatston, Orkney. Although
equipped for deck operations, no Roc ever flew
operationally from a carrier.

In another bid to provide protection to Atlantic
convoys, the British fielded the Catapult Armed
Merchant (CAM) ship, equipped with the Hawker
Sea Hurricane Mk IA, which could be launched by
catapult, the pilot ditching in the sea after the
mission unless he could reach land. Despite the
inherent limitations of the CAM concept, the Sea
Hurricane did at least provide the Fleet Air Arm with
its first modern ship-based fighter. Both Sea

Hurricane Mk IA and IB were intended for use from
CAM ships, and were fitted with catapult spools for
this purpose, although the Mk IB could also be
landed on a carrier deck, thanks to its arrester gear.
The Sea Hurricane Mk II introduced a Roll-Royce
Merlin XX engine. The first operational Sea
Hurricanes were those of No. 804 NAS, deployed
aboard CAM ships from February 1941. In March
1941, No. 880 NAS became the first carrier unit so
equipped, and went into action aboard HMS *Furious*
in the Arctic in July. Thereafter, Sea Hurricanes
served on escort carriers for service in the Arctic and

### ▼ Supermarine Seafire Mk III

*No. 807 NAS, HMS* Hunter, *1945*

While previous Seafires were conversions of Spitfires, the Seafire Mk III was the
first dedicated carrier-borne version, with no direct land-based equivalent, and
featured a Merlin 55 engine, four-blade propeller and folding wings. Note the
extended A-frame arrester hook on this example, and reduced-size roundels.

## Specifications

Crew: 1

Powerplant: 1 x 1182kW (1585hp) Rolls-Royce
Merlin 55 M engine

Maximum speed: 578km/h (348mph)

Range: 825km (359 miles)

Service ceiling: 9753m (32,000ft)

Dimensions: span 11.23m (36ft 10in); length
9.21m (30ft 3in); height 3.40m (11ft 2in)

Weight: 3275kg (7220lb) loaded

Armament: Two 20mm (.79in) Hispano cannon,
four 7.7mm (.303in) M2 Browning machine
guns

Mediterranean, until finally replaced by Seafires and Wildcats in 1943.

## American equipment

Only later in the war did the FAA begin to receive genuinely competitive fighter equipment, comprising the US-supplied Grumman Wildcat and Hellcat and Vought Corsair, and the Supermarine Seafire and Fairey Firefly. The Seafire began life as an adaptation

of the RAF's Spitfire Mk VB, and equipped with an arrester hook, began trials in HMS *Illustrious* in late 1941. The initial production model was the Seafire Mk IB, which retained the Type B wing, while the Seafire Mk IIC appeared in May 1942 with the C Type wing that could accommodate cannon armament, as well as catapult spools, strengthened fuselage and provision for rocket-assisted take-off gear. The Seafire L.Mk IIC was the version with a

### Specifications

Crew: 3

Powerplant: 1 x 1225kW (1640hp) Rolls-Royce Merlin 32 V-12 piston engine

Maximum speed: 340km/h (210mph)

Range: 1165km (725 miles)

Service ceiling: 6585m (21,600ft)

Dimensions: span 14.49m (47ft 6in); length 12.18m (40ft 0in); height 4.6m (15ft)

Weight: 6385kg (14,080lb) loaded

Armament: Two 7.7mm (.303in) Vickers K machine guns; one torpedo or 735kg (1620lb) of bombs

### ▼ Fairey Barracuda Mk II
#### *No. 785 NAS, Crail, 1944*

Depicted with ASV aerial array above the wing and underwing depth bombs, this Barracuda was flown by No. 785 NAS, a dedicated torpedo-bombing/reconnaissance training unit that operated from its Fife base from April 1943 until the end of the war. After just 30 Barracuda Mk Is were delivered to one operational squadron, production switched to the Mk II with Merlin 32 engine, and 10 further squadrons were equipped during 1943.

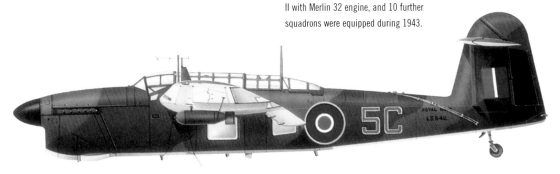

### Specifications

Crew: 3

Powerplant: 1 x 1268kW (1700hp) Wright Cyclone 14-cylinder two-row engine

Maximum speed: 414km/h (257mph)

Range: 4321km (2685 miles)

Service ceiling: 6525m (21,400ft)

Dimensions: span 16.51m (54ft 2in); length 12.42m (40ft 9in); height 4.19m (13ft 9in)

Weight: 7876kg (17,364lb) loaded

Armament: Three 12.7mm (.50in), one 7.7mm (.303in) machine gun in ventral position; bomb load of 1134kg (2500lb)

### ▼ Grumman Avenger Mk I
#### *No. 846 NAS, Machrihanish, 1943*

The Royal Navy received 402 TBF-1Bs, which became the Tarpon Mk I (later Avenger Mk I) in FAA service. The initial operator was No. 832 NAS in January 1943 and early service saw the type employed aboard escort carriers and from shore bases on anti-submarine patrols. This example was active from a shore base in western Scotland. No. 846 NAS also flew its Avengers from HMS *Trumpeter* and provided anti-submarine patrols for the Gibraltar convoys in 1944.

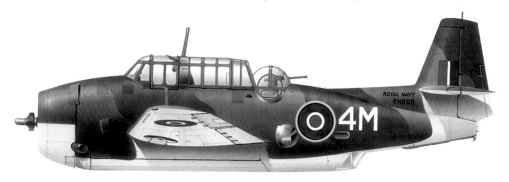

## Specifications

Crew: 3

Powerplant: 1 x 1420kW (1900hp) Wright R-
2600-20 radial piston engine

Maximum speed: 442km/h (275mph)

Range: 1610km (1000 miles)

Service ceiling: 9170m (20,100ft)

Dimensions: span 16.51m (54ft 2in); length
12.48m (40ft 11.5in); height 4.70m (15ft 5in)

Weight: 8115kg (17,893lb) loaded

Armament: One 7.62mm (.30in) nose-mounted

M1919 Browning machine gun; two 12.7mm
(.50in) wing-mounted M2 Browning machine
guns; one 12.7mm (.50in) dorsal-mounted M2
Browning machine gun; up to eight 89mm
(3.5in) Forward Firing Aircraft Rockets, 127mm
(5in) Forward Firing Aircraft Rockets or High
Velocity Aerial Rockets; up to 907kg (2000lb)
of bombs or one 907kg (2000lb) Mark 13
torpedo

### ▼ General Motors Avenger Mk III
#### No. 855 NAS, Hawkinge, 1944

Equivalent to the US Navy's TBM-1, this Avenger Mk III is painted in the invasion
stripes applied for the Allied assault on northwest Europe in mid-1944. JZ490
operated from RAF Hawkinge in June 1944, and later Thorney Island, from where it
was used to patrol the English Channel during the D-Day landings.

## Specifications

Crew: 1

Powerplant: 1 x 895kW (1199hp) Pratt &
Whitney R-1830-76 radial piston engine

Maximum speed: 512km/h (318mph)

Range: 1464km (910 miles)

Service ceiling: 10,363m (34,000ft)

Dimensions: span 11.58m (38ft 0in); length
8.76m (28ft 9in); height 2.81m (9ft 3in)

Weight: 3607kg (7952lb) loaded

Armament: Six 12.7 x 99mm (.50in) Browning
machine guns; one 227kg (500lb) bomb

### ▼ Grumman Martlet Mk I
#### No. 804 NAS, Skaebrae, 1941

The first examples of the Martlet Mk I arrived in the UK in summer 1940 and were
delivered to No. 804 NAS at Hatston, replacing that unit's Sea Gladiators. A pair of
No. 804 NAS Martlet Mk Is operating from Skaebrae was responsible for the first
combat success achieved by the type, a Luftwaffe Ju 88 being claimed off Orkney
on Christmas Day 1940.

low-altitude wing, while the Seafire F.Mk III (and
low-altitude L.Mk III) introduced a manual wing-
fold mechanism. In 1945 the first Griffon-engined
Seafire appeared, with the Mk XV, although this was
just too late to see active service in World War II. Key
actions in which the Seafire was involved included
the Allied landings in North Africa in November
1942, and the subsequent landings at Salerno and in

the south of France. The Seafire also saw active
service in the Pacific theatre.

In FAA service the Wildcat was initially known as
the Martlet, the first examples of the Martlet Mk I
being diverted from a French order of 1939. These
arrived in the UK in July 1940 and saw combat as
early as December that year with No. 804 NAS,
becoming the first US-built fighters to destroy

German aircraft in World War II. The Royal Navy subsequently received General Motors-built FM-1 and FM-2 versions, which saw service with the local designations Wildcat Mk V and Wildcat Mk VI, respectively, the fighter's name having been changed from Martlet to Wildcat in January 1944.

Originally to have received the British service name Gannet, the Hellcat was produced for FAA service as the Hellcat Mk I and Mk II. The first of these arrived under the Lend-Lease scheme in April 1943, the initial operators being Nos 800 and 804 NAS. FAA Hellcat Mk Is saw considerable action off Norway and in the Mediterranean, while the Mks II were operated throughout the East Indies, Malaya, Burma and during the final assault on Japan.

Just over 2000 examples of the Corsair were ultimately supplied to the FAA under Lend-Lease, the British aircraft being modified with clipped wingtips to permit below-decks stowage on smaller carriers, and initial service entry was recorded in June 1943. With F4U carrier operations prohibited by the US Navy, the British were first to take the cranked-

### Specifications

Crew: 1

Powerplant: 1 x 895kW (1200hp) Pratt & Whitney R-1830-S3C4-G radial piston engine

Maximum speed: 512km/h (318mph)

Range: 1464km (910 miles)

Service ceiling: 10,363m (34,000ft)

Dimensions: span 11.58m (38ft 0in); length 8.76m (28ft 9in); height 2.81m (9ft 3in)

Weight: 3607kg (7952lb) loaded

Armament: Six 12.7mm (.50in) Browning machine guns; up to 90kg (200lb) bomb load

### ▼ Grumman Martlet Mk II

**No. 888 NAS, HMS Formidable, 1943**

This Martlet wears hybrid Royal Navy/US Navy markings for participation in Operation Torch, the Allied landings in North Africa in November 1942. Originally delivered to Karachi for Far East operations, AJ108 was aboard *Formidable* for Operation Torch. Subsequently the squadron provided cover for the landings in Sicily in July 1943 and the Salerno landings in September 1943.

## TYPICAL BRITISH LATE-WAR CARRIER AIR GROUPS

| Raids on the Japanese Home Islands | | |
|---|---|---|
| 24–28 July 1945 | | |
| Task Force 37 | | |
| HMS *Formidable* | 'Illustrious' class | |
| 848 NAS | Avenger Mk II | 12 |
| 1841 NAS | Corsair Mk IV | 18 |
| 1842 NAS | Corsair Mk IV | 18 |
| 1848 NAS | Hellcat Mk II | 4 |
| | Hellcat PR.Mk II | 2 |
| | | |
| HMS *Victorious* | 'Illustrious' class | |
| 849 NAS | Avenger Mk II | 16 |
| 1834 NAS | Corsair Mk II/IV | 19 |
| 1836 NAS | Corsair Mk II/IV | 18 |
| Ship's Flight | Walrus | 2 |
| | | |
| HMS *Implacable* | 'Implacable' class | |
| 801 NAS | Seafire L.Mk III | 24 |
| 828 NAS | Avenger Mk II | 21 |
| 880 NAS | Seafire L.Mk III and FR.Mk III | 24 |
| 1771 NAS | Firefly Mk I | 12 |
| | | |
| HMS *Indefatigable* | 'Implacable' class | |
| 820 NAS | Avenger Mk II | 21 |
| 887 NAS | Seafire F.Mk III | 15 |
| | Seafire L.Mk III | 9 |
| 894 NAS | Seafire L.Mk III | 16 |
| 1772 NAS | Firefly Mk I | 12 |

wing fighter into battle from a carrier deck, when Corsair Mk IIs from No. 1834 NAS took part in operations against the *Tirpitz* off Norway on 3 April 1944, flying from HMS *Victorious*. Meanwhile, Corsairs from HMS *Illustrious* were in action off the coast of Sumatra.

## Firefly supreme

Of the British-designed Fleet fighters to see service in the closing stages of the war, the most capable was the two-seat Firefly, first flown in prototype form in December 1941 and originally conceived as a replacement for the Fulmar. The initial-production Firefly Mk I was ready for service in March 1943. The Firefly's baptism of fire came during the attacks on the German battleship *Tirpitz* launched from HMS *Indefatigable*, and the type also saw much use in Norwegian raids. By the end of the war against Japan, five squadrons of Fireflies were in the Pacific, these pressing home attacks against Japanese-occupied islands shortly before VJ-Day.

In terms of bombers, replacements for obsolescent equipment arrived in the form of the American Grumman Avenger and the Fairey Barracuda. In an effort to replace the venerable Swordfish, Fairey had designed a successor, the Albacore, which retained the

biplane configuration of its predecessor, but added an enclosed cabin, a new Bristol Taurus radial engine and aerodynamic refinements. The Albacore entered FAA service in 1940 and first saw combat during the attacks on Boulogne in September that year. Subsequently, the Albacore was widely operated from land bases, but carrier-based examples succeeded in severely damaging the Italian battleship *Vittorio Veneto* during the Battle of Cape Matapan in March 1941, operating from HMS *Formidable*. Subsequently, the type's carrier operations encompassed the Arctic, North Atlantic, Mediterranean and Indian Ocean.

While the Albacore was intended to replace the Swordfish, the nominated successor to the Albacore was the same company's Barracuda, schemed in 1937 as a three-seat naval bomber, this time intended for use as both a torpedo-carrier and a dive-bomber. With high performance entrusted to its monoplane configuration and Rolls-Royce Merlin inline engine, the Barracuda suffered a delayed development, and did not fly until December 1940.

In the event, the performance of the Barracuda left much to be desired, even when the Merlin XXX of the Barracuda Mk I gave way to the more powerful Merlin Mk 32 in the Barracuda Mks II and III. It was not until January 1943 that production deliveries to the FAA began, but the Barracuda went on to play a

### Specifications

| | |
|---|---|
| Crew: 1 | Weight: 7025kg (15,487lb) loaded |
| Powerplant: 1 x 1491kW (2000hp) Pratt & Whitney R-2800-10 or 10W Double Wasp 18-cylinder two-row radial engine | Armament: One 12.7mm (.50in) M2 Browning machine gun, or two 20mm (.79in) cannon, or four 12.7mm (.50in) Browning machine guns; |
| Maximum speed: 603km/h (375mph) | six 127mm (5in) HVARs, or two 298mm (11in) |
| Range: 2559km (1590 miles) | Tiny Tim unguided rockets; one 907kg |
| Service ceiling: 11,705m (38,400ft) | (2000lb) bomb or one Mk.13-3 torpedo |
| Dimensions: span 13.06m (42ft 10in); length 10.24m (33ft 7in); height 3.99m (13ft 1in) | |

▼ **Grumman Hellcat Mk I**

*No. 800 NAS, HMS* Emperor, *1944*

JV131 was a Hellcat Mk I (originally to have been a Gannet Mk I), the Fleet Air Arm equivalent of the F6F-3. The aircraft was likely embarked in HMS *Emperor* on 10 September 1945, when the carrier sailed into Singapore harbour to reinstate British rule there. No. 800 NAS was the first FAA unit to equip with the Hellcat, in July 1943, and provided escort for the attacks against the *Tirpitz* from *Emperor*, shooting down an Fw 190 and two Bf 109Gs on 8 May 1944.

## Specifications

Crew: 1

Powerplant: 1 x 1490kW (2000hp) Pratt & Whitney R-2800-8 (B) radial piston engine

Maximum speed: 671km/h (417mph)

Range: 2425km (1507 miles)

Service ceiling: 11,308m (37,100ft)

Dimensions: span 10.16m (33ft 3in); length 10.02m (33ft 2in); height 4.58m (15ft)

Weight: 6281kg (13,846lb) loaded

Armament: Six 12.7mm (.50in) Browning machine guns

### ▼ Vought Corsair Mk I

*No. 1835 NAS, Brunswick, 1943*

Flying from a land base in Maine, this early Corsair Mk I (F4U-1) demonstrates the original cockpit canopy, albeit fitted with a small bulge, and unclipped wings. No. 1835 NAS was one of the first units to form up on the type in the US, prior to being shipped to the UK aboard Royal Navy escort carriers.

## Specifications

Crew: 2

Powerplant: 1 x 1290kW (1730hp) Rolls-Royce Griffon 74 V-12 piston engine

Maximum speed: 618km/h (386mph)

Range: 2092km (1300 miles)

Service ceiling: 9450m (31,000ft)

Dimensions: span 12.55m (40ft 2in); length 8.51m (27ft 11in); height 4.37m (14ft 4in)

Weight: 7301kg (16,096lb) loaded

Armament: Four 20 (.79in) Hispano-Suiza HS.404 cannons; eight RP-3 27kg (60lb) rockets; two 454kg (1000lb) bombs

### ▼ Fairey Firefly Mk I

*Unknown unit, 1944*

Ordered 'off the drawing board' in 1940, Z2035 was an example of the first batch of Fairey-built Firefly Mk Is, of which 931 were eventually completed, including licensed production by General Aircraft. Initial Firefly Mk Is were powered by the Griffon IIB, replaced in later production by the more powerful Griffon XII.

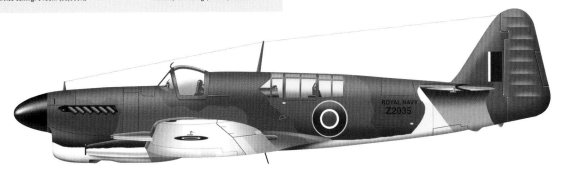

significant role in the Pacific theatre in 1944–45, while closer to home its major success was in the attack on the *Tirpitz* in April 1944.

The US-built Avenger was originally selected for FAA service as the Tarpon. The initial operator was No. 832 NAS, which took the Tarpon Mk I on charge in January 1943. In June that year, No. 832 NAS operated from USS *Saratoga* in support of US Marine landings in the Solomon Islands. In January 1944 the aircraft were renamed as Avengers. Serving from the carriers HMS *Formidable*, *Illustrious*, *Indefatigable* and *Victorious*, the FAA Avengers played

an important role in the final stages of the Pacific War, their targets including Formosa and the Japanese home islands.

Inspired by the US Navy's lead, the Royal Navy began to mount large-scale carrier operations in the Pacific, introducing larger carrier groups equipped with more capable aircraft. By May 1945, Royal Navy carriers were able to field air groups consisting of Barracudas, Corsairs and Seafires, and with Allied aerial supremacy secured in the Pacific, commanders were able to assume the initiative in taking the war to Japan.

# United States
## 1939–45

**With the industrial capacity required to produce carriers in numbers, the US pioneered the carrier task force, outfitting vessels with carrier aircraft that would prove decisive in combat.**

A S THE UNITED States was thrust into World War II by the Japanese attack on Pearl Harbor, the US Navy's carrier air groups found themselves in the midst of a re-equipment process, as units made the transition to more modern equipment.

The Brewster F2A Buffalo that had been the US Navy's first carrier-borne monoplane fighter was giving way to the Grumman F4F Wildcat, while in the dive-bomber category, the Douglas SBD Dauntless was fast establishing itself in the ranks. Although a number of F2As saw operational service in the Pacific, the Buffalo quickly proved itself inferior to contemporary Japanese fighters, being deficient in terms of agility, overall weight and stability. Although phased out of fleet service by that time, the land-based Buffalo survived long enough in the US Marine Corps hands to see action in the Battle of Midway in June 1942.

Quick to appreciate the monoplane fighter, the very last of the Navy's biplane fighters were meanwhile disposed of in June 1941, when VF-5 retired its last F3F-3s. With this passing, the days of biplane fighters on US carriers ended for good.

### Wildcat genesis

Ordered in 1936, the Wildcat was first flown in XF4F-2 prototype form in September 1937, and although a monoplane was derived directly from Grumman's series of biplane naval fighters that had culminated in the F3F; indeed, the original XF4F-1 was to have been a biplane prototype, intended as an insurance should the F3A fail. Although it only offered a marginal increase in speed compared to the F2A-1 when in prototype XF4F-2 form, the production F4F would provide

| US NAVY CARRIER AIR GROUPS – BATTLE OF CORAL SEA | | | |
|---|---|---|---|
| 4–8 May 1942 | | | |
| Task Group 17.5 (Carrier Group) | | | |
| USS *Lexington* (CV-2) | | 'Lexington' class | |
| Lexington Air Group | | | |
| VF-2 | F4F-3/-3A Wildcat | 21 | Lt Cdr Paul H. Ramsey |
| VB-2 | SBD-2/3 Dauntless | 18 | Lt Cdr William L. Hamilton |
| VS-2 | SBD-3 Dauntless | 17 | Lt Cdr Robert E. Dixon |
| VT-2 | TBD-1 Devastator | 13 | Lt Cdr James H. Brett, Jr |
| | | | |
| USS *Yorktown* (CV-5) | | 'Yorktown' class | |
| Yorktown Air Group | | | |
| VF-42 | F4F-3 Wildcat | 18 | Lt Cdr Charles R. Fenton |
| VB-5 | SBD-3 Dauntless | 18 | Lt Wallace C. Short |
| VS-5 | SBD-3 Dauntless | 17 | Lt Cdr William O. Burch, Jr |
| VT-5 | TBD-1 Devastator | 13 | Lt Cdr Joe Taylor |

▲ An F4F-4 Wildcat from 'Fighting Forty-One' (VF-41) in early 1942. Established as VF-4, this unit received F4F-3s in late 1940, and was renamed VF-41 the following year. After combat during the invasion of North Africa, the squadron once again became VF-4.

## Specifications

Crew: 1

Powerplant: 1 x 895kW (1200hp) Pratt & Whitney R-1830-86 radial piston engine

Maximum speed: 528km/h (328mph)

Range: 1360km (845 miles)

Service ceiling: 12,000m (39,500ft)

Dimensions: span 11.58m (38ft 0in); length 8.76m (28ft 9in); height 2.81m (9ft 3in)

Weight: 3698kg (8125lb) loaded

Armament: Four 12.7 x 108mm (.50in) Browning machine guns

### ▼ Grumman F4F-3 Wildcat

*VF-7, NAS Norfolk, 1940*

Shown in service with VF-7, the second US Navy operator of the Wildcat, this F4F-3 was flown from NAS Norfolk, Virginia, in December 1940. The colour scheme includes national insignia worn on the forward fuselage in accordance with a March 1940 directive covering aircraft that were participating in the Neutrality Patrol, and a red lower cowling signifying assignment to VF-7's 1st Flight.

## Specifications

Crew: 1

Powerplant: 1 x 701kW (940hp) Wright R-1820-40 piston engine

Maximum speed: 516km/h (321mph)

Range: 2703km (1680 miles)

Service ceiling: 9100m (30,000ft)

Dimensions: span 10.7m (35ft); length 8.03m

(26ft 4in); height 3.68m (12ft 1in)

Weight: 2867kg (6321lb) loaded

Armament: Two 12.7mm (.50in) nose mounted M2 machine guns, two 12.7mm (.50in) wing-mounted M2 machine guns; two 45kg (100lb) underwing bomb load

942. The F2A-2 odifications included a otation gear. At the flying the F2A, but of this aircraft included n markings.

hter squadrons fic. Re-engined Whitney XR- KF4F-3 finally d was ordered ust 1939. The ghter paid off, on machine in veries followed by December that year, with the initial operators being VF-7 and VF-41. In 1941 a batch of aircraft

was completed with single-stage supercharged R-1830-90 engines, and these entered service as the F4F-3A. By 1942, production had switched to the F4F-4 that offered a six-gun armament, self-sealing tanks and manually folding wings, among other refinements, together with a small batch of a long-range unarmed reconnaissance derivative, the F4F-7.

The first examples of the F4F-4 entered service in November 1941, a month prior to the attack on Pearl Harbor. When General Motors began to build the F4F-4 under contract in summer 1942, this became

## Specifications

Crew: 2

Powerplant: 1 x 746kW (1000hp) Wright R-
1820-52 Cyclone piston engine

Maximum speed: 410km/h (255mph)

Range: 2165km (1345 miles)

Service ceiling: 8260m (27,100ft)

Dimensions: span 12.66m (41ft 6in); length

9.96m (38ft 8in); height 4.14m (13ft 7in)

Weight: 4717kg (10,400lb) loaded

Armament: Two 12.7 x 108mm (.50in) forward-
firing Browning M2 machine guns and two

7.62 x 63mm (.30in) flexible-mounted

Browning machine guns in rear cockpit

### ▼ Douglas SBD-3 Dauntless

**VS-41, USS Ranger, 1942**

This Dauntless was operated by 'Scouting Forty-One' aboard the USS *Ranger* during Operation Torch in November 1942. The SBD-3 version was introduced in March 1941 and featured additional fuel capacity (within self-sealing tanks), armour protection, a bulletproof windscreen and the Wright R-1820-52 engine. The SBD-3 also established the definitive gun armament of two forward-firing 12.7-mm (0.5-in) and two flexible-mounted 7.62mm (.3in) machine guns.

the FM-1, or the FM-2 when equipped with a more powerful Wright Cyclone engine. The F4F-4 version was in large-scale service at the time of the naval battles at Coral Sea, Midway and Guadalcanal, serving with distinction from the USS *Enterprise*, *Hornet* and *Saratoga*. In late 1942, US Navy Wildcats took part in the Allied invasion of North Africa, and the type remained the primary naval fighter until it was replaced by Hellcats in 1943.

By a process of refining the basic concept of the Wildcat, Grumman produced the F6F Hellcat, the most successful naval fighter of all time – based on aerial victories – and the aircraft that succeeded in wresting control of the air over the Pacific from the Japanese. Informed by combat experience with the F4F, a first prototype Hellcat, the XF6F-1, took to the air in June 1942. It was planned to test four different engine installations, but the urgency of the situation saw the most powerful, the Pratt & Whitney R-2800-27 specified, and the first prototype was re-flown in this form in July 1942. The F6F-3 production version of the fighter began to be delivered to VF-9 aboard USS *Essex* in January 1943. In August 1943 the Hellcat saw combat for the first time, in the hands of VF-5 from USS *Yorktown*. Night-fighter variants of the basic model were developed as the F6F-3E and the F6F-3N, with radar carried in an underwing pod.

### Fighter-bomber Hellcat

By mid-1944 production of the F6F-3 series had come to an end, but the Hellcat was now available for fighter-bomber missions, the latest F6F-5 variant adding provision for underwing stores and with optional cannon armament as well as a variety of aerodynamic improvements and water-injection for the powerplant. The F6F-5 began to be issued to service units in spring 1944. In combat, the Hellcat excelled during the Battle of the Philippine Sea, when no fewer than 15 US Navy carriers embarked 480 F6Fs as part of Task Force 58. Within a week of fighting, the Task Force had claimed destruction of over 400 Japanese aircraft and had sunk three carriers. Such was the rate of production – over 2500 examples completed in 1943 – that the F6F had succeeded in replacing the F4F with most units that same year. With an overall tally of 4947 enemy aircraft downed in US Navy and Marine Corps service, the Hellcat claimed around three-quarters of all wartime US air combat victories.

The Vought F4U Corsair that ultimately emerged as the most capable carrier fighter of World War II entered development in 1938 and was first flown in prototype form in May 1940, the aircraft combining a lightweight airframe with the powerful Pratt & Whitney Double Wasp engine. After receiving the production go-ahead in June 1941, the first series-built

F4U-1s began to be delivered to the Navy in July 1942. The bulk of early deliveries went to the US Marine Corps, however, and the Corsair flew its first combat mission from land bases, with VMF-124 employing the fighter over Bougainville in February 1943. In fact, early trials had demonstrated that the Corsair was ill suited to carrier operations, and required modifications to both its cockpit canopy and undercarriage. The optimized aircraft emerged as the F4U-1A, with the first operational Navy unit, VF-17, which had formed in April 1943, being the first to receive the revised version. In order to meet growing operator demands, additional Corsair production lines were established at Brewster and Goodyear, these producing the F3A-1 and the fixed-wing FG-1, respectively. While the F4U-1C added cannon armament, the 'D' model (built as the F4U-1D, F3A-1D and FG-1D) differed in its use of an R-2800-8W engine boosted by water-injection and could carry underwing bombs and rockets.

## Specifications

Crew: 1

Powerplant: 1 x 895kW (1200hp) Pratt & Whitney R-1830-76 radial piston engine

Maximum speed: 512km/h (318mph)

Range: 1464km (910 miles)

Service ceiling: 10,363m (34,000ft)

Dimensions: span 11.58m (38ft 0in); length 8.76m (28ft 9in); height 2.81m (9ft 3in)

Weight: 3607kg (7952lb) loaded

Armament: Six 12.7 x 108mm (.50in) M2 Browning machine guns; up to 90kg (200lb) bomb load

### ▲ Grumman F4F-4 Wildcat

**VGF-28, USS Suwannee, 1942**

This Wildcat wears markings associated with Operation Torch in November 1942, with the standard fighter scheme of non-specular blue/grey and light grey combined with prominent yellow surrounds to the national insignia on the fuselage and under the wings. For a decrease in ammunition capacity, the F4F-4 added two additional wing pylons, giving a total of six.

### ▼ Grumman TBF-1 Avenger

**VT-8, USS Hornet, 1942**

Illustrated is one of the first Avengers to enter service, assigned to VT-8 aboard USS Hornet. Avengers from this unit took part in the type's ill-starred combat debut at the Battle of Midway on 4 June 1942, when the aircraft flew from a land base on Midway Island and operated without fighter cover. The detachment lost five of its six aircraft during the battle, without inflicting any losses on enemy shipping.

## Specifications

Crew: 3

Powerplant: 1 x 1268kW (1700hp) Wright Cyclone 14-cylinder two-row radial engine

Maximum speed: 275km/h (442mph)

Range: 1610km (1000 miles)

Service ceiling: 9170m (30,100ft)

Dimensions: span 16.51m (54ft 2in); length 12.42m (40ft 9in); height 4.19m (13ft 9in)

Weight: 7876kg (17,364lb) loaded

Armament: One 7.62 x 51mm (.30in) nose mounted M1919 Browning machine gun (on early models); two 12.7 x 108mm (.50in) wing-mounted M2 Browning machine guns; one 12.7 x 108mm (.50in) dorsal-mounted M2 Browning machine gun; one 7.62 x 51mm (.30in) ventral-mounted M1919 Browning machine gun

The first US Navy Corsair operations were conducted in the Pacific from April 1944. Last of the major versions to see service in World War II was the F4U-2, a night-fighter that was employed by VFN-75 and VFN-101. By the end of the war in the Pacific the Corsair had, according to Navy records, assembled a kill:loss ratio of 11:1, claiming 2140 victories for only 189 losses of its own.

## Biplane survivor

Among the last of the biplane equipment that served the Navy was the Curtiss SBC-3 Helldiver, which survived in front-line service with VB-8 and VS-8 aboard the USS *Hornet* when America entered the war. There were still 69 examples of the SBC-3 remaining in operation with scouting squadrons into 1942, prior to replacement by the SBD Dauntless. Keenly aware of its limitations, the Navy kept the SBC-3 away from active combat. Similarly, operating from land bases, Vought SB2U-3 Vindicators

survived in service to see participation with the US Marine Corps at Midway, but their vulnerability to Japanese aircraft quickly sealed their withdrawal.

The Douglas SBD Dauntless made the carrier dive-bomber role its own, appearing in service in time for the US entry into the war. The SBD was a further development of the interwar Northrop BT-1, after Northrop was incorporated within the Douglas company; the prototype Dauntless, the XBT-2, was in fact based on a reworked BT-1. The SBD was ordered in April 1939, and production machines began to come off the line in 1940, these encompassing the SBD-1 model for the US Marine Corps and the SBD-2 version for the US Navy scout and bombing squadrons.

The initial Navy operating units had received their equipment by late 1941, VB-6 and VS-6 taking the SBD aboard the USS *Enterprise*, while VB-2 embarked in the USS *Lexington*. By the time of the attack on Pearl Harbor, the Navy had

## US NAVY CARRIER AIR GROUPS – MIDWAY AND ALEUTIANS

| Carrier Striking Force: Midway | | | |
|---|---|---|---|
| **Task Group 17.5 Carrier Group** | | | |
| USS *Yorktown* (CV-5) ('Yorktown' class) | | | |
| VS-5 | SBD-3 Dauntless | 19 | Lt Wallace Clark Short, Jr |
| VF-3 | F4F-3 Wildcat | 27 | Lt Cdr John Smith Thach |
| VB-3 | SBD-3 Dauntless | 18 | Lt Cdr Maxwell Franklin Leslie |
| VT-3 | TBD-1 Devastator | 15 | Lt Cdr Lance Edward Massey |
| **Task Group 16.5 Carrier Group** | | | |
| USS *Enterprise* (CV-6) ('Yorktown' class) | | | |
| Commander Air Group | SBD-3 Dauntless | 1 | Lt Cdr Clarence Wade McClusky Jr |
| VF-6 | F4F-3 Wildcat | 27 | Lt James Seton Gray Jr |
| VS-6 | SBD-3 Dauntless | 18 | Lt Wilmer Earl Gallaher |
| VB-6 | SBD-2/3 Dauntless | 18 | Lt Richard Halsey Best |
| VT-6 | TBD-1 Devastator | 14 | Lt Cdr Eugene Elbert Lindsey |
| USS *Hornet* (CV-8) ('Yorktown' class) | | | |
| Commander Air Group | SBD-3 Dauntless | 1 | Cdr Stanhope Cotton Ring |
| VF-8 | F4F-4 Wildcat | 27 | Lt Cdr Samuel G. Mitchell |
| VS-8 | SBD-3 Dauntless | 16 | Lt Cdr Walter Fred Rodee |
| VB-8 | SBD-3 Dauntless | 18 | Lt Cdr Robert Ruffin Johnson |
| VT-8 | TBD-1 Devastator | 15 | Lt Cdr John Charles Waldron |

## Specifications

Crew: 1

Powerplant: 1 x 1491kW (2000hp) Pratt &
Whitney R-2800-10W

Maximum speed: 611km/h (380mph)

Range: 1521km (945 miles)

Service ceiling: 11,368m (37,300ft)

Dimensions: span 13.0m (42ft 10in); length
10.2m (33ft 7in); height 3.9m (13ft 1in)

Weight: 6990kg (15,413lb) loaded

Armament: Six 7.62mm (.30in) M2 Browning
machine guns; two 298mm (11.75in) Tiny Tim
unguided rockets; one 910kg (2000lb) bomb or
one mk 13-3 torpedo; two 454kg (1000lb)
bombs or four 227kg (500lb) bombs or eight
113kg (250lb) bombs

### ▼ Grumman F6F-3 Hellcat

#### VF-27, USS Princeton, 1944

Armed with underwing High-Velocity Aircraft Rockets (HVARs) and bombs, this
Hellcat served with VF-27, which flew the type from the light carrier USS *Princeton*
between May and October 1944, including the campaign in the Marianas, gaining
134 combat victories in the process.

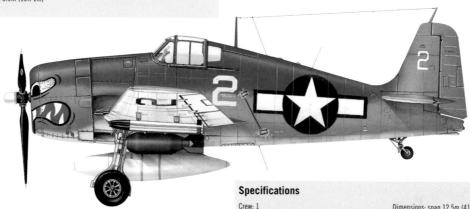

### ▼ Vought F4U-1A Corsair

#### VF-17, 1944

This famous Corsair was the mount of Lieutenant (Junior Grade) Ira C. 'Ike'
Kepford, the leading US Navy ace in the Pacific, who had scored his 16 aerial
victories by early 1944. VF-17 'Jolly Rogers' was the first Navy Corsair unit to go
into combat, and produced 15 aces. Although embarked for carrier training on
board USS *Bunker Hill* in September 1943, VF-17 mainly operated from land
bases, initially at Ondongo, northeast of Guadalcanal in the Solomons.

## Specifications

Crew: 1

Powerplant: 1 x 1678kW (2250hp) Pratt &
Whitney R-2800-8

Maximum speed: 671km/h (417mph)

Range: 1634km (1015 miles)

Service ceiling: 11,247m (36,900ft)

Dimensions: span 12.5m (41ft 0in); length
10.1m (33ft 4in); height 4.9m (16ft 1in)

Weight: 6349kg (14,000lb) loaded

Armament: Six 12.7 x 108mm (.50in) M3
Browning machine guns, 910kg (2000lb)
bomb load

introduced the improved SBD-3 with heavier gun
armament, additional armour protection, self-
sealing tanks and the R-1820-52 engine. Introduced
to the production line in March 1941, an impressive
total of 584 SBD-3s had been received by
December that year. The production standard for
1942 was the SBD-4 with revised electrical

provisions, and built at El Segundo, California,
while the Douglas facility at Tulsa, Oklahoma, built
the SBD-5 and SBD-6, these powered by the R-
1820-60 and -66 engines, respectively. The
Dauntless played a vital role in the naval actions at
Midway, Coral Sea and the Solomons, and its
importance to US Navy carrier air groups in the
Pacific cannot be overstated: the type was
responsible for sinking a greater tonnage of Japanese
shipping than any other aircraft. Reflecting the
excellence of the basic design, the SBD remained a
useful asset for both the US Navy and Marine Corps

## Specifications

Crew: 3

Powerplant: 1 x 1420kW (1900hp) Wright R-
2600-20

Maximum speed: 444km/h (276mph)

Range: 1626km (1010 miles)

Service ceiling: 9174m (30,100ft)

Dimensions: span 16.5m (54ft 2in); length
12.4m (40ft 11in); height 5.0m (16ft 5in)

Weight: 8115kg (17,893lb) loaded

Armament: One 7.62mm (.30in) nose-mounted
M1919 Browning machine gun; two 12.7mm
(.50in) wing-mounted M2 Browning machine
guns; one 12.7mm (.50in) dorsal-mounted
M2 Browning machine gun; up to eight 89mm
(3.5in) Forward Firing Aircraft Rockets or
127mm (5in) Forward Firing Aircraft Rockets;
up to 907kg (2000lb) of bombs or one 907kg
(2000lb) Mark 13 torpedo

### ▼ General Motors TBM-3 Avenger

**USS Ranger, 1945**

Part of the air group of USS *Ranger* in January 1945, this TBM was assigned to
Task Force 58. General Motors' Eastern Division had assumed responsibility for a
second Avenger production line in September 1942, building the TBM series. By
the time the production line had closed in June 1945, General Motors had
produced over 7500 Avengers for US and Royal Navy service.

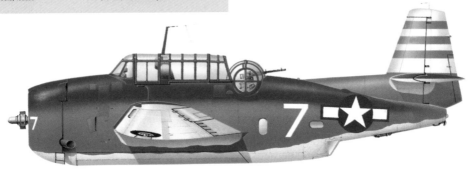

## Specifications

Crew: 2

Powerplant: 1 x 1417kW (1900hp) Wright R-
2600-20 Cyclone radial engine

Maximum speed: 475km/h (295mph)

Range: 1876km (1165 miles)

Service ceiling: 8870m (29,100ft)

Dimensions: span 15.17m (49ft 9in); length
11.18m (36ft 8in); height 4.01m (13ft 2in)

Weight: 4853kg (10,700lb) loaded

Armament: Four 12.7mm (.50in) guns mounted
in the wings, one 7.62mm (.30in) dorsal gun;
up to 1 x 907kg (2000lb) bomb

### ▼ Curtiss SB2C-1 Helldiver

**VB-8, USS Bunker Hill, 1944**

VB-8 was one of the first units to be equipped with the Helldiver, completing
carrier qualification with the SBD-5 before receiving its new equipment on the US
East Coast in July 1943. In March 1944 'Bombing Eight' took over from VB-17
aboard USS *Bunker Hill*, and remained with the carrier until October. It was a
costly cruise, however, with the unit losing 38 men, 35 of them in combat.

until late 1944, after which time it finally gave way
to the more modern SB2C Helldiver.

Continuing the tradition of Curtiss-built aircraft
named Helldiver, design of the SB2C dated back to
1938 and the aircraft was intended to undertake the
scout-bomber role, replacing the same company's
SBC Helldiver. The aircraft was first flown in
XSB2C-1 prototype form in December 1940. Large-

scale production had been authorized even before the
first prototype flew, although it was not until June
1942 that the first production aircraft was rolled out.

Although over 7000 examples were completed, to
make it the most prolific of all US Navy dive-
bombers, the SB2C did not enjoy a particularly good
reputation. The first Navy unit to equip with the
SB2C was VS-9 in December 1942, but development

## US NAVY CARRIER AIR GROUPS – BATTLE OF THE PHILIPPINE SEA

Task Force 58 (TF58)

### TF58.1

USS *Hornet* (CV-12) ('Essex' class)

| F6F Hellcat | 41 |
| SB2C Helldiver | 33 |
| TBF Avenger | 18 |

USS *Yorktown* (CV-10) ('Essex' class)

| F6F Hellcat | 46 |
| SB2C Helldiver | 40 |
| TBF Avenger | 17 |
| SBD Dauntless | 4 |

USS *Belleau Wood* (CVL-24) ('Independence' class)

| F6F Hellcat | 26 |
| TBF Avenger | 9 |

USS *Bataan* (CVL-29) ('Independence' class)

| F6F Hellcat | 24 |
| TBF Avenger | 9 |

### TF58.2

USS *Bunker Hill* (CV-17) ('Essex' class)

| F6F Hellcat | 42 |
| SB2C Helldiver | 33 |
| TBF Avenger | 18 |

USS *Wasp* (CV-18) ('Essex' class)

| F6F Hellcat | 39 |
| SB2C Helldiver | 32 |
| TBF Avenger | 18 |

USS *Cabot* (CVL-28) ('Independence' class)

| F6F Hellcat | 26 |
| TBF Avenger | 9 |

USS *Monterey* (CVL-26) ('Independence' class)

| F6F Hellcat | 21 |
| TBF Avenger | 8 |

### TF58.3

USS *Enterprise* (CV-6) ('Yorktown' class)

| F6F Hellcat | 31 |
| F4U Corsair | 3 |
| SBD Dauntless | 21 |
| TBF Avenger | 14 |

USS *Lexington* (CV-16) ('Essex' class)

| F6F Hellcat | 41 |
| SBD Dauntless | 34 |
| TBF Avenger | 18 |

USS *San Jacinto* (CVL-30) ('Independence' class)

| F6F Hellcat | 24 |
| TBF Avenger | 8 |

USS *Princeton* (CVL-23) ('Independence' class)

| F6F Hellcat | 24 |
| TBF Avenger | 9 |

### TF58.4

USS *Essex* (CV-9) ('Essex' class)

| F6F Hellcat | 42 |
| SB2C Helldiver | 36 |
| TBF Avenger | 20 |

USS *Langley* (CVL-27) ('Independence' class)

| F6F Hellcat | 23 |
| TBF Avenger | 9 |

USS *Cowpens* (CVL-25) ('Independence' class)

| F6F Hellcat | 23 |
| TBF Avenger | 9 |

continued and it was not until late 1943 that it was deemed ready for combat service. Helldivers gradually replaced the SBD through 1944, and saw widespread action across the Pacific theatre. The very first operation in which the SB2C took part was an attack on Rabaul on 11 November 1943 by VB-17.

The US Navy's first carrier-based monoplane, the Douglas TBD, emerged from a 1934 design competition that sought to field a torpedo-bomber to equip the forthcoming carrier USS *Ranger*, due to be commissioned that year, and other new carriers. The Douglas XTBD-1 prototype first flown in April 1935 saw off competition from a rival Great Lakes biplane, thereby firmly establishing the pre-eminence of the monoplane in US Navy service.

After successful Navy trials, the TBD-1 was ordered into production in February 1936, with deliveries beginning in June 1937. In October 1937 the first Navy unit re-equipped with the TBD-1, when examples were taken on charge by VT-3. In the following year VT-2, VT-5 and VT-6 were similarly equipped. The TBD remained in service until after Midway, this battle having demonstrated the type's

obsolescence when 35 were shot down by Zeroes and naval artillery in a confrontation on 4 June 1942.

## Ultimate torpedo-bomber

Designated replacement for the TBD was the Grumman TBF Avenger, which made its mark as the definitive US Navy torpedo-bomber of World War II. After development had been initiated in early 1940, the prototype XTBF-1 made a maiden flight in August 1941, by which time production orders had already been issued. The initial production aircraft was the TBF-1 that entered the Navy inventory in January 1942, and which initially served with VT-8, which received its first examples in May 1942. When first thrown into combat in the Battle of Midway, the TBF suffered heavy losses, five from six VT-8 aircraft launched at the height of the fighting on 4 June 1942 failing to return. These aircraft had been intended to go aboard USS *Hornet* to reinforce VT-8's TBD-1s, but in the event had been operated from Midway Island. Despite an inauspicious debut, the Navy remained convinced of the Avenger's capabilities, and in order to boost production capacity, General Motors began to build the Avenger as the TBM, beginning with the TBM-1, a direct equivalent to the TBF-1. Specialist versions fielded during the war included the TBF-1C with increased gun armament, the TBF-1D and -1E that were equipped with ASV radar, and the TBF-1L that carried a searchlight in the bomb bay. General Motors also built these derivatives, with equivalent designations in the TBM sequence. The ultimate versions were the TBM-3 series that appeared in April 1944. These introduced the R-2800-20 engine and were also produced in equivalent sub-variants.

### Specifications

Displacement: 27,100 tons standard, 36,380 tons full load

Length: 250m (820ft) waterline, 266m (872ft) overall

Beam: 28m (93ft) waterline, 45m (147ft 6in) overall

Draught: 8.66m (28ft 5in) light, 10.41m (34ft 2in) full load

Speed: 61km/h (33 knots)

Range: 37,000km (20,000nm) at 28 km/h (15 knots)

Aircraft: 90–100 aircraft

1 x deck-edge elevator

2 x centerline elevators

Armament: four x twin 127mm (5in) 38 calibre guns, four x single 127mm (5in) 38 calibre guns, eight x quadruple 40mm (1.57in) 56 calibre guns, 46 x single 20mm (0.78in) 78 calibre guns

Complement: 2600 officers and enlisted

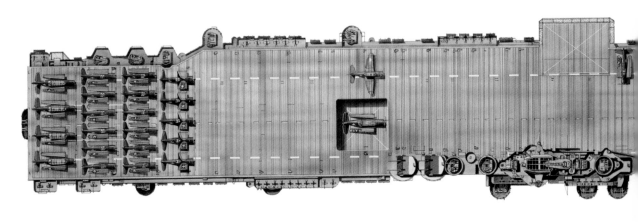

## Specifications

Crew: 2

Powerplant: 1 x 1417 kW (1900hp) Wright R-2600-20 Cyclone radial engine

Maximum speed: 295mph (475km/h)

Range: 1876km (1116 nautical miles)

Service ceiling: 8870m (29,100ft)

Dimensions: span 15.17m (49ft 9in); length 11.18m (36ft 8in); height 4.01m (13ft 2in)

Weight: 4794kg (10,547lb) empty

Armament: 2 x 20mm (.79in) cannon in the wings; 900kg (2000lb) of bombs or one Mark 13-2 torpedo

### ▼ Curtiss SB2C-3 Helldiver

*VB-3, USS Yorktown, 1945*

This Helldiver served with VB-3, arguably the premier US Navy bombing squadron of the war. The SB2C-3 was the second major production version, with a more powerful engine driving an improved four-blade Curtiss Electric propeller, and with other, detail refinements. A total of 1112 examples was built.

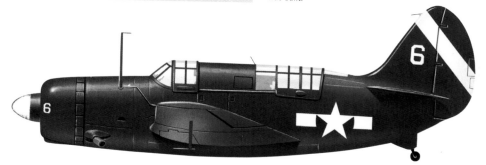

## Specifications

Crew: 1

Powerplant: 1 x 678kW (2250hp) Pratt & Whitney R-2800-8W radial engine

Maximum speed: 684km/h (425mph)

Range: 1633km (1015 miles)

Service ceiling: 11,200m (36,900ft)

Dimensions: span 12.5m (41ft); length 10.1m (33ft 4in); height 4.90m (16ft 1in)

Weight: 6300kg (14,000lb) loaded

Armament: 4 x 12.7mm (.50in) M2 Browning machine guns; 4 x 12.7mm (.50in) High Velocity Aircraft Rockets

### ▼ Vought F4U-1D Corsair

*USS Essex, 1945*

Serving aboard USS *Essex* in April 1945, this Corsair is armed with rockets for 'softening-up' attacks on Okinawa. The F4U-1B sub-variant was the first with hardpoints under the inner wings, these capable of mounting two 606-litre (160-US gal) drop tanks or 454kg (1000lb) bombs. The 'D' also featured water injection on its R-2800 engine, and was also built by Brewster and Goodyear.

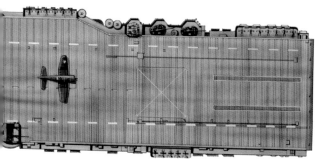

### ◀ USS *Intrepid*

The USS *Intrepid* (CV-11) is depicted as she appeared from June 1944, having been repaired and outfitted with additional anti-aircraft guns prior to returning to the Pacific. The *Intrepid* was the third ship in the 'Essex' class, the largest class of major warships ever built. In terms of aircraft complement, carriers of the 'Essex' class could accommodate a nominal air group of 82, but by 1945 it was common to embark as many as 108 aircraft of various types. Eleven 'Essex'-class vessels were ordered in 1940 and a further 13 carriers were completed during World War II, with an average of just 17.5 months required to build each vessel.

# Chapter 3

# The Cold War (1945–89)

While the major carrier powers of the victorious Allies would see their fleets contract in the years after 1945, the surplus of vessels meant that new operators could establish their own carrier capabilities. Carrier airpower was thrown into various Cold War conflicts, whether during the post-colonial wars that dogged former empires, or the battles fought between Eastern and Western power blocs in Korea and Vietnam. Meanwhile, the emergence of the nuclear missile submarine and the shift towards amphibious warfare saw the aircraft carrier adopt new roles, as dedicated anti-submarine and assault carriers, with air groups tailored to hunting and destroying underwater threats, or delivering amphibious troops to their objectives.

◀ **HMS *Ark Royal***

In the 1970s the Royal Navy's conventional carrier capability reached its height with the introduction of the Phantom, which provided fleet defence alongside Buccaneer strike aircraft. Both were fully committed to the support of NATO operations in the Atlantic and Mediterranean. Here HMS *Ark Royal* is seen off the coast of Florida during her final cruise in August 1978, with the Phantom FG.Mk 1s of No. 892 NAS.

# Argentina
## 1959–83

**With the aim of establishing itself as the leading military power in the region, Argentina introduced its first carrier in 1959, while a new carrier saw service in the Falklands War.**

THE ARGENTINE NAVY'S first aircraft carrier was the 'Colossus'-class ARA *Independencia* (previously HMS *Warrior* in Royal Navy service) that was commissioned in 1959. Initial equipment for the carrier included the Vought F4U-5 Corsair, received in 1956, and followed by deliveries of the Grumman F9F Panther. However, the jet fighter did not embark operationally in the carrier, and only one landing was made aboard the *Independencia*, in July 1963. The initial air wing therefore comprised F4Us and carrier-configured North American Texans, the latter used for training and light attack. In 1962 the Navy acquired a carrier-based anti-submarine capability, with receipt of six examples of the Grumman S-2A Tracker. In 1965 the Corsair was replaced by the North American T-28 Trojan, which took over the ground-attack role and served alongside the Texan.

Although the *Independencia* was equipped with a partially angled deck, the carrier was not deemed capable of embarking jet aircraft, and it was eventually paid off in 1970. The successor was ARA *25 de Mayo*, another 'Colossus'-class light fleet carrier, which had previously served as HMS *Venerable* and with the Netherlands as the *Karel Doorman*. By 1972 the Argentine Navy had inducted the Douglas A-4Q (upgraded A-4B) Skyhawk jet fighter-bomber and the Sikorsky S-61D Sea King anti-submarine warfare (ASW) helicopter.

### Fight for the Malvinas

Immediately prior to the outbreak of the Falklands (Malvinas) War in 1982, the air wing of the *25 de Mayo* consisted of A-4Qs tasked with air defence, ground-attack and anti-shipping strike, Trackers for submarine and surface vessel surveillance, and Sea Kings for ASW and transport duties. In addition, a single Alouette III was normally embarked in the carrier for plane-guard and liaison. The Dassault Super Étendard, 14 of which had been ordered as the ultimate replacement for the Skyhawk, had been introduced to service in 1981, but was not yet operating from the carrier. The original S-2As had by now given way to more capable S-2E Trackers, six of which were delivered in 1978.

As part of Task Force 20, *25 de Mayo* set sail for the Falkland Islands on 28 March 1982, just prior to the

---

### Specifications

Crew: 1

Powerplant: 1 x 34.7kN (7800lbf) J65-W-16A turbojet

Maximum speed: 1078km/h (670mph)

Range: 1480km (1000 miles)

Service ceiling: 14,935m (49,000ft)

Dimensions: span 8.38m (27ft 6in); length 12.22m (40ft 1.5in); height 4.66m (15ft 3in)

Weight: 12,437kg (27,420lb) loaded

Armament: Two 20mm (.78in) Mk 12 cannons; five external hardpoints with provisions for 2268kg (5000lb) of stores, including air-to-surface missiles, bombs, rocket-launcher pods, cannon pods, drop tanks and ECM pods

---

### ▼ Douglas A-4Q Skyhawk

*3a Escuadrilla Aeronaval de Caza y Ataque, Comandante Espora, 1972*

Acquired in 1970–71, the Argentine Navy Skyhawk fleet comprised 16 A-4Bs reworked as A-4Qs, and eight standard A-4Bs. When not embarked, the aircraft operated from Comandante Espora air base, near Buenos Aires. Following the Falklands War, a number of A-4Qs adopted this medium-grey scheme.

### ◄ 25 de Mayo

The deck of the *25 de Mayo* in the mid-1980s supported A-4Q Skyhawk and Super Étendard aircraft. Note the steam from the catapult, indicating that an aircraft has just left the flight deck.

Argentine assault. After covering the invasion and providing transport to Marines using its S-61s, the carrier returned to Argentina. Now under the flag of Task Force 79, the carrier prepared to face the British Task Force that was headed towards the Falklands. The British arrived on station on 30 April, and the following day both sides launched strikes. Initially, however, aircraft from *25 de Mayo* were not involved, but on 2 May, the carrier's Trackers were ordered to locate the British Task Force, while eight Skyhawks were readied for combat. Although one of the Trackers detected the Royal Navy's presence, it eventually lost contact with the ships, and with limited wind over the deck of their carrier, the A-4Qs were unable to launch. When a Royal Navy submarine sank the Argentine cruiser ARA *General Belgrano* later the same day, the High Command made the decision to withdraw *25 de Mayo* from the combat zone. Thereafter, the air wing continued to take part in the conflict, but was restricted to operations from land bases. With four out of five aircraft available, the Super Étendards flew five missions against the British Task Force, sinking HMS *Sheffield* and the MV *Atlantic Conveyor* on 4 May. Flying from Rio Grande, the eight A-4Qs that had been aboard the carrier carried out 39 attack missions between 21 May and 12 June, and were responsible for sinking HMS *Ardent*, for the loss of three of their own number. Another Skyhawk and pilot were lost after an unsuccessful ejection at Rio Grande. The Trackers that had been carrier-embarked operated from Rio Gallegos for the remainder of the war, establishing numerous contacts with British ships.

It was not until after the war that the Super Étendards embarked in *25 de Mayo* for the first time, going aboard in April 1983, by which time all 14 aircraft had been delivered.

### Specifications

Crew: 4

Powerplant: 2 x 1137kW (1525hp) Wright R-1820-82WA radial engines

Maximum speed: 450km/h (280mph)

Range: 2170km (1350 miles)

Service ceiling: 6700m (22,000ft)

Dimensions: span 22.12m (72ft 7in); length 13.26m (43ft 6in); height 5.33m (17ft 6in)

Weight: 10,630kg (23,435lb) loaded

Armament: 2200kg (4800lb) bomb payload; Mk 34, Mk 41, Mk 43 or Mk 44 torpedoes; Mk 54 depth charges

### ▼ Grumman S-2E Tracker

*Escuadrilla Aeronaval Antisubmarina, Comandante Espora, 1976*

After operating S-2As between 1969 and 1978, the *25 de Mayo* began to embark the S-2E version, which saw active service during the Beagle Channel Crisis with Chile and the Falklands War. This is the last of six S-2Es delivered.

2-AS-26

# Australia
## 1948–82

**The first carrier for the Royal Australian Navy was provided by the UK, and the 'Majestic'-class light fleet carrier HMAS _Sydney_ (the incomplete HMS _Terrible_) entered service in 1948.**

WITH ONE CARRIER in service, the RAN set about establishing two Carrier Air Groups, and selected British equipment in the form of the Hawker Sea Fury and Fairey Firefly, as well Supermarine Sea Otters for plane-guard and rescue. The initial 20th CAG was formed in the UK in August 1948, receiving two former FAA units, Nos 805 and 806 Squadrons, with Sea Furies and Fireflies, respectively.

In February 1949 aircraft were embarked for the first time in _Sydney_, and by 1950 a second air group had been established, as the 21st CAG (Nos 808 and 817 Squadrons, again with Sea Furies and Fireflies). With the war raging in Korea, the RAN sent _Sydney_ to relieve HMS _Glory_ on station in October 1951. In total, the carrier completed seven Korean War patrols, initially embarking an enlarged air group with one Firefly and two Sea Fury squadrons. A single Royal Navy or US Navy helicopter was normally embarked as a plane-guard.

Between August 1951 and January 1952, the _Sydney_ Air Group flew over 2300 operational sorties over Korea. Meanwhile, a second 'Majestic'-class carrier, HMAS _Melbourne_, was being completed with an angled deck, to allow operations by jet aircraft. With _Sydney_ in Korea, HMAS _Vengeance_ was loaned

| Royal Australian Navy air units, 1960 | |
|---|---|
| **Carrier-deployable units** | |
| _Melbourne_ Air Group | |
| 805 Squadron | Sea Venom FAW.Mk 53 |
| 816 Squadron | Gannet AS.Mk 1 |
| **Shore-based units**  RANAS Nowra | |
| 723 Squadron | Firefly Mk 5/6, Sycamore HR.Mk 50/51, Auster |
| 724 Squadron | Sea Venom FAW.Mk 53 |
| 725 Squadron | Sea Fury FB.Mk 11, Gannet AS.Mk 1/T.Mk 2, Auster, Dakota |

▲ **Hawker Sea Fury FB.Mk 11**

_No. 724 Squadron, RANAS Nowra, 1955–56_

Resplendent in a non-standard midnight blue scheme applied for display flying in the late 1950s, this Sea Fury was operated by No. 724 Squadron, which operated from Nowra as a second-line formation between 1955–56. In total, the RAN put no fewer than 99 Sea Furies into service between 1948 and 1962.

**Specifications**

Crew: 1

Powerplant: 1 x 1850kW (2480hp) Bristol Centaurus XVIIC 18-cylinder twin-row radial engine

Maximum speed: 740km/h (460mph)

Range: 1127km (700 miles)

Service ceiling: 10,900m (35,800ft)

Dimensions: span 11.7m (38ft 4.75in); length 10.6m (34ft 8in); height 4.9m (16ft 1in)

Weight: 5670kg (12,500lb) loaded

Armament: Four 20mm (.79in) Hispano Mk V cannon; twelve 76.2mm (3in) rockets; 907kg (2000lb) bomb load

## Specifications

Crew: 1

Powerplant: 1 x 41kN (9,300lbf) Pratt & Whitney J52-P8A engine

Maximum speed: 1078km/h (670mph)

Range: 1480km (920 miles)

Service ceiling: 12,192m (40,000ft)

Dimensions: span 8.41m (27ft 6in); length 13.41m (44ft 0in); height 4.57m (15ft)

Weight: 11,113kg (24,500lb) loaded

Armament: Two 20mm (.79in) Colt Mk 12 cannon; Four 127mm (5in) Mk 23 Zuni rockets; Four air-to-air AIM-9 Sidewinder missiles; air-to-surface missiles including AGM-12 Bullpup, AGM-45 Shrike anti-radar missiles

### ▼ Douglas A-4G Skyhawk

**VF805, HMAS Melbourne, 1977**

Wearing the squadron badge and the chequered tail markings of VF805, this A-4G was operated by the single operational squadron established on the Skyhawk. No. 805 Squadron became VF805 from 1969, while the fleet support and training unit was No. 724 Squadron (later designated VC724).

by the Royal Navy, filling the intervening carrier gap within the RAN.

HMAS *Melbourne* was finally commissioned in 1955, and its air group was based around the de Havilland Sea Venom FAW.Mk 53 fighter and the Fairey Gannet AS.Mk 1 anti-submarine aircraft.

HMAS *Sydney* was paid off into the reserve in 1958. Two years later, however, the government decided to convert the Fleet Air Arm to an all-rotary-wing organization. *Melbourne* was due to become a helicopter carrier, embarking Westland Wessex Mk 31As tasked with anti-submarine warfare, which had been acquired in 1962.

### New fixed-wing equipment

Increasing tensions in Southeast Asia in 1963 saw a reversal of policy. The original decision saw the disbandment of the front-line Sea Venom squadron, but now examples of this type would remain attached to the front-line Gannet squadron until 1967. New fixed-wing equipment was ordered by the RAN in 1964, with a contract signed for Grumman S-2E Tracker ASW aircraft, followed by an order for Douglas A-4G Skyhawks the following year. The A-4G model, of which eight were ordered, was similar to the A-4F. The eight single-seaters were supported by two TA-4G two-seat trainers, while follow-on orders were placed in 1970 for a similar batch of eight ex-US Navy A-4Fs and

TA-4Fs – these were similarly converted to A-4G/TA-4G standard.

*Sydney* remained in service at this time, primarily as a troop carrier, a role in which it served during the Vietnam War. The earlier carrier also embarked a flight of Wessex helicopters for ASW protection. *Sydney* was finally decommissioned in 1973.

The *Melbourne* was refitted in time to begin its first cruise with the revised air group in 1969. In 1976 a new ASW helicopter was acquired in the form of the Westland Sea King Mk 50. In 1976, orders were placed for an additional 16 S-2Gs, after a

| Royal Australian Navy air units, 1970 | | |
|---|---|---|
| **Carrier-deployable units** | | |
| *Melbourne* Air Group | | |
| VF805 | A-4G Skyhawk | |
| VS816 | S-2E Tracker | |
| HS817 | Sea King Mk 50 | |
| **Shore-based units** | RANAS Nowra | |
| HT723 | Scout AH.Mk 1, UH-1B Iroquois | |
| VC724 | TA/A-4G Skyhawk, Sea Vampire T.Mk 22, Sea Venom FAW.Mk 53/TT.Mk 53, Dakota | |
| HT725 | Wessex Mk 31 | |
| VC851 | S-2E Tracker, HS748, Dakota | |

## Specifications

Crew: 2–4

Powerplant: 2 x 1238kW (1660hp) Rolls-Royce
Gnome H 1400 turbshaft engines

Maximum speed: 230km/h (143mph)

Range: 1229km (764 miles)

Service ceiling: 4480m (14,700ft)

Dimensions: Rotor diameter 18.9m (62ft 0in);
length 17.04m (55ft 9in); height 5.21m (17ft
1in)

Weight: 9525kg (21,000lb) loaded

Armament: Four Mk 44, Mk 46 or Sting Ray
torpedos, or four depth charges

### ▼ Westland Sea King Mk 50

**HS817, RANAS Nowra, 1980**

Shore-based at RANAS Nowra, New South Wales, this is one of the RAN's Sea King Mk 50s that began to be received in 1976 and undertook the anti-submarine role. The Sea King superseded the Wessex in this capacity, although examples of the latter survived in use for carrier-based search and rescue.

number of the original batch of S-2Es had been destroyed in a hangar fire. Skyhawks continued to operate from *Melbourne* until 1979, when problems with the carrier's arrester wires and catapult saw A-4 operations restricted to land bases. The carrier entered

### ▼ HMAS *Melbourne*

Flagship of the Royal Australian Navy, HMAS *Melbourne* is seen entering Pearl Harbor in June 1958. The air group at this time comprised 27 aircraft including Sea Venom fighters and Gannet anti-submarine aircraft.

refit in 1980, before being decommissioned in 1982. As replacement, the RAN hoped to receive the Royal Navy's HMS *Invincible*, although the Falklands War saw this offer retracted.

Instead, *Melbourne* looked set to return to service, before a change of government in Australia announced an end to carrier operations. As a result, the carrier was decommissioned for good, and RAN fixed-wing aircraft operations came to an end in June 1984, with the retirement of the A-4s and S-2s.

# Brazil
## 1956–96

**After taking on the former Royal Navy and RAN carrier *Vengeance*, Brazil established a carrier air group that included both Air Force (fixed-wing) and Navy (rotary-wing) components.**

BRAZIL'S FIRST CARRIER was the former HMAS *Vengeance*, which became surplus to RAN requirements when HMAS *Melbourne* became available. The former HMAS *Vengeance* (previously HMS *Vengeance*) was duly returned to the UK, and the 'Colossus'-class carrier was then sold to Brazil in 1956. In Brazilian Navy service, the carrier was named Navio Aeródromo Ligeiro (Light Aircraft Carrier, NAeL) *Minas Gerais* (A-11). After modernization in the Netherlands, the vessel arrived in Rio de Janeiro in 1960.

The first equipment for the air group of the *Minas Gerais* was provided by the Dutch, with the carrier sailing to Brazil with three TBM-3 Avengers on board. In the event, these aircraft remained land-based, while the Brazilian Air Force (Força Aérea Brasileira, FAB) prepared to form operational units to embark on the new carrier. At the time of the carrier's acquisition, all military aircraft were operated by Brazil's air force, rather than the Navy.

This situation began to change once the carrier had arrived. The Navy duly established its first operational unit equipped with fixed-wing aircraft, when 1° Esquadrão de Aviões Anti-Submarino (1st Anti-Submarine Squadron) was equipped with North American T-28 Trojans in 1963. This unit was subsequently renamed as 1° Esquadrão Mixto de Aviões Anti-Submarino e de Ataque (1st Mixed Anti-Submarine and Attack Squadron). The six Trojans were supplied by the US, but saw only brief service until the decision was made to prohibit the Navy from operating fixed-wing types. When embarked in the *Minas Gerais*, the T-28s were primarily used for pilot training. The Brazilian Navy eventually acquired further examples of the Trojan from French stocks, although these never made it into service.

### Inter-service rivalry

While the Navy attempted to add to its first six Trojans, the FAB became increasingly hostile to the developing situation. As early as 1957, the Navy had made efforts to create another operational, carrier-

### Specifications

Crew: 4

Powerplant: 2 x 1121kW (1525hp) Wright R-1820-82WA

Maximum speed: 404km/h (251mph)

Range: 1481km (920 miles)

Service ceiling: 6126m (21,100ft)

Dimensions: span 22.1m (72ft 7in); length 13.2m (43ft 6in); height 5.0m (16ft 7in)

Weight: 12,184kg (26,867lb) loaded

Armament: 2200kg (4800lb) bomb payload, provision for Mk 41, 43, 34 and 44 torpedoes, or Mk 54 depth charges and naval mines

### ▼ Grumman S-2E Tracker
#### *1° GAE 'Cardeal', Santa Cruz*

In Brazilian service from 1961, the S-2E received the local designation P-16E. Uniquely, the Tracker was operated on board the *Minas Gerais* by the Brazilian Air Force and the aircraft were shore-based at Santa Cruz. The 21 aircraft procured included 13 S-2As and eight S-2Es.

The first crews trained on the type with the US Navy at Key West, Florida.

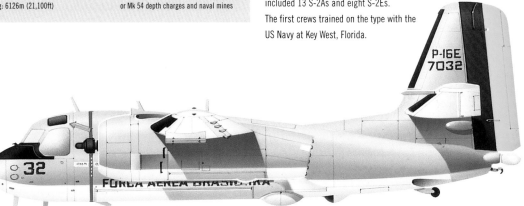

## Specifications

Crew: 2

Powerplant: 1 x 559kW (750hp) Alvis Leonides
Major 755 14-cylinder two-row radial engine

Maximum speed: 175km/h (109mph)

Range: 534km (334 miles)

Service ceiling: 3960m (13,000ft)

Dimensions: Rotor diameter 16.15m (53ft 0in);
length 12.72m (41ft 8.5in); height 4.76m
(15ft 7in)

Weight: 3538kg (7800lb) loaded

Armament: 1 x Mark 30 or Mark 44 torpedo or
depth charges

### ▼ Westland Whirlwind Series 3

*HU-1, 1967*

Brazil's first Whirlwind Series 1 helicopters were brought to Brazil aboard the *Minas Gerais*, arriving in Brazil in January 1961. These were joined by another two examples acquired from a Canadian civil operator. Two surviving helicopters were sent to Westland in 1966–68 to be converted to Series 3 standard, including this aircraft, serial number N-7027. In 1966 another five new-build Series 3 aircraft were also acquired.

embarked unit, under 1° Grupo de Aviação Embarcada (1st Carrier Air Group). In 1961, the unit began to receive the Grumman S-2A/E Tracker for anti-submarine work. A total of 21 ex-US Navy Trackers was acquired, comprising 13 S-2As and eight of the improved S-2Es, although all served under the local designation P-16. The S-2E represented the definitive production configuration for the Tracker, with a new tactical navigation suite.

After crews were trained in the US, 1° GAE was established with the type at Santa Cruz, operating in the ASW and reconnaissance roles. Santa Cruz was equipped with its own dummy deck for carrier practice, and when embarked in the *Minas Gerais*, the Trackers typically operated as detachments of four or five aircraft.

In 1965 the situation was resolved, with a government edict stating that all fixed-wing aircraft would in future be operated by the FAB. The Navy, meanwhile, could still operate helicopters, and the

## Brazilian Navy/Air Force carrier air units

Carrier-deployable units, 1963–70

| Força Aérea Naval | ForAeNav |
|---|---|
| 1° Grupo de Aviação Embarcada (1st Carrier Air Group) | |
| 1° Esquadrão de Aviões Anti-Submarino (1st Anti-Submarine Squadron)* | Avenger, T-28 Trojan, S-2A/E Tracker |
| * renamed as 1° Esquadrão Mixto de Aviões Anti-Submarino e de Ataque (1st Mixed Anti-Submarine and Attack Squadron) | |
| 1° Esquadrão de Helicópteros Anti-Submarinos (1st Squadron of Anti-submarine Helicopters, HS-1) | SH-34J Seabat, SH-3A Sea King |
| 1° Esquadrão de Helicópteros de Instrução (1st Helicopter Training Squadron, HI-1) | Bell 47, Hughes 269 |
| 1° Esquadrão de Helicópteros de Emprego Geral (1st Utility Helicopter Squadron, HU-1) | Widgeon, Bell 47G/J, Whirlwind/S-55C, Wasp, Hiller FH-1100 |
| **Força Aérea Brasileira** | FAB |
| 1° Grupo de Aviação Embarcada (1st Carrier Air Group) | S-2A/E Tracker |

## Specifications

Crew: 4

Powerplant: 2 x 1040kW (1400hp) General
Electric T58-GE-10 turboshaft engines

Maximum speed: 267km/h (166mph)

Range: 1000km (621 miles)

Service ceiling: 4481m (14,700ft)

Dimensions: Rotor diameter 19m (62ft 0in);
length 16.7m (54ft 9in); height 5.13m (16ft
10in)

Weight: 8449kg (18,626lb) loaded

Armament: 2 x Mk 46 torpedoes

### ▼ Sikorsky S-61D-3 Sea King

*HS-1, São Pedro da Aldeia, 1977*

In 1970, HS-1 (1° Esquadrão de Helicópteros Anti-Submarinos) began to replace its SH-34J Seabat ASW helicopters with the first Brazilian Navy Sea Kings. The initial deliveries comprised six Sikorsky-built S-61D-3s, with serial numbers from N-3007 to N-3012. After two helicopters were written off, four survivors were then upgraded to ASH-3D standard by Agusta in Italy.

*Minas Gerais* therefore went to sea with a joint-force air group. The former Navy Trackers were integrated within FAB structure, remaining with 1° GAE. One Tracker was upgraded to P-16H standard featuring an improved mission avionics suite and Pratt & Whitney PT6A-67-CF turboprops, with a view to installing this equipment fleet-wide. Although test-flown in 1990, the P-16H modifications were not adopted for service. The FAB remained responsible for Tracker operations until 1996, when the type was finally retired, leaving the *Minas Gerais* with helicopter equipment only.

## First-generation helicopters

The Navy's first helicopter equipment comprised two Westland Widgeon 2s received in 1958, although these did not go to sea with the *Minas Gerais*. The first helicopter to regularly embark in the carrier was the Westland Whirlwind, the first five of which served with HU-1 between 1961 and 1968. In the late 1960s five new turbine-powered Whirlwind Series 3s were purchased, and two of the earlier Series 2 helicopters were upgraded to the same standard. The primary roles of the carrier-based Whirlwind were search and rescue and transport.

The Whirlwind was joined in 1965 by six examples of the Sikorsky SH-34J Seabat, provided under the Mutual Defense Assistance Programme (MDAP), and which remained the primary ASW

helicopter in Brazilian service until 1975, the aircraft being passed to the Navy after operating within the FAB's 1° GAE. Replacement for the Seabat in the carrier-based ASW role was the Sea King, which began to arrive in service in 1970. The first of the Brazilian Navy Sea Kings were six Sikorsky S-61D-3s, equivalent to the US Navy SH-3D and delivered between 1970 and 1972. Four Italian-built Agusta-Sikorsky AS-61D-3s and two ex-US Navy SH-3Ds (provided as spares) supplemented these initial deliveries. Four surviving S-61D-3 aircraft were upgraded by Agusta in Italy in 1984, becoming ASH-3Ds in the process, and broadly equivalent to the US Navy's SH-3H then in service.

Ten Westland Wasps were acquired by the Navy from 1965. Although mainly operated from smaller warships, from 1977 they were in service with HU-1 and their work included detachments aboard *Minas Gerais*, when they were used for general-purpose duties until replaced by the Helibras Esquilo.

The Navy's primary land-based facility for helicopter operations was, and remains, São Pedro da Aldeia in the state of Rio de Janeiro. This base was home to, among others, the SH-34Js and the Sea Kings of HS-1, together with HU-1, responsible for operating the Wasp and the Whirlwind. Also at the base was training squadron HI-1, and HA-1, the latter established in 1978 to provide Westland Lynx helicopter detachments for smaller warships.

# Canada
## 1946–70

**During World War II the Royal Canadian Navy had jointly operated two escort carriers with the Royal Navy, although aircrew and aircraft were the responsibility of the British.**

POST-WAR CANADA RECEIVED two light fleet carriers, HMS *Warrior* and *Magnificent*, from the UK. The 'Colossus'-class HMCS *Warrior* duly entered service in 1946, remaining in use until 1948, when it was superseded by the 'Majestic'-class HMCS *Magnificent*. Both these carriers employed air groups based around the Sea Fury fighter and the Avenger anti-submarine aircraft.

The RCN operated a total of 74 Sea Furies from 1948, with deliveries continuing until 1953. The initial operator was 803 Squadron, later renumbered as 870 Squadron and finally being designated as VF 870, under the US Navy-style unit names system. The final examples were retired in 1956.

The RCN Avengers were ex-Royal Navy TBM-3Es, the first of which were taken on charge in 1950,

| Typical Royal Canadian Navy carrier air group, mid-1960s | | |
|---|---|---|
| *Bonaventure* air wing, 1965 | | |
| VS 880 | CS2F-3 Tracker | 12 |
| HS 50 | CHSS-2 Sea King | 6 |
| HU 21 | HO4S-3 | 1 |
| VU 32 | CS2F Tracker (COD) | 1 |

the initial 75 aircraft being modified by Fairey Aviation as Avenger A.S. 3 Mk 1s. In addition to the primary ASW role, a total of eight Avengers were operated for airborne early warning (AEW), these being the Avenger 3W2 variant with AN/APS-20 search radar.

With a further 50 Avengers ordered in 1952, the RCN eventually possessed a total of 125, making it the third largest operator of the type. A number of improvements produced the Avenger A.S. 3M Mk 1,

▼ **Magestic class**
Grumman Avengers sit on the deck of HMCS *Magnificient*, a 'Majestic' class aircraft carrier, somewhere in the North Atlantic, 1952.

▲ **de Havilland Canada (Grumman) CS2F Tracker**
The Tracker ASW aircraft was licence-built by de Havilland Canada, which completed 99 aircraft – these being joined by a single Grumman-built machine and one aircraft briefly loaned from the US Navy. Displaying the wing fold to advantage, these aircraft are being prepared for launch from the HMCS *Bonaventure*.

while the final incarnation was the A.S. 3M Mk 2, of which just two were completed.

## A new carrier

In 1957, HMCS *Magnificent* was returned to the UK, and its place taken by HMCS *Bonaventure*, an unfinished 'Majestic'-class ship that was modernized and fitted with an angled deck. The new carrier introduced new aircraft equipment, and the Sea Fury and Avenger were replaced by the McDonnell F2H Banshee and Grumman Tracker, respectively.

Ordered in 1952, the F2H enjoyed only a brief carrier with the RCN, and was retired in 1962, without replacement. A total of 39 ex-US Navy F2H-3 versions were procured, with deliveries between 1955 and 1958, and these saw service with VF 870 and VF 871, operating from Shearwater naval air station when not embarked in *Bonaventure*. The RCN's only jet equipment, the Banshee could be armed with AIM-9 Sidewinder air-to-air missiles and was also assigned to the NORAD defence network. The Tracker was licence-built by de Havilland Canada

as the CS2F and a total of 100 examples were eventually acquired, beginning with the CS2F-1 in 1957, the aircraft first embarking in *Bonaventure* in early 1959, with VS 880. From 1960 the CS2F-2 began to be introduced, with improved magnetic anomaly detection (MAD) gear. By 1966 the survivors had been modified to the definitive CS2F-3 standard, with Julie and Jezebel ASW systems, Doppler radar and a new tactical navigation suite.

The fixed-wing Tracker remained in use, although from 1964 it was joined in the ASW role by the CHSS-2 Sea King, 41 of which were acquired. By the mid-1960s, the typical *Bonaventure* air group consisted of 12 Trackers, six Sea Kings, a single Sikorsky HO4S-3 for plane-guard duties, and one Tracker equipped for carrier onboard delivery.

In 1964 the Canadian armed forces began the process of unification, and despite cutbacks the *Bonaventure* was refitted, and remained in commission until 1970. After unification both the Trackers (becoming CP-121s) and Sea Kings (now as CH-124s) continued in service.

# France
## 1946–60

**After establishing a carrier arm shortly after the end of World War II, the French Navy would find itself deploying carrier aircraft in combat on a number of occasions during the 1950s.**

THE FIRST TRUE French aircraft carrier was provided by the UK, the former HMS *Biter*, an escort carrier, entering Marine Nationale service as the *Dixmude* in 1945. In 1946 a second carrier was accepted, with the former HMS *Colossus* being commissioned as *Arromanches*. Together with the ships, the UK provided Supermarine Seafire Mk III fighters to form their initial aircraft component. By 1946, the first four carrier aviation units had been established, equipped with the Seafire, Dauntless dive-bomber (two squadrons) and one training unit operating both types. Shore-based at Hyères, they were joined by an additional Seafire unit in 1948.

The carrier *Dixmude* was first to see combat duty during the French war in Indochina, sailing to the region in 1947, with Dauntless dive-bombers embarked, although these chiefly operated from shore bases when in theatre. Between 1948–49 the *Arromanches* operated in Indochina, with an air group of Seafires and Dauntless, the latter seeing considerable service in the ground-attack role.

Although more capable Seafire Mk 15s were provided in 1949, they were too few in number to equip front-line units. New equipment was urgently required by the early 1950s, and when *Arromanches* next operated in Indochina, between 1951–53, it was with an air group comprising Aéronavale F6F-5 Hellcats and SB2C-5 Helldivers, which saw much action in the close support role. On its return to France in 1953, the *Arromanches* left its air group to operate from land bases. A new carrier, *La Fayette*, arrived on station to relieve *Arromanches*, this being the former US Navy light fleet carrier USS *Langley* (CVL-27). Again, Hellcats and Helldivers were embarked. By the time of the decisive battle at Dien Bien Phu in 1954, the *Arromanches* was on station to provide support using its Hellcats and Helldivers, which sustained heavy losses in the process. Towards the end of this operation the Aéronavale introduced the Corsair, these operating from land bases. The carrier *Bois Belleau* (the former USS *Belleau Wood*, CVL-24) relieved *Arromanches* in May 1954, but

### Specifications

Crew: 1

Powerplant: 1 x 1491kW (2000hp) Pratt & Whitney R-2800-10W 'Double Wasp' two-row radial engine with a two-speed two-stage supercharger

Maximum speed: 610km/h (380mph)

Range: 1520km (945 miles)

Service ceiling: 11,370m (37,300ft)

Dimensions: span 13.06m (42ft 10in); length 10.24m (33ft 7in); height 3.99m (13ft 1in)

Weight: 5714kg (12,598lb) loaded

Armament: Either six 12.7mm (.50in) M2 Browning machine guns, or two 20mm (.79in) cannons and four 12.7mm (.50in) Browning machine guns

▼ **Grumman F6F-5 Hellcat**

*Escadrille 1F, Arromanches, 1954*

France received a total of 124 F6F-5s and 15 F6F-5N night-fighters, although five of the latter were later converted to day-fighter standard. Escadrille 1F (later named Flottille 11F) was the first operator of the type, converting to the Hellcat in March 1950. Later in the same year Flottille 12F similarly re-equipped and both units were shore-based at Hyères. Flottille 11F embarked in *Arromanches* in August 1951 for deployment to Indochina.

reinforcements were not enough to prevent a French surrender at Dien Bien Phu.

## Opération Mousequetaire

French carrier aviation was again in combat during the Suez campaign of October–November 1956. Under Opération Mousequetaire, *Arromanches* and *La Fayette* were on station with Corsairs, TBM Avengers and Piasecki HUP-2 Retriever plane-guard and search and rescue helicopters. The Aéronavale was a major employer of the Avenger, with deliveries encompassing TBM-3E, TMB-3S/3S2, TBM-3U and TBM-3W2 variants. During the Suez action, embarked Avengers included hunter-killer teams of TBM-3W2 and TMB-3S aircraft that were employed against Egyptian naval vessels. Corsairs, meanwhile, were employed in attacks against Egyptian airfields and shipping, as well as providing close support to the Allied troops before the operation ended.

The next conflict in which Aéronavale carrier aircraft found themselves employed was in Algeria. Beginning in 1956, Corsairs were stationed in Algeria to support ground forces, together with Sud-Est Aquilons, representing the French Navy's first jet fighters. The Aquilon was a licence-built version of the de Havilland Sea Venom, and was produced in both single- and two-seat forms, latterly with American AN/APQ-605 radar and Nord 5103 guided missiles. TBM-3E Avengers also operated

| French Navy carrier air units | | |
|---|---|---|
| Carrier-deployable units, 1961 | | |
| Flottille 4F | Alizé | Hyères |
| Flottille 6F | Alizé | Hyères |
| Flottille 9F | Alizé | Hyères |
| Flottille 11F | Aquilon | Karouba |
| Flottille 12F | Corsair | Karouba |
| Flottille 14F | Corsair | Hyères |
| Flottille 15F | Corsair | Hyères |
| Flottille 16F | Aquilon | Hyères |
| Flottille 17F | Corsair | Karouba |
| Flottille 31F | HSS-1 | Lartigue |
| Flottille 32F | HSS-1 | Lartigue |
| Flottille 33F | HSS-1 | Lartigue |
| Escadrille 10S | various types | Saint-Raphaël |
| Escadrille 20S | various helicopter types | Saint-Raphaël |
| Escadrille 23S | HUP-2, Alouette II | Saint-Mandrier |
| Escadrille 56S | Alizé | Lann-Bihoué |
| Escadrille 57S | Zéphyr | Port-Lyautey |
| Escadrille 59S | Zéphyr, Aquilon | Hyères |

from shore bases, in a maritime patrol capacity. Algeria was the first conflict in which concerted combat use was made of helicopters, and the

### Specifications

Crew: 1

Powerplant: 1 x 1715kW (2300hp) Pratt & Whitney R-2800-43W radial piston engine

Maximum speed: 708km/h (440mph)

Range: 1802km (1120 miles)

Service ceiling: 11,308m (41,500ft)

Dimensions: span 12.5m (41ft 0in); length 10.1m (33ft 4in); height 4.5m (14ft 9in)

Weight: 8798kg (19,398lb) loaded

Armament: Four 20mm (.79in) M3 cannons; up to 2268kg (5000lb) bombs or rockets

### ▽ Vought F4U-7 Corsair

*Flottille 12F, Algeria*

The F4U-7 version of the Corsair was designed to a French requirement, combining the airframe of the post-war AU-1 with the powerplant of the earlier F4U-4. A first prototype took to the air in July 1952, and a total of 94 aircraft were completed. France supplemented these aircraft with 24 AU-1s delivered by the US Navy as a stopgap measure, and eventually received a further 66 examples.

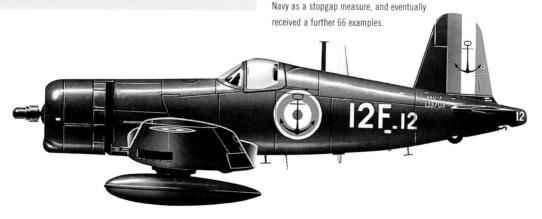

## Specifications

Crew: 2

Powerplant: 1 x 1417kW (1900hp) Wright
R-2600-20 engine

Maximum speed: 439km/h (272mph)

Range: 1819km (1130 miles)

Service ceiling: 7090m (23,261ft)

Dimensions: span 16.51m (54ft 3in); length

12.19m (39ft 10in); height 5.00m (16ft 4in)

Weight: 8286kg (18,267lb) loaded

Armament: Wing and tail mounted 7.7mm
(.303in) Browning machine guns; 89mm
(3.5in) or 127mm (5in) forward firing rockets,
up to 907kg (2000lb) bomb load or one 907kg
(2000lb) Mark 13 torpedo

### ▼ Curtiss SB2C-5 Helldiver

*Flottille 3F, Arromanches, 1954*

This Helldiver is depicted as it appeared during Indochina operations in 1954. The replacement for the Dauntless in French Navy service, the first batch of 54 SB2C-5s was delivered between 1949 and 1950, with follow-on deliveries in 1952 (44 aircraft) and 1955 (10). The initial operators were Flottilles 3F and 4F, which embarked in the carriers *Arromanches* and *Bois Belleau*. The aircraft of 4F were later handed over to a third unit, Flottille 9F.

## Specifications

Crew: 1

Powerplant: 1 x 23.4kN (5150lbf) de Havilland
Ghost 48 turbojet

Maximum speed: 1030km/h (640mph)

Range: with drop tanks 1730km (1075 miles)

Service ceiling: 14,630m (48,000ft)

Dimensions: span 12.7m (41ft 8in); length
10.38m (32ft 4in); height 1.88m (6ft 2in)

Weight: 6945kg (15,310lb) loaded

Armament: Four 20mm (.79in) Hispano 404
cannons; two wing pylons for Nord
5103(AA.20) air-to-air missiles

### ▼ Sud-Est Aquilon 203

*Escadrille 59S*

A single-seat derivative of the two-seat Aquilon 202, the Aquilon 203 was equipped with an American AN/APQ-65 radar. From late 1958 it received missile armament, in the form of the Nord 5103 command-guided air-to-air missile. In total, 25 Aquilon 202s were completed, together with 40 Aquilon 203s. These had been preceded by 20 production versions of the original Aquilon 20 model.

Aéronavale first employed Sikorsky S-55s (licence-built by SNCASE) in theatre in a trials capacity. Large-scale use was made of Piasecki H-21C Shawnees for troop transport from 1956, with Sikorsky H-19D and Sikorsky HSS-1 Seabat units arriving in 1957 and 1958, respectively. Eventually operated under the command of a single unit (GHAN 1), the Aéronavale helicopters were widely used for commando assault and were soon equipped with an array of weaponry for ground support.

A crisis in Tunisia in 1961 saw the involvement of French carrier aircraft, once again operating from land bases in North Africa. Corsairs provided combat air patrols to protect the entry of French forces into the country, and were joined by Aquilons to conduct a number of strikes against Tunisian positions.

By the end of the 1950s, the Aéronavale was well versed in helicopter operations, having begun with detachments of Sikorsky S-51s (aboard *Arromanches*) and then HUP-2s for carrier-based search and rescue and plane-guard duties. In addition, rotorcraft began to assume the anti-submarine role, first with the Westland-built WS-55 (on an experimental basis) and later the HSS-1.

## Specifications

Crew: 2

Powerplant: 1 x 1137kW (1525hp) Wright R-1820-84 radial engine

Maximum speed: 198km/h (123mph)

Range: 293km (182 miles)

Service ceiling: 3960m (13,000ft)

Dimensions: Rotor diameter 17.07m (56ft 0in); length 17.28m (56ft 8.5in); height 4.85m (15ft 11in)

Weight: 6350kg (14,000lb) loaded

Armament: Up to three M60 or M60D machine guns

### ▼ Sikorsky HSS-1 Seabat

**Escadrille 20S, Saint-Raphaël**

While early HSS-1s were provided by the US, subsequent production was handled locally by Sud-Aviation. The HSS-1 was used for both anti-submarine and transport duties, and served in the latter role during the war in Algeria, where it was also fitted with 20mm (0.78in) cannon for fire support missions. This aircraft was operated by Escadrille 20S, responsible for ASW trials with the Seabat.

# France
## 1961–89

**By 1961 the French Navy was preparing for overhaul, with the receipt of the first of a new class of purpose-built carrier that would project naval airpower until the end of the Cold War.**

FRANCE'S NEW AIRCRAFT carrier *Clémenceau* was commissioned in 1961, and was followed by a sister vessel, *Foch*, in 1963. These powerful new ships demanded fully revamped air components in order to meet the demands of service in the 1960s and beyond. Three primary aircraft would outfit the air groups deployed on the two carriers: the F-8 Crusader for air defence, the Étendard IVM for attack and Étendard IVP for reconnaissance, and the Alizé for anti-submarine warfare and surveillance.

The Alizé emerged from the prototype Breguet Vultur that was first flown in 1951, and was developed as three-seat turboprop for anti-submarine missions, with a retractable search radar and an internal weapons bay. After a first flight in October 1956, a first production Alizé was delivered to Flottille 6F in October 1959. Three front-line units operated the type, and in 1977, 28 survivors from the

original total of 75 aircraft were modernized with a new Iguane radar and an electronic surveillance system. By this stage, helicopters had taken over most of the ASW mission, and the Alizé would see out its service in the surveillance role.

The Étendard was developed to meet an original NATO requirement for a lightweight tactical strike aircraft and was first flown in Étendard IV prototype form in July 1956. Although it lost out in the NATO requirement, the Étendard IV was selected by the Aéronavale in December 1956, and was developed as the Étendard IVM for carrier operations. The Étendard IVM first flew in May 1958 and, powered by a single Atar turbojet, entered operational service with Flottille 15F in June 1962. The aircraft featured folding wingtips, an in-flight refuelling probe and Aïda fire-control radar. In addition to 69 production Étendard IVMs for three front-line units, the type

71

was adapted for the reconnaissance role, with 21 Étendard IVPs having provision for up to six cameras in a re-profiled nose and a centreline pod.

In order to succeed the Aquilon, the Aéronavale settled on the Vought F-8E(FN) Crusader, an adaptation of the US Navy carrier fighter for French service, and featuring a redesigned wing to allow operations from smaller carriers. Two squadrons eventually equipped with the Crusader, with 42 aircraft being procured between 1964–65. The aircraft was equipped to carry French-made missiles, the R.530 later giving way to the R.550 Magic.

For a major cruise to the Indian and Pacific Oceans in the mid-1960s, the *Foch* air group comprised 12 Alizés, eight Étendard IVMs, four Étendard IVPs, 10 HSS-1s, six Alouette IIs and six Alouette IIIs. While the two new carriers replaced the *La Fayette* and *Bois Belleau* in service, the *Arromanches* soldiered on until finally being withdrawn in 1974, latterly being used for training.

### Étendard reborn

The Aéronavale expected to replace the Étendard with a navalized version of the Anglo-French SEPECAT Jaguar strike/attack aircraft, but this was abandoned in favour of an evolutionary development of the earlier jet, as the Super Étendard, introduced to service in 1979 after three prototypes had been completed using IVM airframes. The new type eventually equipped three front-line Flottilles and the final Étendard IVM was retired from first-line duties in 1980. Key changes included introduction of the

| French Navy carrier air units | | |
|---|---|---|
| Carrier-deployable units, 1971 | | |
| Flottille 4F | Alizé | Lann-Bihoué |
| Flottille 6F | Alizé | Nîmes-Garons |
| Flottille 9F | Alizé | Lann-Bihoué |
| Flottille 11F | Étendard IVM | Landivisiau |
| Flottille 12F | F-8E(FN) Crusader | Landivisiau |
| Flottille 14F | F-8E(FN) Crusader | Landivisiau |
| Flottille 16F | Étendard IVP | Landivisiau |
| Flottille 17F | Étendard IVM | Hyères |
| Flottille 31F | HSS-1 | Saint-Mandrier |
| Flottille 32F | Super Frelon | Lanvéoc-Poulmic |
| Flottille 33F | HSS-1 | Saint-Mandrier |
| Escadrille 10S | various types | Saint-Raphaël |
| Escadrille 20S | various helicopter types | Saint-Raphaël |
| Escadrille 22S | Alouette II, Alouette III | Lanvéoc-Poulmic |
| Escadrille 23S | Alouette II, Alouette III | Saint-Mandrier |
| Escadrille 27S | Super Frelon, Alouette III | Hao |
| Escadrille 59S | Zéphyr, Étendard IVM | Hyères |

Agave radar that allowed it to launch the AM.39 Exocet anti-ship missile, and the ASMP nuclear-armed cruise missile was another weapons option.

Renewal of the Aéronavale helicopter fleet included the 1978 introduction of the Westland

### Specifications

Crew: 3

Powerplant: 1 x 1565W (2100hp) Rolls-Royce Dart RDa.7 Mk 21 turboprop

Maximum speed: 518km/h (322mph)

Range: 2500km (1553 miles)

Service ceiling: 8000m (26,250ft)

Dimensions: span 15.60m (51ft 2in); length 13.86m (45ft 5.75in); height 5.00m (16ft 5in)

Weight: 8200kg (18,078lb) loaded

Armament: Torpedoes, depth charges, rockets, missiles and bombs

### ▼ Breguet Alizé

*Flottille 4F, 1990*

Flottille 4F re-equipped with the Alizé in 1960 and continued to operate the type until 1997, before becoming the French Navy E-2C operator. The Iguane surveillance radar in the rear fuselage is seen here retracted.

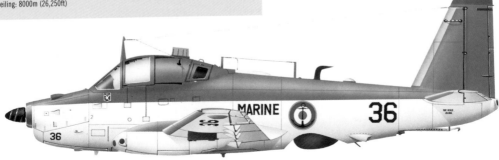

## Specifications

Crew: 1

Powerplant: 1 x 43.15kN (9700lbf) TPA
SNECMA Atar 8B

Maximum speed: 1093km/h (679mph)

Range: 1700km (1056 miles)

Service ceiling: 13,700m (44,947ft)

Dimensions: span 9.60m (31ft 5in); length
14.69m (48ft 2in); height 3.79m (12ft 43in)

Weight: 8170kg (18,011lb) loaded

Armament: None

### ▼ Dassault Étendard IVP

*Flottille 16F, 1973*

In 1968 four Étendard IVMs were converted to become IVP reconnaissance aircraft, including this example, 162. As such, they joined 21 production aircraft previously completed. Flottille 16F was the primary operator, a dedicated naval reconnaissance unit, but examples were also detached to 15F and 17F.

## Specifications

Crew: 1

Powerplant: 1 x 80kN (18,000lbf) Pratt &
Whitney J57-P-20A afterburning turbojet

Maximum speed: 1827km/h (1135mph)

Range: 966km (600 miles)

Service ceiling: 17,680m (58,000ft)

Dimensions: span 10.87m (35ft 8in); length

16.61m (54ft 6in); height 4.8m (15ft 9in)

Weight: 13,000kg (29,000lb) loaded

Armament: Four 20mm (.79in) M39 cannons;
provision for up to 2268kg (5000lb) of stores,
including two Matra air-to-air missiles or
eight 127mm (5in) rockets

### ▼ Vought F-8E(FN) Crusader

*Flottille 12F, 1972*

Seen here armed with Matra R.550 Magic missiles, this Crusader was operated by Flottille 12F, which was re-established with the new type at Lann-Bihoué in 1964, after an initial cadre of pilots had received training in the US. In 1968 12F, and the second operational unit, 14F, relocated to Landivisiau. Throughout their service, the F-8E(FN)s carried only defensive weaponry.

## Specifications

Crew: 1

Powerplant: 1 x 49kN (11,023lb) SNECMA Atar
8K-50 turbojet

Maximum speed: 1180km/h (733mph)

Range: 850km (528 miles)

Service ceiling: 13,700m (44,950ft)

Dimensions: span 9.6m (31ft 6in); length

14.31m (46ft 11in); height 3.86m (12ft 8in)

Weight: 12,000kg (26,455lb) loaded

Armament: Two 30mm (1.18in) cannons;
provision for up to 2100kg (4630lb) of stores,
including nuclear weapons and Exocet air-to-
surface missiles

### ▼ Dassault Super Étendard

*Flottille 11F, 1983*

This Super Étendard was flown by the first unit to be equipped with the type, Flottille 11F becoming fully operational with the new aircraft in February 1979. The aircraft is shown wearing the two-tone disruptive camouflage scheme that was adopted for combat service over Lebanon, replacing the earlier dark blue/white colours.

### ▲ Westland Lynx HAS.Mk 2(FN)

*Flottille 34F, 1985*

Although more often embarked in frigates and destroyers, the Lynx made occasional visits to French carrier decks after its introduction in 1978. For its ASW role on smaller warships, the Lynx was armed with Mk 46 torpedoes (as seen here). However, aboard carriers, the aircraft served in the SAR and plane-guard role, pending the availability of the Eurocopter Dauphin.

### Specifications

Crew: 2–3

Powerplant: 2 x 846kW (1135hp) Rolls-Royce
Gem 42-1 turboshaft engines

Maximum speed: 232km/h (144mph)

Range: 178km (111 miles)

Service ceiling: 3960m (13,000ft)

Dimensions: Rotor diameter 12.8m (42ft 0in);
length 11.92m (39ft 1.25in);

height 3.48m (11ft 5in)

Weight: 4763kg (10,500lb) loaded

Armament: Pylons for two Mk 46 Stingray
torpedoes, two Mk 11 depth charges, plus one
FN HMP 12.7mm (.50in) machine gun for self
protection

Lynx, which replaced the HSS-1 and Sud Aviation Alouette III in the ASW roles. The Alouette III survived in the search and rescue (SAR) and carrier-borne utility roles, however, and examples were embarked for every cruise of the *Clémenceau* and

### ▼ Étendard IVM

A 17F Étendard IVM drops its catapult bridle as it leaves the deck of a French carrier. Between 1962 and 1980 the Étendard IVM was France's primary carrier-borne attack aircraft, and its weapons options included Matra rockets, AS.20 and AS.30 air-to-surface missiles, Sidewinders and the AN.52 tactical nuclear bomb.

*Foch*. Another periodic visitor to the decks of the carriers was the Sud Aviation Super Frelon, mainly for commando transport and long-range SAR.

During the Lebanon crisis in the early 1980s, Aéronavale aircraft again flew combat missions. Following an attack on the French embassy in Beirut in September 1983, Super Étendards from the *Foch* flew missions against artillery positions. In October Super Étendards flew from *Clémenceau* to attack a rebel barracks, with Crusaders providing escort.

# India
## 1957–87

**A 'Majestic'-class light fleet carrier, HMS *Hercules* was purchased by India as INS *Vikrant* (R11) in 1957, and was completed with an angled deck, steam catapult and other modern features.**

COMMISSIONED IN 1961, the carrier embarked an air wing comprised of Hawker Sea Hawk fighters and Alizé anti-submarine aircraft.

India's first 46 Sea Hawks consisted of both new-build aircraft and a variety of ex-Royal Navy versions, all brought up to a common FGA.Mk 6 standard prior to delivery, which began in 1960. In 1965 an order was placed for 10 ex-German Navy Sea Hawk Mk 100s and 18 radar-equipped Mk 101s, although these were embargoed and not delivered until after the 1965 Indo-Pakistan War. All were operated by INAS 300, shore-based at INS Hansa in Goa.

The Sea Hawks first saw action, from their shore base, during the Indian liberation of Goa in 1961, when they flew defensive air patrols. During the 1965 war with Pakistan, the *Vikrant* was being refitted and was unavailable to participate, but Sea Hawks operated from Jamnagar, flying air defence missions.

Twelve Alizés were acquired to serve with INAS 310, and these again saw land-based service during the Indian operations in Goa, flying electronic warfare and reconnaissance missions.

*Vikrant* was back in commission during the 1971 Indo-Pakistan War, with both Sea Hawks and Alizés

on board. The Sea Hawks flew numerous ground-attack sorties, attacking targets in East Pakistan, including airfields and other installations at Cox's Bazaar and the port and airfields of Chittagong. Sea Hawks also provided ground support to Indian troops and covered an amphibious landing.

### Alizé at war

After the delivery of three attrition replacements from French Navy stocks in 1966, the Alizés played a significant role in the 1971 war, flying from *Vikrant* and launching attacks on naval vessels and ground targets alike, and helping enforce a maritime blockade. In total, the air group launched 291 Sea Hawk and Alizé sorties during the conflict, with radar-equipped Alizés flying most night missions.

The Sea Hawk survived in service until December 1983, when a final official flight was conducted, and in the same month the type's replacement, the BAe Sea Harrier, embarked in *Vikrant* for the first time.

The Alizé remained in use aboard *Vikrant* until 1987, serving alongside the Sea Harrier and Westland Sea King Mk 42, before its ASW role was assumed by the Sea King. Subsequently, Alizés operated from

### Specifications

| | |
|---|---|
| Crew: 1 | Dimensions: span 11.89m (39ft 0in); length |
| Powerplant: 1 x 23.1kN (5200lbf) Rolls-Royce | 12.09m (39ft 8in); height 2.64m (8ft 8in) |
| Nene 103 turbojet | Weight: 5996kg (13,220lb) loaded |
| Maximum speed: 965km/h (600mph) | Armament: Four 20mm (.79in) Hispano Mk V |
| Range: 770km (480 miles) | cannons; 20 x 27kg (60lb) unguided rockets; |
| Service ceiling: 13,564m (44,500ft) | four 227kg (500lb) bombs |

### ▼ Hawker Sea Hawk FGA.Mk 6

***INAS 300 'White Tigers', INS* Vikrant, *1971***

Former Royal Navy WF293 was part of the initial batch of 46 Sea Hawks received by India from UK stocks. Wearing the 'W' deck code for *Vikrant*, the aircraft was built as a Sea Hawk FB.Mk 3 but was refurbished to FGA.Mk 6 standard prior to delivery. The first aircraft to be received were nine modernized FB.Mk 3s that were delivered from January 1960. Indian Navy Sea Hawks saw combat in successive wars against Pakistan in 1965 and 1971.

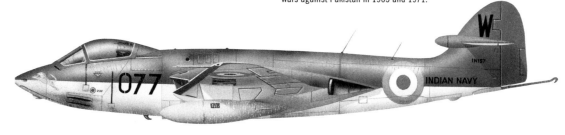

## Specifications

Crew: 1

Powerplant: 1 x 95.6kN (21,500lbf) Rolls-Royce
  Pegasus vectored thrust turbofan

Maximum speed: 1110km/h (690mph)

Range: 740km (460 miles)

Service ceiling: 15,545m (51,000ft)

Dimensions: span 7.7m (25ft 3in); length

14.5m (47ft 7in); height 3.71m (12ft 2in)

Weight: 11,884kg (26,200lb) loaded

Armament: Two 30mm (1.18in) cannons,
  provision for AIM-9 sidewinder or Matra
  Magic air-to-air missiles, and two Harpoon or
  Sea Eagle anti-shipping missiles; up to a
  total of 3629kg (8000lb) bombs

### ▼ BAe Sea Harrier FRS.Mk 51

*INAS 300 'White Tigers'*

A peculiarity of the Sea Harrier in Indian Navy service was the selection of the French-made Matra R.550 Magic as the primary short-range missile armament. This aircraft carries the Magic on underwing launchers, with the removable twin 30mm (1.18in) ADEN cannon pods carried under the fuselage.

## Typical Indian Navy carrier air group, early 1970s

| INS *Vikrant* air wing, Indo-Pakistan War, 1971 | | |
|---|---|---|
| INS *Vikrant* (R11) | 'Majestic' class | |
| 4–14 December 1971 | | |
| INAS 300 'White Tigers' | Sea Hawk | 10 |
| INAS 310 'Cobras' | Alizé | 4 |
| Ship's Flight | Alouette III | 2 |

### ▼ INS *Vikrant*

An Alizé with wings folded aboard INS *Vikrant*, together with its replacement in the ASW role, the Sea King Mk 42. The Alizé finally left carrier service in 1987.

shore bases in the ASW and anti-surface vessel role until 1991–92. The Sea King had begun to enter service with INAS 330 in 1971, the first six aircraft operating from shore bases during the war with Pakistan. Another six Sea Kings arrived in 1973. The next three deliveries in 1980 were Mk 42As, for operations from smaller warships, while the 12 Mk 42Bs delivered from 1985 featured uprated engines, composite main rotors and improved avionics. The last three Sea Kings to be delivered from Westland production were Mk 42Cs equipped for SAR and utility. The other main helicopter embarked in *Vikrant* was the Alouette III, and later the licence-built HAL Chetak derivative, for liaison and SAR.

# Netherlands
## 1945–68

**The aircraft of the Marine Luchvaartdienst (Naval Air Service) served aboard two successive carriers of the Dutch Navy until the late 1960s, latterly in the anti-submarine warfare role.**

THE NETHERLANDS HAD operated with the Royal Navy in World War II, its pilots serving aboard British carriers, and in 1945 the Dutch were working up to operate a new carrier in the Far East, with aircrew already training to operate the Fairey Barracuda for its new air group. The end of the war put paid to this, but the Dutch negotiated with the British to operate the escort carrier HMS *Nairana*, acquired on a two-year lease.

The initial air group for the carrier, which was renamed Hr.Ms. *Karel Doorman* when commissioned in 1946, was the Firefly Mk 1, 30 examples of which were delivered to 860 Squadron beginning the same year. The squadron sailed with *Karel Doorman* to the Far East in 1946, and its Fireflies went ashore, remaining in the area to see active service during policing actions conducted in the Dutch East Indies during 1947–48.

In May 1948 the original Hr.Ms. *Karel Doorman* was returned to the UK after its loan period expired, and it was replaced by a second vessel of the same name, the former HMS *Venerable* of the 'Colossus' class being taken on charge the same day. The air group for the new carrier was to be based around 40 of the more capable Firefly FR.Mk 4s and over 40 Sea Furies. The first Firefly FR.Mk 4s began to be delivered in 1947, the 40 aircraft from the original order being supplemented by 14 NF.Mk 5 variants from 1949. Another four aircraft (both Mk 4s and 5s) were received from the Royal Canadian Navy in 1952. The first Sea Furies to arrive, in 1948, were 10 FB.Mk 50s, followed by 12 FB.Mk 60s, an export version of the FB.Mk 11, these being taken on hand by 1950. There followed 25 Sea Fury FB.Mk 51s that were licence-built by Fokker.

### Far East service

For its first cruise to the Far East in 1950, *Karel Doorman* embarked Firefly FR.Mk 4s, and squadrons operating this type represented the primary aircraft equipment until 1954. From that year, the carrier began to operate the Sea Fury FB.Mk 51, together with the Avenger. Fulfilling the ASW role, the Avenger was operated as a hunter-killer team involving the TBM-3W2 and TBM-3S2 variants. In total, the Dutch received 24 TBM-3W2 (hunter) and

**Specifications**

Crew: 1

Powerplant: 1 x 1850kW (2480hp) Bristol Centaurus XVIIC 18-cylinder twin-row radial piston engine

Maximum speed: 740km/h (460mph)

Range: 1127km (700 miles)

Service ceiling: 10,900m (35,800ft)

Dimensions: span 11.7m (38ft 4.75in); length 10.6m (34ft 8in); height 4.9m (16ft 1in)

Weight: 5670kg (12,500lb) loaded

Armament: Four 20mm (.79in) Hispano Mk V cannons, twelve 76.2mm (3in) rockets or 907kg (2000lb) bomb load

▼ **Hawker Sea Fury FB.Mk 60**

*Unknown unit*

The Netherlands received 22 Hawker-built Sea Fury FB.Mk 50/60 aircraft for use on board the carrier Hr.Ms. *Karel Doorman*. The first batch comprised 10 FB.Mk 50s equivalent to the Royal Navy's F.Mk X fighter, delivered in 1948. There followed a second batch, consisting of 12 FB.Mk 60s, export versions of the FB.Mk 11 fighter-bomber, delivered in 1950. In 1951 the surviving Mk 50s were rebuilt by Hawker to Mk 60 standard.

## Specifications

Crew: 3

Powerplant: 1 x 1397kW (1900hp) Wright R-
2600 Cyclone engine

Maximum speed: 444km/h (276mph)

Range: 1818km (1130 miles)

Service ceiling: 7132m (23,400ft)

Dimensions: span 16.52m (54ft 2in); length
12.47m (40ft 9in); height 4.24m (13.9ft)

Weight: 7444kg (16,412lb) loaded

Armament: Three 12.7mm (.50in) machine
guns and up to 907kg (2000lb) of ordnance

### ▼ Grumman TBM-3E2 Avenger

*Valkenburg*

Unlike the TBM-3W2 and TBM-3S2 hunter-killer team, the TBM-3E2 was not
embarked in *Karel Doorman*, with operations instead being carried out from
Valkenburg. The TBM-3E and TBM-3E2 were both provided by the Royal Navy in
1958 and were used for short-range coastal patrol work along the Dutch coast.
After a brief period of service, the last examples were withdrawn in late 1961.

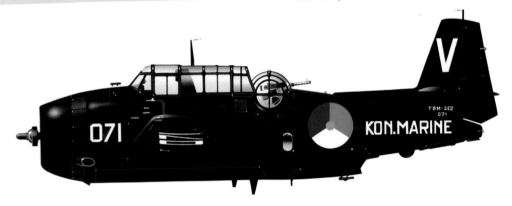

34 TBM-3S2 (killer) models between 1953 and
1954. In 1954 the *Karel Doorman* began regular
helicopter operations, initially with a single example
of the Sikorsky S-51. In 1953 the type was

superseded by three examples of the Sikorsky
HO4S-3. Both types were used for SAR, utility
transport and plane-guard duties.

By 1958 the *Karel Doorman* had been modified
with an angled deck, steam catapult and mirror
landing system, paving the way for jet operations.
These began in earnest in 1957, when the first
example of the Sea Hawk FGA-50, as it was locally
designated, was delivered. The 22 Sea Hawks were
taken on charge between 1957 and 1958 and were
equivalent to the Royal Navy's FGA.Mk 6 version.
The Sea Hawks were capable of conducting both air
defence and ground-attack missions, with AIM-9
Sidewinder missiles available for the former.

Initially, the Sea Hawks operated alongside
Avengers, but after a final cruise in 1960, the jet
fighters saw out their service from land bases only. A
replacement for the HO4S-3 was embarked from
1960, in the form of the first of an eventual 10
examples of the Sikorsky HSS-1N (later designated
SH-34J), which for the first time added the ASW role
to the helicopter's duties. After 1966, six of the HSS-
1Ns were modified to UH-34J standard, to fulfil the
utility role, with ASW equipment removed.

### Anti-submarine warfare carrier

With the Sea Hawks removed from the air group,
*Karel Doorman* assumed anti-submarine warfare as its
primary mission, and therefore embarked a squadron

| Royal Netherlands Navy carrier air units | | |
|---|---|---|
| Carrier-deployable units, 1946–68 | | |
| 1 Squadron | Firefly Mk 1 | 1952 |
| 2 Squadron | Firefly Mk 1 | 1950 |
| | Firefly FR.Mk 4/5 | 1951, 1954 |
| | TBM-3S2 Avenger | 1954, 1955, 1958–60 |
| | TBM-3W2 Avenger | 1954, 1955, 1958–60 |
| 4 Squadron | Firefly FR.Mk 4/5 | 1948–54 |
| | TBM-3S2 Avenger | 1954, 1955, 1958–60 |
| | TBM-3W2 Avenger | 1954, 1955, 1958–60 |
| | S2F-1 Tracker | 1962–68 |
| 8 Squadron | HO4S-3 | 1954, 1955, 1958–60 |
| | HSS-1N | 1960–68 |
| 860 Squadron | Firefly Mk 1 | 1946 |
| | Sea Fury FB.Mk 51 | 1954, 1955 |
| | Sea Hawk FGA-50 | 1958–60 |
| 861 Squadron | Firefly Mk 1 | 1947–50 |

of S2F-1 Trackers between 1962 and 1968. The Netherlands received 26 S2F-1s in 1960, with another two examples arriving in 1962, these replacing the Avenger. A number of (C)S-2A aircraft were also obtained in the early 1960s, but these only saw use from land bases. After an overhaul in 1966, the *Karel Doorman* suffered a major fire in the engine room in 1968 and it was judged uneconomical to complete the required repairs. Originally planned to decommission in 1970, this was brought forward, and the carrier was formally retired from service in October 1968.

The *Karel Doorman* was survived by the Trackers that had constituted its air group during its final years of operation as an ASW carrier. Between 1968 and 1970 a total of 18 surviving S2F-1 (S-2A) models were converted to S-2N standard. The Tracker remained in service in a shore-based capacity until 1975, flying from bases both in the Netherlands and in the Dutch Antilles. The final Trackers in Dutch service were a pair of US-2N target-tug adaptations that were finally withdrawn in October 1975. *Karel Doorman* was sold to Argentina, where she was recommissioned as the *25 de Mayo* in 1969.

## Specifications

Crew: 1

Powerplant: 1 x 24kN (5400lbf) Rolls-Royce Nene 103 turbojet

Maximum speed: 969km/h (602mph)

Range: 370km (230 miles)

Service ceiling: 13,565m (44,500ft)

Dimensions: span 11.89m (39ft 0in); length 12.09m (39ft 8in); height 2.64m (8ft 8in)

Weight: 7348kg (16,200lb) loaded

Armament: Four 20mm (.79in) Hispano cannons; provision for four 227kg (500lb) bombs and twenty 76mm (3in) or sixteen 127mm (5in) rockets

### ▼ Hawker Sea Hawk FGA-50

*860 Squadron, Karel Doorman*

860 Squadron was the initial operator of the Sea Hawk within the Marine Luchtvaartdienst, the unit taking on its first example in July 1957. By early 1958, all 22 Sea Hawks had been delivered. In addition to carrying Sidewinders for the air defence role, Dutch Sea Hawks could be equipped with 227kg (500lb) bombs and rocket projectiles for ground-attack work.

## Specifications

Crew: 4

Powerplant: 2 x 1137kW (1525hp) Wright R-1820-82WA radial engines

Maximum speed: 450km/h (280mph)

Range: 2170km (1350 miles)

Service ceiling: 6700m (22,000ft)

Dimensions: span 22.12m (72ft 7in); length 13.26m (43ft 6in); height 5.33m (17ft 6in)

Weight: 11,860kg (26,147lb) loaded

Armament: Two torpedoes

### ▼ Grumman S-2N Tracker

*Valkenburg*

With its 'V' tailcode signifying assignment to the Dutch Navy base at Valkenburg, this Grumman Tracker is one of 18 that were brought up to S-2N standard from 1968. The aircraft were originally delivered under the Military Defense Assistance Program in the early 1960s and were embarked in the *Karel Doorman* between 1962 and 1968. They later served from land bases.

# Soviet Union
## 1967–89

**Although the Soviet Union did not put a conventional aircraft carrier into front-line service during the Cold War, it nonetheless fielded both helicopter and VTOL 'carrier-cruisers'.**

THE SOVIET UNION gained its first experience in sustained aviation operations at sea with its Project 1123 Kondor vessels, which received the Western codename 'Moskva' class after the lead ship. Classified as 'anti-submarine cruisers with aircraft armament', the *Moskva* and *Leningrad* entered service in 1968 and 1969 respectively, and in addition to their own ASW and air defence armament they typically embarked 12 Kamov Ka-25PL anti-submarine helicopters and a pair of Ka-25PS search and rescue helicopters.

The Ka-25 utilized co-axial main rotors as part of its compact design, and was first flown in 1961. Of the 275 production examples completed between 1965 and 1977, the major carrier-based version was the initial Ka-25PL for the ASW mission, equipped with search radar and sonobuoys with optional dipping sonar and MAD gear. The Ka-25PL typically operated as a hunter-killer team, with a pair of helicopters equipped with sonobuoys, sonar and MAD supported by two helicopters carrying internal torpedoes and depth charges. The Ka-25Ts version was embarked in missile-carrying warships and was fitted with targeting radar to provide target acquisition and mid-course 'over the horizon' missile guidance. The Ka-25PS was an unarmed search and rescue version, used for carrier-based utility and plane-guard duties. The first operational Ka-25s embarked in *Moskva* in 1967, and the type was declared fully operational in 1971.

### VTOL carriers

The first Soviet warships capable of embarking fixed-wing aircraft were the 'heavy aircraft-carrying cruisers' of the Project 1143 ('Kiev' class) that yielded *Kiev* and *Minsk*. A new vertical take-off and landing jet fighter was developed to serve on these ships, although for its primary ASW role it would continue to rely upon helicopters and its own missile armament and sensors. The first efforts towards fielding a VTOL fighter were realized in the experimental Yakovlev Yak-36, an experimental type that was ordered into production in 1967 and which made its maiden flight in Yak-36M form in 1971.

The production version of the Yak-36 was the Yak-36MP, which was entirely redesigned for operational use. At the same time as this work was being

### Specifications

Crew: 1

Powerplant: 2 x 29.9kN (6724lbf) Rybinsk RD-36-35VFR lift turbojets; one 6950kN (15,322lbf) Tumanskii R-27V-300 vectored-thrust turbojet

Maximum speed: 1280km/h (795mph)

Range: 1300km (807 miles)

Service ceiling: 11,000m (36,089ft)

Dimensions: span 7.32m (24ft 0in); length 16.37m (50ft 1in); height 4.25m (14ft 5in)

Weight: 11,300kg (28,700lb) loaded

Armament: Four external hardpoints with provision for 2000kg (4409lb) of stores, including missiles, bombs, pods and drop tanks

▼ **Yakovlev Yak-38**

*Soviet Navy*

The Yak-38 was the first carrier-based fixed-wing aircraft to enter operational service with the Soviet Navy, serving with units of the Northern and Pacific Fleets, and even being tested under combat conditions in Afghanistan. The basic mission avionics included a simple gun sight, while the pilot was provided with an automatic flight-control system.

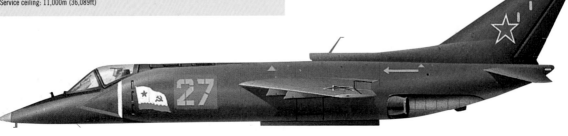

### Typical Soviet Navy carrier air groups

| Project 1123 Kondor ('Moskva' class) air group | | Project 1143.3 and 1143.4 (*Novorossiysk* and *Baku/Admiral Gorshkov*) | |
|---|---|---|---|
| Ka-25PL | 12 | Yak-38 | 28 |
| Ka-25PS | 2 | or | |
| | | Ka-25PL/Ka-27PL | 28 |
| Project 1143 (*Kiev* and *Minsk*) | | Ka-25PS/Ka-27PS | 2 |
| Yak-38 | 20 | | |
| or | | | |
| Ka-25PL/Ka-27PL | 20 | | |
| Ka-25PS/Ka-27PS | 2 | | |

| Carrier-deployable units, 1968–89 | | | |
|---|---|---|---|
| Black Sea Fleet | | | |
| 78th OKPLVP | Ka-25 | Donuzlav, Crimea | *Moskva, Leningrad* |
| 872nd OKPLVP | Ka-25 | Kacha, Crimea | *Moskva* |
| Northern Fleet | | | |
| 279th OKShAP | Yak-38 | Saki, Severomorsk-3 | *Kiev, Baku/Admiral Gorshkov* |
| 830th OKPLVP | Ka-25, Ka-27 | Severomorsk-2 | *Kiev, Baku/Admiral Gorshkov* |
| Pacific Fleet | | | |
| 311th OKShAP | Yak-38 | Knevichi, Vladivostok | *Minsk, Novorossiysk* |
| 710th OKPLVP | Ka-25, Ka-27 | Novonezhino, Vladivostok | *Minsk, Novorossiysk* |

conducted, it was hoped the design of the Project 1123 could be modified to permit limited fixed-wing operations. In the event, the new aircraft required an entirely new class of ship, the Project 1143, work on which began in 1968. However, the first deck landing by a Yak-36MP took place on *Moskva* in November 1972. The Yak-36MP was powered by an R-27V-300 turbojet for lift and cruise, supplemented by a pair of RD-36 lift engines. Tailored for the air defence and light attack missions, the aircraft could carry guided and unguided weapons on four underwing pylons, including Kh-23 (AS-7 'Kerry') command-guided air-to-surface missiles.

After pilot training on the type began in March 1975, the first Yak-36MP landing on board *Kiev* was completed in May that year, and the first two vessels of the class would thereafter go to sea with a typical air group of either 20 Yak-36MPs or a similar number of Ka-25s, but not a combination of both. A pair of Ka-25PS rescue helicopters was always embarked, while up to three Ka-25Ts helicopters provided mid-course guidance for the ships' surface-to-surface missiles.

On being officially commissioned to service in 1976, the Yak-36MP was re-designated as the Yak-38. In service, the Yak-38 proved to offer only limited capabilities (it lacked radar and carried only a very restricted weapons load), and initially suffered from poor serviceability. After difficulties in operations in hot climates, the Yak-38 was modified to allow it to complete running take-offs, and these were introduced in 1980, on board *Minsk*. A total of 231 aircraft were completed between 1973 and 1987, including 38 two-seat Yak-38U pilot trainers. From 1982, production switched to the Yak-38M with uprated engines for an increased take-off weight. After training with the 33rd Centre for Combat Training and Aircrew Conversion in Ukraine, the Yak-38 saw front-line service with two Independent Shipborne Attack Aviation Regiments, the 279th OKShAP in the Crimea and the 311th OKShAP near Vladivostok. These were respectively assigned to the *Kiev* and *Minsk* with the Northern and Pacific Fleets.

Authorized in 1974, two improved versions of the 'Kiev' class were also commissioned, as the

▲ **Yakovlev Yak-38**
Although offering strictly limited combat capabilities, the Yak-38 did serve to familiarize the Soviet Navy with fixed-wing aviation operations on board its carriers.

*Novorossiysk* (Project 1143.3) in 1983 and *Baku* in 1987 (Project 1143.4, later renamed *Admiral Gorshkov*). These vessels were somewhat larger and incorporated revised weapons and sensors. The air group was also enlarged, with a maximum of 30–36 embarked aircraft, although in practice 28 aircraft was the more usual number, supported by two SAR helicopters.

### New rotorcraft

A successor to the Ka-25 series was fielded on board the 'Kiev' class from the early 1980s. A further development of its predecessor, the Ka-27 featured an enlarged fuselage and uprated engines driving a new main rotor, allowing a 50 per cent increase in take-off weight despite similar overall dimensions. The basic ASW version was the Ka-27PL, with surveillance radar, sonobuoys and either dipping sonar or MAD 'bird' stowed in the rear fuselage. The Ka-27PS was the unarmed SAR version that operated from carriers

in a utility transport and plane-guard capacity. Operated by a crew of two or three, the Ka-27 first went to sea in *Minsk* in 1978, and was officially commissioned to service in 1981.

The Yak-38 was meanwhile to be superseded by a new vertical/short take-off and landing (V/STOL) design, the Yak-41. The new aircraft entered much-delayed flight test in 1987. By then, production of the Yak-38 had ended, and the V/STOL concept was falling from favour. Early problems dogged the promising Yak-41, which offered supersonic performance, radar and multi-role capability. A second flight was achieved in 1989, but in 1991 tests aboard *Admiral Gorshkov* ended in a heavy landing for one of the prototypes, and funding for the project was withdrawn in 1992.

The 'Kiev' class were not true aircraft carriers according to Western understanding, but the Soviet Union was working on a new generation of conventional carriers, still under the 'heavy aircraft-carrying cruiser' designation. The first of these, *Tbilisi*, was to replace the limited Yak-38 with newly developed conventional take-off and landing aircraft, which would be launched with the aid of a ski jump ramp and recovered using arrester gear. The new class of carrier was first proposed in 1973 as the Project 1160 Oriol, which were to employ nuclear powerplants and carry 70 aircraft. The Oriol 'super-carrier' was superseded by the somewhat smaller Project 1153 Oriol in 1976, with an air wing reduced to 50, but the whole project was finally shelved in 1976. Instead the more modest, conventionally powered Project 1143.5 would be developed as a follow-on to the 'Kiev' design.

## Specifications

Crew: 4

Powerplant: 2 x 728kW (975hp) Glushenkov GTD-3F turboshaft engines

Maximum speed: 209km/h (130mph)

Range: 400km (247 miles)

Service ceiling: 3350m (10,990ft)

Dimensions: Rotor diameter 15.74m (51ft 7.75in); length 9.75m (31ft 11.75in); height 5.37m (17ft 7.5in)

Weight: 7500kg (16,535lb) loaded

Armament: Two 450mm (18in) ASW torpedoes, nuclear or conventional depth charges

### ▶ Kamov Ka-25PS

*Soviet Navy*

The search and rescue and utility transport version of the Ka-25, dubbed 'Hormone-C' by NATO, was initially finished in this red and white scheme to reflect its non-combatant role. Two examples of the Ka-25PS were employed aboard each of the 'Moskva'-class helicopter cruisers and the early 'Kiev'-class aviation cruisers, for liaison, SAR and plane-guard duties.

## Specifications

Crew: 1–3

Powerplant: 2 x 1660kW (2225hp) Isotov turboshaft engines

Maximum speed: 270km/h (166mph)

Range: 980km (605 miles)

Service ceiling: 5000m (16,400ft)

Dimensions: Rotor diameter 15.80m (51ft 10in); length 11.30m (37ft 1in); height 5.50m (18ft 1in)

Weight: 11,000kg (24,200lb) loaded

Armament: One torpedo or 36 RGB-NM & RGB-NM-1 sonobouys

### ▼ Kamov Ka-27PL

*710th OKPLVP, Novorossiysk*

The successor to the Ka-25PL as the standard Soviet shipborne ASW helicopter was the Ka-27PL 'Helix-A'. Equipped with an Osminog computerized search/attack system, the Ka-27PS was equipped with dipping sonar or MAD, plus radio sonobuoys. Using a datalink, flights of helicopters could work together in their hunt for underwater targets, feeding information back to the ship and to other Ka-27s in the vicinity.

# Spain
## 1967–89

**Spain has operated two successive carriers, the first of these being the wooden-decked *Dédalo* that was in service from 1967 until 1989, latterly as the first true 'Harrier carrier' V/STOL ship.**

AFTER OPERATING A flying-boat tender between the wars, Spain began to plan the establishment of an aircraft carrier arm in 1951. Initial plans focused on the conversion of an Italian cruiser for aircraft operations, but this was shelved, together with plans to acquire an 'Essex'-class carrier from the US, the latter abandoned on cost grounds.

Spain had to wait until 1967 before introducing a true aircraft carrier, with the transfer of the SNS *Dédalo* (PH 01) in August that year. The *Dédalo* was the former USS *Cabot*, an 'Independence'-class light carrier, with a wooden flight deck that was retained in Spanish service. In the meantime, an initial carrier aviation unit had been established in November 1954, as 1a Escuadrilla at Marin in northwest Spain. Initial equipment comprised three Bell 47G-2 helicopters.

In 1957 operations of the Arma Aérea, Spanish Naval Aviation, had been centred upon Rota naval air station. The units at this base formed an air group, known as the Unidad Aérea Embarcada when operating from the carrier. A first ASW unit was established as 2a Escuadrilla, equipped with the Sikorsky HRS-2, while 3a Escuadrilla stood up in

1964, operating the Agusta-Bell AB204A. It was an AB204A that completed the first landing and take-off on the *Dédalo*, in December 1967. In total, four AB204As were used, their primary role being ASW, for which they were equipped with dipping sonar, torpedoes and depth charges. The AB204As were retired in 1978–79.

### Helicopter revamp

In 1978 a new unit was created to operate the Hughes 500, 6a Escuadrilla receiving 14 of these helicopters, equipped for anti-submarine operations as the Model 500M-ASW. The Hughes 500s primarily operated from the Navy's FRAM destroyers, but were frequently embarked in small numbers on the *Dédalo*, mainly for liaison duties. Initially supplied under the Military Defense Assistance Program, Spain purchased the *Dédalo* outright in 1973. By this time, the Sikorsky SH-3D Sea King was well established as the Spanish Navy's primary ASW helicopter, while the AB212ASW had replaced the AB204 as the standard light ASW helicopter. The AB212 joined 3a Escuadrilla in 1974, with 14 aircraft being acquired up to 1980. The

### Specifications

Crew: 1

Powerplant: 1 x 105kN (23,500lbf) Rolls-Royce F402-RR-408 vectored-thrust turbofan engine

Maximum speed: 1070km/h (662mph)

Range: 2200km (1400 miles)

Dimensions: span 9.25m (30ft 4in); length 14.12m (46ft 4in); height 3.55m (11ft 8in)

Weight: 10,410kg (22,950lb) loaded

Armament: 2 x 30mm (1.2in) cannon mounted under fuselage; provisions for up to 5988kg (13,200lb) payload including rockets, air-to-air missiles, air-to-surface missiles and guided and unguided bombs

### ▼ McDonnell Douglas AV-8S Matador

*8a Escuadrilla, Rota, 1994*

With poor relations with the UK at the time, Spain acquired its Harriers through US channels, although subsequently the Spanish and British enjoyed the benefits of joint training. The AV-8S Matador also had a reconnaissance capability, using the F95 camera that was fitted behind an aperture in the port side of the nose. 8a Escuadrilla flew the Matador until August 1996.

## Specifications

Crew: 4

Powerplant: 2 x 1400kW (1877hp) General Electric T58-GE-10 turboshaft

Maximum speed: 267km/h (166mph)

Range: 1000km (621 miles)

Service ceiling: 4481m (14,700ft)

Dimensions: Rotor diameter 19m (62ft 0in); length 16.7m (54ft 9in); height 5.13m (16ft 10in)

Weight: 8449kg (18,626lb) loaded

Armament: B-57 depth charge; door guns and gun turrets

### ▼ Sikorsky SH-3D Sea King

*5a Escuadrilla, 1967*

The SH-3D was delivered for service with 5a Escuadrilla, which had originally been established at NAS Key West in Florida in November 1965. The first three SH-3Ds then arrived at Rota in Spain during the course of 1966. As originally delivered, Spain's SH-3Ds wore a gloss sea blue colour scheme, which later gave way to a low-visibility grey.

SH-3D began to equip 5a Escuadrilla in 1966, and 18 examples were taken on charge until 1981.

In order to introduce a fixed-wing component to its carrier arm, Spain ordered the Harrier V/STOL fighter, and became the first operator to routinely embark the jet on a carrier. Spain placed orders for the Harrier via the US government, with a contract covering six single-seat AV-8S that were locally designated VA.1 Matador, plus a pair of two-seat TAV-8S, designated as the VAE.1 Matador. Subsequently, a further five AV-8S aircraft were added to the order. The Matador pilots were trained in the US, and embarked in the *Dédalo* in US waters in 1976, returning to Rota before the end of the year. The Matadors were primarily used for air defence, armed with AIM-9 Sidewinders and two 30mm (1.2in) cannon, but could also carry bombs and rockets for air-to-ground duties. With the addition of a fixed, removable refuelling probe, the Matadors could be refuelled in flight, and this was conducted using Spanish Air Force KC-130H and KC-707 tankers. Until 1984, Matador pilots were trained by the Royal Air Force's 233 Operational Conversion Unit.

8a Escuadrilla was commissioned with the Matador in September 1976, and the aircraft first went to sea aboard *Dédalo* the following year. With the addition of the Matador, the designation of SNS *Dédalo* was revised to PA 01, reflecting its new fixed-

wing aviation capability. The carrier also required some modifications to operate Matadors, receiving a strengthened flight deck and elevators, and other upgrades. The carrier's ultimate air group typically comprised six Matadors and up to 20 helicopters, including SH-3s, AB212s and Hughes 500s. 2a Escuadrilla was disbanded in 1978, while 1a Escuadrilla followed suit in 1987.

With the arrival of a new carrier, the *Principe de Asturias*, in 1988, the time had come to withdraw *Dédalo*, and the vessel was duly decommissioned in August 1989. The AV-8A Matador unit, 8a Escuadrilla, was subsequently disbanded in August 1996, and its surviving aircraft were sold to Thailand.

## Arma Aérea de la Armada

| Carrier-deployable units, 1954–86 | HQ Rota |
| --- | --- |
| 1a Escuadrilla | Bell 47G-2/OH-13 |
| 2a Escuadrilla | HRS-2 |
| 3a Escuadrilla | AB.204AS, AH-1G Cobra (Det), AB.212ASW |
| 5a Escuadrilla | SH-3D Sea King |
| 6a Escuadrilla | Hughes 369M |
| 7a Escuadrilla | AH-1G Cobra |
| 8a Escuadrilla | AV-8S/TAV-8S Matador |

# United Kingdom
## 1946–59

**The Fleet Air Arm played a crucial role in carrier-based power projection during the immediate inter-war period, with successive campaigns waged over Korea, Malaya and the Canal Zone.**

BY THE END of World War II, the Royal Navy possessed a carrier arm second only in size to that of the United States. At VJ-Day, the Royal Navy could call upon 34 carriers of various types in the Far East alone, and 72 front-line squadrons that included Seafire, Corsair and Hellcat fighters, and Barracuda, Firefly and Avenger multi-purpose types. However, post-war cutbacks saw a number of incomplete carriers transferred to other navies, while planned new carriers were cancelled. As such, the Royal Navy entered the immediate post-war period with the 'Colossus' class light fleet carrier as its most important aircraft carrier class. Since these carriers were relatively small, they were limited to embarking two front-line squadrons each.

By 1950, US-supplied Lend-Lease types had been disposed of, and the Fleet Air Arm's front-line strength now included three carrier-deployable squadrons of Sea Fury fighter-bombers, four of Seafire fighters, two of Sea Hornet fighters and night-fighters, five of Firefly night-fighter and anti-submarine aircraft, one of Blackburn Firebrand torpedo-fighters and one of Barracuda torpedo-reconnaissance aircraft.

Originally conceived as a cannon-armed carrier-based interceptor, the Firebrand went into service with No. 813 NAS as a torpedo-fighter, but proved to be too unwieldy for successful carrier operations, although it fared better than the twin-engined de Havilland Sea Mosquito that equipped No. 811 NAS, but which was restricted to operations from land bases. More successful was the Sea Hornet, a conceptual development of the Mosquito, which served in carriers in day-fighter, night-fighter and photo-reconnaissance roles. Powered by two Rolls-Royce Merlins, the Sea Hornet first saw service with No. 801 NAS, established at RNAS Ford in June 1947, and first deployed in HMS *Implacable* in 1949. The ultimate FAA piston-engined type, however, was the Sea Fury, which entered service in 1947, and which became the standard carrier-based strike fighter across the Commonwealth.

Production of the Sea Fury, the Royal Navy's last piston-engined fighter, concentrated on the FB.Mk 11, which superseded the wartime FB.Mk X, orders for which were slashed after the end of hostilities. The 50 Sea Fury FB.Mk Xs first saw service with No. 807

### Specifications

| | |
|---|---|
| Crew: 1 | Dimensions: span 15.62m (51ft 3.5in); length 12m (39ft 1in) |
| Powerplant: 1 x 1865kW (2500hp) Bristol Centaurus IX 18-cylinder radial engine | Weight: 7100kg (15,671lb) loaded |
| Maximum speed: 560km/h (350mph) | Armament: Four 20mm (.79in) Hispano Mk II cannons; two 454kg (1000lb) bombs or one 840kg (1850lb) Mark XVII torpedo |
| Range: 2000km (1250 miles) | |
| Rate of climb: 13.2m/s (2600ft/min) | |

### ▼ Blackburn Firebrand TF.Mk V

**No. 703 NAS**

EK747 was an example of the Firebrand TF.Mk V, the definitive version of the aircraft, and the second to see front-line service, after the TF.Mk IV. Both variants were powered by the Centaurus IX engine, the Mk V being a conversion of the earlier model. No. 703 NAS was one of six second-line Firebrand units.

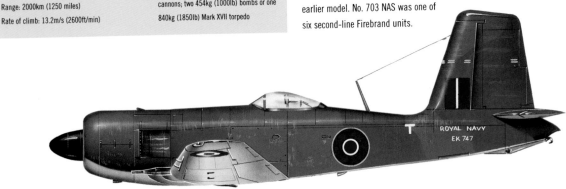

| Typical Royal Navy carrier air group, Korean War | |
| --- | --- |
| Carrier Air Group 14 | |
| HMS *Glory* (R62) | 'Colossus' class |
| April 1951 to May 1952 | |
| 804 NAS | Sea Fury FB.Mk 11 |
| 812 NAS | Firefly FR.Mk 5 |

NAS in August 1947, but were soon superseded by the definitive FB.Mk 11, a fighter-bomber with a pair of underwing pylons and provision for rocket-assisted take-off gear. No. 802 NAS was the first to receive the FB.Mk 11, in May 1948, and the 615 production aircraft completed to this standard saw service with the Royal Australian and Canadian navies, as well as with eight front-line FAA squadrons, and two Reserve squadrons.

The Firefly was the standard fighter-reconnaissance, night-fighter and anti-submarine warfare type within the FAA into the early 1950s. By 1950 there was just one front-line squadron equipped with the wartime Firefly F.Mk 1. The next production model was the FR.Mk 4 with an improved Griffon engine and wing-mounted radiators, while the FR.Mk 5 of 1948 was a multi-role type with a 'universal' fuselage. The Mk 5 was issued to first-line squadrons from early 1949 and was followed by the Firefly AS.Mk 6 introduced in

1951, a dedicated ASW aircraft with detection gear including sonobuoys. The first operator of the Firefly AS.Mk 6 was No. 814 NAS in January 1951, and the type went on to equip five front-line squadrons before being handed over to Reserve units.

## War in Korea

When war broke out in Korea in 1950, the Royal Navy sent the 'Colossus'-class HMS *Triumph* to the area, and at this time the carrier embarked an air group of Seafire FR.Mk 47s and Firefly FR.Mk 1s and NF.Mk 1s, these flying their first strikes over Korea on 3 July 1950. A Commonwealth carrier would be on station until the end of the fighting, with HMS *Theseus* replacing *Triumph* in October 1950 and introducing an air group of Sea Fury FB.Mk 11s and Firefly FR.Mk 5s of the 17th Carrier Air Group, which would eventually complete almost 3500 sorties during a seven-month deployment. These two types became the standard for the rest of the war, supported by the Sikorsky S-51 Dragonfly for plane-guard work, the helicopter replacing the Supermarine Sea Otter amphibian in this role from 1951. Other Royal Navy carriers involved in the Korean effort were HMS *Glory*, first on station with the 14th CAG from April 1951, and HMS *Ocean*, which arrived in May 1952 with the 17th CAG. By the time hostilities ended in July 1953, FAA aircraft had flown almost 23,000 sorties

### Specifications

Crew: 1

Powerplant: 1 x 1850kW (2480hp) Griffon 87/88 radial engine

Maximum speed: 740km/h (460mph)

Range: 1127km (700 miles)

Service ceiling: 10,900m (35,800ft)

Dimensions: span 11.7m (38ft 4.75in); length 10.6m (34ft 8in); height 4.9m (16ft 1in)

Weight: 5670kg (12,500lb) loaded

Armament: Four 20mm (.79in) Hispano Mk V cannons; twelve 76.2mm (3in) rockets, 907kg (2000lb) bomb load

▼ **Supermarine Seafire FR.Mk 47**

**No. 800 NAS, HMS *Triumph*, *1950***

This Seafire was one of those embarked on HMS *Triumph* for the carrier's contribution to the UN effort in the Korean War. No. 800 NAS was the second and final unit to be equipped with the Seafire FR.Mk 47, and its aircraft flew 300 sorties over Korea between July and September 1950. The FR.Mk 47 was the ultimate mark of Seafire, with a Griffon 87/88 engine driving a contra-rotating propeller and with provision for rocket-assisted take-off gear.

## Specifications

Crew: 2

Powerplant: 1 x 1678kW (2250hp) Rolls-Royce
Griffon 74 V-12 piston engine

Maximum speed: 618km/h (386mph)

Range: 2092km (1300 miles)

Service ceiling: 9450m (31,000ft)

Dimensions: span 12.55m (41ft 2in); length
8.51m (27ft 11in); height 4.37m (14ft 4in)

Weight: 7301kg (16,096lb) loaded

Armament: Four 20mm (.79in) Hispano
cannons; up to 907kg (2000lb) of bombs or
1627kg (3587lb) rockets

### ▼ Fairey Firefly FR.Mk 5
#### No. 821 NAS, HMS Glory, 1953

Seen with undercarriage deployed and with a rocket projectile underwing, this
Firefly is depicted as it appeared in March 1953, during a Korean combat cruise
aboard HMS *Glory* that had begun in September 1952. Introduced to production in
1948, the FR.Mk 5 was the most important post-war mark of Firefly, and could be
configured to carry out a range of missions. Three FAA squadrons flew the FR.Mk 5
on combat tours during the Korean conflict.

## Specifications

Crew: 1

Powerplant: 1 x 1850kW (2480hp) Bristol
Centaurus XVIIC 18-cylinder twin-row
radial engine

Maximum speed: 740km/h (460mph)

Range: 1127km (700 miles)

Service ceiling: 10,900m (35,800ft)

Dimensions: span 11.7m (38ft 4.75in); length
10.6m (34ft 8in); height 4.9m (16ft 1in)

Weight: 5670kg (12,500lb) loaded

Armament: Four 20mm (.79in) Hispano Mk V
cannons; Twelve 76.2mm (3in) rockets; 907kg
(2000lb) bomb load

### ▼ Hawker Sea Fury FB.Mk 11
#### No. 802 NAS, HMS Ocean, 1952

This famous Sea Fury was the mount of Lieutenant Peter Carmichael when he
downed a MiG-15 jet fighter over Korea on 9 August 1952. Despite tangling with
MiGs, the Sea Fury's primary role in Korea was ground attack, for which it could
carry 227kg (500lb) or 454kg (1000lb) bombs or rocket projectiles. No. 802 NAS
was the second front-line operator, and received its first
Sea Furies in April 1948, initially operating the
FB.Mk X version.

and had lost 22 pilots in operations, as well as
another 13 in non-combat accidents.

The Royal Navy deployed carriers to participate in
other actions in the 1950s, notably in Malaya. As
early as August 1949, HMS *Triumph* was deployed to
the Far East Station, with Seafire FR.Mk 47s and
Firefly FR.Mk 1s and NF.Mk 1s flying raids against
bandit positions from October 1949 to January
1950. HMS *Glory* and *Ocean* were also involved in
the Malayan Emergency from 1952, while HMS

*Warrior* launched its Fireflies to attack Malayan
communists in 1954.

## New carrier classes

Although only piston-engined types would be flown
in combat in Korea, the FAA entered the jet age in
1951, and the first generation of these aircraft were
employed by the four new 'Centaur'-class light fleet
carriers (HMS *Centaur*, *Albion*, *Bulwark* and
*Hermes*), as well as HMS *Eagle*, a fleet carrier of the

'Audacious' class. In December 1945, Lieutenant Commander Eric Brown had successfully landed a naval-adapted de Havilland Vampire on the deck of HMS *Ocean*, but it was not until 1952 that the first jet entered front-line FAA service. The FAA's first operational jet, the Supermarine Attacker of No. 800 NAS, embarked in HMS *Eagle* in March 1952. The Attacker had originally been designed as a Royal Air Force day fighter, the prototype of 1946 being navalized and returning to the air in June 1947 before embarking in HMS *Illustrious* for carrier trials in October that year. The initial-production Attacker F.Mk 1 was powered by a Rolls-Royce Nene engine, and 52 examples were completed, together with eight Attacker FB.Mk 2s that had underwing pylons for offensive stores. The final Attacker FB.Mk 2 entered production in 1952 and was powered by a new Nene Mk 102 turbojet, 85 examples of this version being delivered to the FAA by 1953. Alongside No. 800 NAS, Nos 803 and 890 NAS were the only front-line units, and its service was destined to be brief, the fighter being superseded by the Hawker Sea Hawk as the standard FAA day fighter from 1954.

Powered by a Rolls-Royce Nene turbojet, the initial-production Sea Hawk F.Mk 1 variant was first flown in November 1951 and subsequently entered service with No. 806 NAS in March 1953, going to sea aboard *Eagle* in the Mediterranean less than a year later, in February 1954. After 35 examples of the F.Mk 1 had been completed, production switched to the F.Mk 2, with 60 of this model being built, featuring power-assisted ailerons. The Sea Hawk FB.Mk 3 optimized the design for the ground-attack role, with a strengthened wing to carry bomb or rocket armament. Four front-line units were flying the FB.Mk 3 by the end of 1954, when the Sea Hawk FGA.Mk 4 was introduced, this being tailored for the close air support role. The final production model was the similar Sea Hawk FGA.Mk 6, this utilizing a new Nene 103 engine. The Sea Hawk FB.Mk 5 was the Mk 3 refitted with the same engine. As the pre-eminent FAA day fighter during the 1950s, the Sea Hawk saw the decade out in front-line service, the final operational unit, No. 806 NAS, disbanding in December 1960.

### ▼ De Havilland Sea Hornet F.Mk 20

Representing the first generation of new carrier aircraft to be introduced by the FAA after World War II, these Sea Hornet F.Mk 20s were operated by No. 801 NAS, shore-based at RNAS Ford, the only front-line unit to be equipped with this version of the fighter. First deployment was in HMS *Implacable* in 1949.

In 1954 the FAA received its first radar-equipped jet, with the de Havilland Sea Venom two-seat all-weather fighter entering service with No. 890 NAS at RNAS Yeovilton in March.

The Sea Venom replaced the piston-engined Sea Hornet, with the initial service version being the FAW.Mk 20, which began trials in HMS *Illustrious* in July 1951. Fifty examples of the initial production model were completed before the appearance of the Sea Venom FAW.Mk 21 with AI.M 21 radar and more powerful Ghost Mk 104 engine. After 167 FAW.Mk 21s, 39 of the definitive Sea Venom FAW.Mk 22 were completed, with Ghost Mk 105 and AI.Mk 22 radar. From 1958 this version became the first operational British fighter with missile armament, when it received the de Havilland Blue Jay (later Firestreak) guided weapon. Operating units comprised seven front-line squadrons by the time of the Suez Crisis, all of which operated the FAW.Mk 21. The Sea Venom FAW.Mk 22 served with three operational units from 1957.

At the same time as the Sea Hawk and Sea Venom were swelling the ranks, the FAA was introducing an airborne early warning capability to its air groups, with the Douglas Skyraider AEW.Mk 1 that entered service with No. 849 NAS in July 1952, the initial operational assignment being completed by the squadron's 'A' Flight, aboard HMS *Eagle*. Thereafter, the squadron provided four flights for deployment in carriers at sea, while the HQ flight operated from RNAS Culdrose. In an effort to expand its attack capabilities, the FAA introduced to service the turboprop-powered Westland Wyvern strike aircraft as a replacement for the Firebrand from 1953, although by now the specialist torpedo-carrying role had been abandoned in favour of more general attack duties. No. 813 NAS, the first operational Wyvern S.Mk 4 unit, stood up in May 1953, going aboard HMS *Albion* in the Mediterranean in September. Despite its troubled development, with three different engines trialled before the Armstrong Siddeley Python was selected, the Wyvern was adopted by four front-line squadrons. The type proved its worth in the Suez campaign, in the course of which 79 sorties were flown by No. 813 NAS for the loss of two aircraft in combat.

## British innovations

In order to employ the first generation of turbine-powered carrier aircraft to best effect, the Royal Navy adapted its aircraft carriers accordingly, introducing the angled deck, first tested in 1951 and swiftly adopted by the US Navy and other nations. While earlier carriers were retrofitted, HMS *Ark Royal* of 1955 became the first carrier to be completed with an angled deck. Other British developments in carrier design improved the margin of safety, and included the mirror landing system (replacing the batsman previously used to guide pilots during a deck landing), while the use of steam-powered catapults, incorporated in the fleet from 1955, allowed heavier aircraft to be launched.

### Specifications

Crew: 1

Powerplant: 1 x 24kN (5395lb) Rolls-Royce Nene Mk 103

Maximum speed: 965km/h (600mph)

Range: 772km (417 miles)

Service ceiling: 13,564m (44,000ft)

Dimensions: span 11.9m (39ft); length 12.3m (40ft 4in); height 3m (9ft 9in)

Weight: 7500kg (16,535lb) loaded

Armament: 4 x 20mm (.79in) Hispano Mk V cannons; 6 x underwing hardpoints with provisions to carry combinations of 20 x 27kg (60lb) rockets or 16 x 127mm (5in) unguided rockets; 4 x 500lb (227kg) bombs

### ▼ Armstrong Whitworth (Hawker) Sea Hawk FGA.Mk 4

**No. 810 NAS, HMS Albion, 1956**

Armed with underwing rocket projectiles, this Sea Hawk FGA.Mk 4 flew from HMS *Albion* during Operation Musketeer, the British military response to Egypt's nationalization of the Suez Canal in 1956. The FGA.Mk 4 version was tailored to the close air support mission, and was delivered to units from 1954. After 97 examples had been built, production switched to the definitive FGA.Mk 6, with the more powerful Nene Mk 103 turbojet engine.

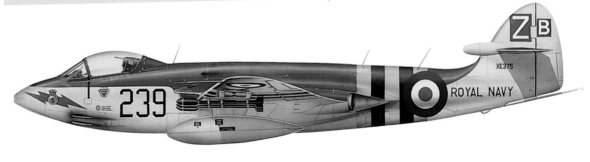

### ▼ Westland Dragonfly HR.Mk 3

#### *HMS* Ark Royal, *1952*

A licence-built version of the Sikorsky S-51, the Westland Dragonfly was the first
FAA helicopter to make regular deployments aboard warships. The initial-
production Dragonfly HR.Mk 1 was in service from January 1950, before being
superseded by the HR.Mk 3 that incorporated metal rotor blades. The final variant
to see service with the FAA was the Dragonfly HR.Mk 5, with minor improvements,
and which was similarly assigned to ship's flights.

#### Specifications

Crew: 1–3

Powerplant: 1 x 403kW (540hp) Alvis Leonides
50 radial piston engine

Maximum speed: 153km/h (95mph)

Range: 483km (300 miles)

Service ceiling: 3780m (12,400ft)

Dimensions: Rotor diameter 14.63m (48ft 0in);
length 17.54m (57ft 6.5in); height 3.95m
(12ft 11.5in)

Weight: 2663kg (5870lb) loaded

Armament: None

### ▼ Blackburn Firebrand TF.Mk 5

Four carriers played host to two front-line Firebrand squadrons. These No. 813 NAS Mk Vs enjoyed short periods aboard HMS *Implacable* between 1947 and 1950.

**◄ de Havilland Sea Venom FAW.Mk 21**

After sustaining damage from anti-aircraft fire over Egypt's Almaza airfield on 2 November 1956, this No. 893 NAS Sea Venom FAW.Mk 21 was lucky to return safely to *Eagle* for a belly landing. During the Suez Crisis, Sea Venoms from Nos 809, 892 and 893 NAS were responsible for flying rocket and bomb attacks against Egyptian airfields, supply columns and armour. The aircraft were embarked in HMS *Albion* and *Eagle*.

In order to tackle the growing threat posed by submarines, the FAA initially relied upon American-supplied Avengers. A new, dedicated anti-submarine aircraft was available from 1955, with the Fairey Gannet. Powered by a unique twin-propeller turbine unit, the Armstrong Siddeley Double Mamba, the initial Gannet AS.Mk 1 accommodated a crew of three and was equipped with a capacious weapons bay as well as retractable radar scanner, meaning that the hunter and killer roles could be undertaken by the same aircraft. An order for 100 Gannet AS.Mk 1s was placed in March 1951, and in January 1955 the type entered front-line service with No. 826 NAS, which embarked in *Eagle* for a Mediterranean cruise in June

1955. In the mid-1950s another five operational carrier-borne squadrons were equipped with the Gannet AS.Mk 1, and in April 1956 a new production version was introduced. The Gannet AS.Mk 4 differed in its use of a more powerful Double Mamba 104 powerplant.

## Dawn of the helicopter

The Gannet would soon be supported – and eventually replaced – in its ASW role by helicopters. After early trials work from 1945 involving Sikorsky Hoverflies, the first helicopter to see regular service from Royal Navy carrier decks was the Dragonfly, which equipped No. 705 NAS from 1950, but its size

### Specifications

| | |
|---|---|
| Crew: 1 | 12.09m (39ft 8in); height 2.64m (8ft 8in) |
| Powerplant: 1 x 24kN (5400lbf) Rolls-Royce Nene 103 turbojet | Weight: 7348kg (16,200lb) loaded |
| | Armament: Four 20mm (.79in) Hispano |
| Maximum speed: 969km/h (602mph) | cannons; provision for four 227kg (500lb) |
| Range: 370km (230 miles) | bombs, or two 227kg (500lb) bombs and |
| Service ceiling: 13,565m (44,500ft) | twenty 89mm (3.5in) or sixteen 127mm |
| Dimensions: span 11.89m (39ft 0in); length | (5in) rockets |

**▼ Armstrong Whitworth (Hawker) Sea Hawk FB.Mk 3**

*No. 802 NAS, HMS Albion, 1956*

The FB.Mk 3 was the first Sea Hawk to introduce a genuine ground-attack capability, with a strengthened wing and associated hardpoints for the carriage of bombs or rockets. As well as operating the Mk 3 during the Suez Crisis, No. 802 NAS employed the Mk 1, 2, 4 and 5 versions between 1955 and 1960.

limited it to light utility and plane-guard work. More capable was the Sikorsky S-55 that arrived in 1952, and which was licence-built as the Westland Whirlwind, which served in the SAR, transport and, latterly the ASW roles. The Whirlwind was the first Royal Navy helicopter to be routinely employed in combat operations, and served as an assault transport in Malaya from 1953. The honour fell upon No. 848 NAS, which had been established in October 1952 with a complement of 10 Sikorsky HRS-2s, which operated under the British designation Whirlwind HAR.Mk 21. The helicopters embarked in HMS *Perseus* and sailed to the Far East before the end of 1952, and the unit served for three years in the campaign against the communist guerrillas.

Following on from the US-supplied Whirlwind HAR.Mk 21, the HAR.Mk 1 was the British-built equivalent, examples being delivered to No. 705 NAS in October 1954 for SAR duties. Some of the 10 Mk 1s were also used by No. 848 NAS, flying anti-terrorist missions in Malaya. The next model was the Sikorsky-built Whirlwind HAS.Mk 22, the first of the FAA Whirlwinds to assume an ASW role. The 15 HAS.Mk 22s were taken on charge by No. 845 NAS in March 1954, and featured dipping sonar. The HAS.Mk 22 was pressed into the commando transport role during the Suez campaign, operating from *Theseus*. The Westland-built HAR.Mk 3 (20 built) was the first Whirlwind to regularly embark on carriers, undertaking SAR and communications

duties in HMS *Albion*, *Ark Royal*, *Bulwark*, *Eagle* and *Warrior* from 1955 to 1959. Only seven HAR.Mk 5s were completed, but these were the first to introduce a British powerplant, with the Alvis Leonides major engine. The HAS.Mk 7 was the major ASW model, 120 examples equipping 11 front-line units from August 1957 and carrying radar, dipping sonar and homing torpedoes.

## Suez Crisis

By the time of the Suez Crisis in 1956 the FAA maintained 23 front-line squadrons, most of which were now equipped with jet equipment, and two of which were operating helicopters. Britain's response to the nationalization of the Suez Canal by Egypt's President Nasser in 1956 included a naval task force under Operation Musketeer. Together with France and Israel, the UK launched attacks on Egypt on 1 November 1956, and aircraft from the carriers HMS *Eagle*, *Albion* and *Bulwark* played a significant role. Sea Hawks, Sea Venoms and Wyverns all flew strikes against Egyptian airfields before extending their range of targets to include Egyptian armour, naval vessels and other military objectives. In the first five days of fighting, FAA aircraft generated almost 1300 sorties. On 5 November, a joint French/British airborne assault was launched on Port Said, with Sea Hawks and Sea Venoms flying standing patrols to cover the paratroopers. The following day Whirlwinds from HMS *Ocean* and *Theseus*

<table>
<tr><td colspan="2">**Specifications**</td></tr>
<tr><td>Crew: 2</td><td>Dimensions: span 13.06m (42ft 10in); length</td></tr>
<tr><td>Powerplant: 1 x 23.6kN (5300lbf) de Havilland</td><td>11.15m (36ft 7in); height 2.60m (8ft 6in)</td></tr>
<tr><td> Ghost 105 turbojet</td><td>Weight: 7167kg (15,800lb) loaded</td></tr>
<tr><td>Maximum speed: 927km/h (575mph)</td><td>Armament: Four 20mm (.79in) Hispano Mk V</td></tr>
<tr><td>Range: 1135km (705 miles)</td><td>cannons, eight RP-3 27kg (60lb) rockets, two</td></tr>
<tr><td>Service ceiling: 12,040m (39,500ft)</td><td>450kg (1000lb) bombs</td></tr>
</table>

▼ **de Havilland Sea Venom FAW.Mk 21**

*No. 809 NAS, HMS Albion, 1956*

British tactical aircraft involved in Operation Musketeer generally received the yellow and black recognition stripes worn by this No. 809 NAS Sea Venom FAW.Mk 21, embarked in HMS *Albion*. No. 809 NAS completed 138 combat sorties during the Suez Crisis, with typical targets including Egyptian airfields, tanks and other military vehicles. The Sea Venom FAW.Mk 21 introduced AI.Mk 21 radar.

transported Royal Marines in the first large-scale heliborne assault to be launched. Despite the capture of Port Said, international pressure brought an end to the campaign, and a ceasefire was imposed.

The final major conflict in which FAA airpower was involved was the Iraqi coup of July 1958, when HMS *Eagle* sailed to the Mediterranean where its aircraft provided cover for an airlift into the Jordanian capital, Amman. Skyraiders provided AEW coverage while Sea Hawks and Sea Venoms flew defensive sorties to cover the airlift effort.

## New-generation jets

By 1959, HMS *Hermes*, the last 'Centaur'-class carrier was put into service and HMS *Victorious* (originally laid down during World War II) was returned to service in modernized form, these advanced new carriers featuring angled decks and increased capacity in order to operate a new generation of heavier, high-performance aircraft, typified by the Supermarine Scimitar and de Havilland Sea Vixen, which would replace the Sea Hawk and Sea Venom, respectively, in the coming years. With new fleet carriers coming on line, the Royal Navy could transfer HMS *Bulwark* to the assault carrier role, and it would be joined as a commando carrier by HMS *Albion*.

| Royal Navy carrier air wings, Suez Crisis, 1956 | |
| --- | --- |
| HMS *Albion* (R07) | 'Centaur' class |
| 800 NAS | Sea Hawk FGA.Mk 4/6 |
| 802 NAS | Sea Hawk FB.Mk 3 |
| 809 NAS | Sea Venom FAW.Mk 21 |
| 849 NAS (C Flight) | Skyraider AEW.Mk 1 |
| | |
| HMS *Bulwark* (R08) | 'Centaur' class |
| 804 NAS | Sea Hawk FGA.Mk 6 |
| 810 NAS | Sea Hawk FGA.Mk 4 |
| 895 NAS | Sea Hawk FB.Mk 3 |
| | |
| HMS *Eagle* (R05) | 'Audacious' class |
| 830 NAS | Wyvern S.Mk 4 |
| 892 NAS | Sea Venom FAW.Mk 21 |
| 893 NAS | Sea Venom FAW.Mk 21 |
| 897 NAS | Sea Hawk FGA.Mk 6 |
| 899 NAS | Sea Hawk FGA.Mk 6 |
| 849 NAS (A Flight) | Skyraider AEW.Mk 1 |
| | |
| HMS *Theseus* (R64) | 'Centaur' class |
| 845 NAS | Whirlwind HAS.Mk 22 |

### Specifications

Crew: 1

Powerplant: 1 x 2736kW (3667hp) Armstrong Siddeley Python 3 axial flow turboprop engine

Maximum speed: 613km/h (383mph)

Range: 1446km (904 miles)

Service ceiling: 8537m (28,000ft)

Dimensions: span 13.42m (44ft 0in); length 12.88m (42ft 3in); height 4.57m (15ft)

Weight: 9636kg (21,200lb) loaded

Armament: Four 20mm (.79in) Hispano Mk V cannons; up to 1364kg (3000lb) bomb load or one Mk 15/17 torpedo or sea mine

### ▼ Westland Wyvern S.Mk 4
**No. 830 NAS, HMS Eagle, *1956***

Seen as it appeared during Operation Musketeer, the British participation in the Suez intervention, this Wyvern carries underwing rocket projectiles and fuel tanks, with a bomb on the centreline station. The Wyvern suffered from a protracted development and enjoyed only a brief front-line career. No. 830 NAS received its first Wyverns in 1955 and was the only unit to take the aircraft to war. Once HMS *Eagle* returned to the UK after the Suez operation, the squadron was disbanded in 1957.

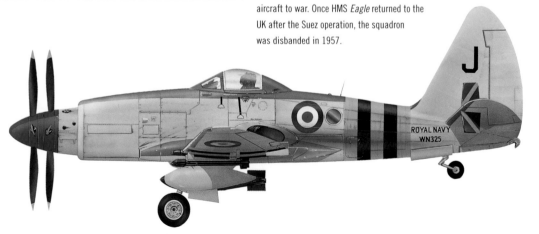

The Scimitar arrived in service in June 1958, the swept-wing fighter powered by two Rolls-Royce Avon engines and armed with four 30mm (1.2in) cannon plus bombs, rockets and (later) Sidewinder missiles carried underwing. The initial operational unit was No. 803 NAS, which embarked in *Victorious* in 1958. Although originally schemed as a fighter, the Scimitar later found its forte in the low-level strike role, and was assigned responsibility for tactical nuclear weapons delivery. When *Hermes* commissioned towards the end of 1959, the carrier embarked an advanced air group of No. 804 NAS Scimitar F.Mk 1s and No. 890 NAS Sea Vixen FAW.Mk 1s.

The twin-boomed, twin-Avon Sea Vixen was a two-seater, with an observer to operate the guided weapons system, which was linked to the carrier's long-range surveillance radar and which also included Firestreak infrared-homing missiles.

## Specifications

Crew: 1

Powerplant: 1 x 2013kW (2700hp) Pratt & Whitney R-3350 radial piston engine

Maximum speed: 518km/h (322mph)

Range: 2115km (1316 miles)

Service ceiling: 8685m (28,500ft)

Dimensions: span 15.25m (50ft 0in); length 11.84m (38ft 10in); height 4.78m (15ft 8in)

Weight: 8213kg (18,106lb) loaded

Armament: Four 20mm (.79in) M2 cannons; up to 3600kg (8000lb) of ordnance including bombs, torpedoes, mine dispensers, unguided rockets or gun pods

### ▼ Douglas Skyraider AEW.Mk 1

**No. 849 NAS, HMS Eagle, 1956**

Wearing the markings of 'A' Flight No. 849 NAS, and identification stripes for the Suez operation, this Skyraider AEW.Mk 1 carries the deck letter 'J' to indicate assignment to HMS *Eagle*. The Skyraider provided a useful stopgap in the airborne early warning role prior to the arrival of the Gannet AEW.Mk 3, serving until 1960.

## Specifications

Crew: 3

Powerplant: 1 x 2200kW (2950hp) Double Mamba 100 turboprop engine

Maximum speed: 499km/h (310mph)

Range: 1111km (690 miles)

Service ceiling: 7620m (25,000ft)

Dimensions: span 16.54m (54ft 4in); length 13.11m (43ft 0in); height 4.18m (13ft 9in)

Weight: 8890kg (19,600lb) loaded

Armament: Up to 907kg (2000lb) of torpedoes, mines, bombs or depth charges

### ▼ Fairey Gannet AS.Mk 1

**No. 815 NAS, HMS Ark Royal**

The Gannet AS.Mk 1 anti-submarine warfare aircraft was powered by an ingenious twin-propeller turbine, with two separate engine 'halves', one of which could be shut down for economical cruising, for example when tracking a submerged contact. Weaponry (typically two torpedoes) was carried within a large internal weapons bay, while immediately behind this was the retractable radar antenna. Rockets could be carried underwing.

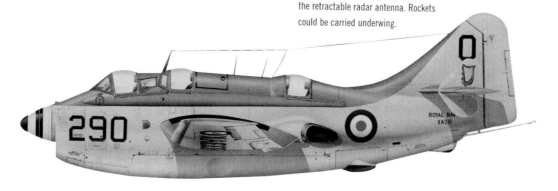

# United Kingdom
## 1960–89

**The once-impressive Royal Navy carrier arm began to contract from the early 1960s, but would rise from the ashes in time for the Falklands War, with a new generation of V/STOL carriers.**

THE FLEET AIR ARM began the new decade with the introduction of two important new types, the Wessex HAS.Mk 1 to replace the Whirlwind HAS.Mk 7 and Gannet AS.Mk 4 in the carrier-based anti-submarine role, and the Gannet AEW.Mk 3 to succeed the Avenger AEW.Mk 1 for airborne early warning. The Gannet AEW.Mk 3 was an almost entirely new design, with an uprated Double Mamba engine, and an enclosed cabin in the fuselage to accommodate two operators for the AN/APS-20F radar. The operational unit for the type was No. 849 NAS, which established its 'A' Flight in February 1960, before providing four carrier-based flights of three or four aircraft each. The Gannet AEW.Mk 3 remained a valuable asset until the final withdrawal of HMS *Ark Royal*, and the last operator, 'B' Flight, was stood down in December 1978.

### Whirlwind replacement

A Westland-built version of the Sikorsky S-58, the turbine-powered Wessex HAS.Mk 1 entered service with No. 815 NAS in July 1961, and its arrival allowed the Whirlwind HAS.Mk 7 to be re-roled for the commando transport role – in this capacity, they

▲ **Supermarine Scimitar**

Photographed in 1959, Scimitar F.Mk 1s share the crowded flight deck of HMS *Victorious* with Sea Venom FAW.Mk 22s of No. 893 NAS and Skyraider AEW.Mk 1s of 'B' Flight, No. 849 NAS. The Scimitars were operated by No. 803 NAS, the first operational unit, which began to receive the fighters in June 1958 before embarking in *Victorious* for a cruise of the Mediterranean in September.

▼ **de Havilland Sea Vixen FAW.Mk 1**

**No. 890 NAS, HMS** Ark Royal, *1961*

The Sea Vixen FAW.Mk 1 was the original version of this powerful all-weather interceptor, with provision for in-flight refuelling and armament of Firestreak missiles or four packs of Microcell unguided rockets. A former Sea Venom operator, No. 890 NAS received the Sea Vixen FAW.Mk 1 in February 1960, and deployed on HMS *Hermes* and, during the Beira Patrol, on HMS *Ark Royal*.

### Specifications

| | |
|---|---|
| Crew: 2 | Dimensions: span 15.54m (51ft 0in); length |
| Powerplant: 2 x 49.9kN (11,230lbf) Rolls-Royce | 17.02m (55ft 7in); height 3.28m (10ft 9in) |
| Avon 208 turbojets | Weight: 18,858kg (41,575lb) loaded |
| Maximum speed: 1110km/h (690mph) | Armament: Four Red Top air-to-air missiles; on |
| Range: 1126km (700 miles) | outer pylons 454kg (1000lb) bombs, Bullpup |
| Service ceiling: 21,790m (48,000ft) | air-to-surface missiles or equivalent stores |

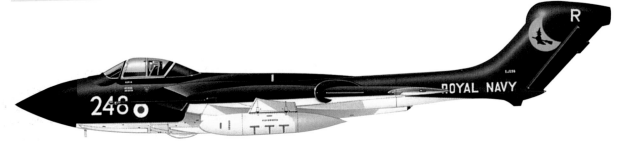

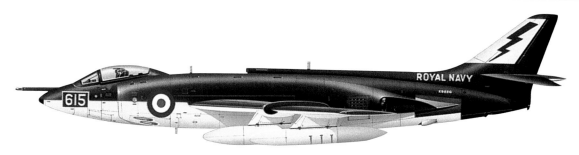

▲ **Supermarine Scimitar F.Mk 1**

*No. 736 NAS, RNAS Lossiemouth*

No. 736 NAS served as the Scimitar training unit for most of the aircraft's front-line career. Only 76 Scimitars were completed, all to F.Mk 1 standard, these equipping four front-line squadrons together with training and service trials units. In addition to bombs and rockets, AIM-9B Sidewinder missiles could be carried.

### Specifications

Crew: 1

Powerplant: 2 x 50.1kN (11,250lbf) Rolls-Royce
Avon 202 turbojet

Maximum speed: 1185km/h (736mph)

Range: 2289km (1422 miles)

Service ceiling: 14,000m (46,000ft)

Dimensions: span 11.33m (37ft 2in); length

16.84m (55ft 3in); height 5.28m (17ft 4in)

Weight: 15,513kg (34,200lb) loaded

Armament: Four 30mm (1.18in) ADEN cannons; capacity for four 454kg (1000lb) bombs or four AIM-9B Sidewinder air-to-air missiles, or up to sixteen 50mm (2in) or 76.2mm (3in) unguided rockets

were later joined and then replaced by the Wessex HU.Mk 5, a dedicated assault transport version, together with Wessex HAS.Mk 1s similarly adapted for the role, and flown by No. 845 NAS.

Operated by three front-line carrier-going and one HQ squadron, the Wessex HAS.Mk 1 typically undertook ASW missions as hunter-killer pairs, with one helicopter using sonar and Doppler, and the other prosecuting contacts with torpedoes. After 129 examples of the Wessex HAS.Mk 1 had been built, a significant number were converted to HAS.Mk 3 standard from 1966, these having the more powerful Gazelle 165 engine and a dorsal radome containing a search radar. Powered by Roll-Royce Gnome engines, the Wessex HU.Mk 5 was based on a Royal Air Force transport version and could carry 16 troops or equivalent loads of cargo. A total of 101 were built, and these saw service from 1964, initially with No. 848 NAS. By 1970 the ASW versions had given way to the Sea King in all but one squadron, although the Wessex HU.Mk 5 remained in use with the commando assault force, embarking in the assault carriers HMS *Bulwark* and *Albion*, and other ships.

| Royal Navy carrier air wings, 1960 | |
|---|---|
| HMS *Albion* (R07) | 'Centaur' class |
| 815 NAS | Whirlwind HAS.Mk 7 |
| 849 NAS (C Flight) | Gannet AEW.Mk 3 |
| 894 NAS | Sea Venom FAW.Mk 22 |
| | |
| HMS *Ark Royal* (R09) | 'Audacious' class |
| 800 NAS | Scimitar F.Mk 1 |
| 807 NAS | Scimitar F.Mk 1 |
| 820 NAS | Whirlwind HAS.Mk 7 |
| 824 NAS | Whirlwind HAS.Mk 7 |
| 892 NAS | Sea Vixen FAW.Mk 1 |
| Ship's Flight | Dragonfly HR.Mk 5 |
| | |
| HMS *Bulwark* (R08) | 'Centaur' class |
| 848 NAS | Whirlwind HAS.Mk 7 |
| | |
| HMS *Centaur* (R06) | 'Centaur' class |
| 801 NAS | Sea Hawk FGA.Mk 6 |
| 810 NAS | Gannet AS.Mk 4 |
| 849 NAS (D Flight) | Skyraider AEW.Mk 1 |
| Ship's Flight | Dragonfly HR.Mk 5 |
| | |
| HMS *Eagle* (R05) | 'Audacious' class |
| 806 NAS | Sea Hawk FGA.Mk 6 |
| | |
| HMS *Victorious* (R38) | 'Illustrious' class |
| 803 NAS | Scimitar F.Mk 1 |
| 831 NAS (A Flight) | Gannet ECM.Mk 6 Avenger AS.Mk 6B |
| 831 NAS (B Flight) | Sea Venom FAW.Mk 21(ECM) |
| 849 NAS (B Flight) | Gannet AEW.Mk 3 |
| Ship's Flight | Dragonfly HR.Mk 5 |

**▲ HMS *Eagle***

Seen leaving Wellington, New Zealand, in the late 1960s, HMS *Eagle* embarks an air wing of Buccaneer S.Mk 2s from No. 809 NAS and Sea Vixen FAW.Mk 2s from No. 899 NAS on deck. The array of aircraft is headed by the ship's single Gannet AS.Mk 4(COD), adapted for the carrier onboard delivery role.

A new version of the Sea Vixen entered service in 1963, the FAW.Mk 2 introducing Red Top missile armament and extended tail booms that housed additional fuel. Following the manufacture of 114 Sea Vixen FAW.Mk 1s, production switched to the FAW.Mk 2 in 1963, with 29 new-build airframes being supplemented by another 67 that were converted from Mk 1s between 1963 and 1968. By early 1961 all four front-line Sea Vixen units were operational, and, led by No. 899 NAS in 1964, all four would eventually re-equip with the FAW.Mk 2 version. No. 899 NAS was also the last squadron to

## Specifications

| | |
|---|---|
| Crew: 2 | Weight: 28,000kg (62,000lb) loaded |
| Powerplant: 2 x 49kN (11,100lbf) Rolls-Royce | Armament: Capacity for four Matra rocket pods |
|   Spey Mk 101 turbofans |   with eighteen SNEB 68mm (2.6in) rockets |
| Maximum speed: 1074km/h (667mph) |   each, two AIM-9 Sidewinders, two AS-30L air- |
| Range: 3700km (2300 miles) |   to-ground missiles, two AS-37 Martel anti- |
| Service ceiling: 12,200m (40,000ft) |   radar missiles, two Sea Eagle missiles; |
| Dimensions: span 13.41m (44ft 0in); length |   various unguided and laser guided bombs as |
|   19.33m (63ft 5in); height 4.97m (16ft 3in) |   well as WE.177 tactical nuclear bombs |

## ▼ Blackburn Buccaneer S.Mk 2

### *No. 809 NAS, HMS* Ark Royal, *1976*

The Buccaneer saw out its career with the FAA as the strike/attack platform for the *Ark Royal*, embarking with No. 809 NAS. First going aboard the carrier in June 1970, No. 809 NAS would eventually complete 21 cruises in the 'Ark' before finally disbanding in December 1978. In addition to offensive duties, the Buccaneers could be equipped as 'buddy' refuelling tankers.

take the Sea Vixen to sea, completing a final cruise aboard *Eagle* in 1971, disbanding the following year.

## Crisis in Kuwait

In June 1961 another crisis erupted in Iraq, and Royal Navy carriers were on hand to defend neighbouring Kuwait. HMS *Victorious* and *Centaur* were on station with their embarked Scimitars and Sea Vixens, while *Bulwark* launched Whirlwinds for a heliborne landing by Royal Marines. Carriers were once again called upon during the Indonesian Confrontation from 1962, with HMS *Albion* launching a heliborne landing in defence of Brunei, using its Wessex and Whirlwind helicopters. Both types played a significant role throughout the campaign that followed, operating from *Albion* and *Bulwark* and from land bases. Policing of the airspace over the Indonesian border involved Sea Vixens and Gannet AEW.Mk 3s from fleet carriers. In response to the coup in Yemen in 1962, Wessex HAS.Mk 1s brought troops ashore from *Centaur* to pursue rebels in the Radfan mountains in December 1963. Rhodesia's declaration of independence in November 1965 was met by a blockade of the port of Beira, which involved *Eagle* and *Ark Royal*. The same year saw the retirement of HMS *Centaur*, leaving the fleet carriers *Ark Royal*, *Eagle*, *Hermes* and *Victorious*.

Powerful new strike equipment was provided by the Blackburn Buccaneer S.Mk 1, which joined the

| Royal Navy carrier air wings, 1970 | |
|---|---|
| HMS *Albion* (R07) | 'Centaur' class |
| 845 NAS | Wessex HU.Mk 5 |
| | Wasp HAS.Mk 1 |
| | |
| HMS *Ark Royal* (R09) | 'Audacious' class |
| 809 NAS | Buccaneer S.Mk 2 |
| 892 NAS | Phantom FG.Mk 1 |
| | |
| HMS *Bulwark* (R08) | 'Centaur' class |
| 848 NAS | Wessex HU.Mk 5 |
| | Wasp HAS.Mk 1 |
| | |
| HMS *Eagle* (R05) | 'Audacious' class |
| 800 NAS | Buccaneer S.Mk 2 |
| 826 NAS | Wessex HAS.Mk 3 |
| 849 NAS (D Flight) | Gannet AEW.Mk 3 |
| 899 NAS | Sea Vixen FAW.Mk 2 |
| Ship's Flight | Wessex HAS.Mk 1 |
| | |
| HMS *Hermes* (R12) | 'Centaur' class |
| 801 NAS | Buccaneer S.Mk 2 |
| 814 NAS | Wessex HAS.Mk 3 |
| 849 NAS (A Flight) | Gannet AEW.Mk 3 |
| 893 NAS | Sea Vixen FAW.Mk 2 |
| Ship's Flight | Wessex HAS.Mk 1 |

## Specifications

Crew: 2

Powerplant: 2 x 1150kW (1535hp) Rolls-Royce Gnome turboshaft engines

Maximum speed: 212km/h (133mph)

Range: 772km (480 miles)

Service ceiling: 3050m (10,000ft)

Dimensions: Rotor diameter 17.07m (56ft 0in); length 20.3m (65ft 8in); height 4.93m (16ft 2in)

Weight: 6123kg (13,500lb) loaded

Armament: Up to three M60 or M60D 7.62mm (.308in) machine guns

▼ **Westland Wessex HU.Mk 5**

*No. 847 NAS, 1982*

Wessex XS518, originally delivered in 1964, is depicted as it appeared during the Falklands campaign, when it served with No. 847 NAS. The HU.Mk 5 variant entered service in 1964 with No. 848 NAS and equipped three other commando assault transport units.

## Specifications

Crew: 2

Powerplant: 2 x 91.2kN (20,515lb) Rolls-Royce
Spey 202 turbofans

Maximum speed: 2230km/h (1386mph)

Range: 2817km (1750 miles)

Service ceiling: 18,300m (60,000ft)

Dimensions: span 11.7m (38ft 5in); length
17.55m (57ft 7in); height 4.96m (16ft 3in)

Weight: 26,308kg (58,000lb) loaded

Armament: Four AIM-7 Sparrow; provision for
20mm (0.79in) M61A1 cannon; wing pylons for
stores to a maximum of 7257kg (16,000lb)

### ▼ McDonnell Douglas Phantom FG.Mk 1

**No. 892 NAS, HMS Ark Royal, 1976**

As what was then the FAA's last operational fixed-wing unit to be established, No. 892 NAS adorned its Phantom carrier-based interceptors with the omega motif on the tailfin – the final letter of the Greek alphabet.

fleet in 1963 and which ultimately replaced the Scimitar. Designed to meet a carrier-based, low-level strike/attack requirement, the Buccaneer could carry a single Red Beard, or later WE177, tactical nuclear store in its rotary bomb bay.

First flown in April 1958, the original Buccaneer S.Mk 1 suffered from a lack of power, and during its initial service had to be launched from HMS *Eagle* with a reduced fuel load, before topping up from Scimitars equipped with 'buddy' refuelling stores. A specialist Scimitar tanker unit was dedicated to the task, when No. 800B NAS was formed in 1964. The S.Mk 1's deficiencies were addressed in the S.Mk 2, with twin Rolls-Royce Spey engines replacing the de Havilland Gyron Junior Mk 101s of the previous model. The Buccaneer S.Mk 1 entered operational service with No. 801 NAS at RNAS Lossiemouth in June 1962, and embarked in *Ark Royal* in 1963.

After two front-line units and one HQ squadron had been formed using 40 S.Mk 1s, the Buccaneer S.Mk 2 began to be introduced in October 1965, with 84 of this definitive version being produced for the Royal Navy. The final operator was No. 809 NAS, which provided Buccaneers for the *Ark Royal*, and from 1972 these included the upgraded S.Mk 2D variant that could launch the Martel TV-guided anti-ship missile.

The Royal Navy hoped to commission a new class of carrier, known as CVA-01 after the lead ship, from the early 1970s, in order to replace *Victorious*, *Ark Royal* and *Eagle*. Planned from 1963, the new carrier was cancelled under the 1966 Defence White Paper.

Meanwhile, the existing carrier fleet was to be run down, based on the government decision to withdraw all forces from 'east of Suez'. The first to go was *Victorious*, paid off in 1967.

The abortive new carriers were to have embarked air groups that included McDonnell Douglas F-4K Phantom IIs re-engined with the British Spey, as well as the Hawker Siddeley P.1154 supersonic V/STOL fighter. The latter was cancelled in 1964, but the Phantom was ordered in the same year as a replacement for the Sea Vixen in the all-weather fleet interceptor role. By the time the Phantom FG.Mk 1 was ready for operational service in 1969, the Royal Navy possessed just one carrier that was suitable to operate it. A total of 50 Phantoms were delivered for front-line service with No. 892 NAS, although 14 were diverted to the Royal Air Force.

Designated as the Phantom FG.Mk 1 in FAA service, the aircraft featured a number of modifications for British use. In addition to the British-specified Spey engines, the Phantom was fitted with strengthened undercarriage, leading-edge flaps with boundary layer control, a folding radome and an extended nose gear oleo. Primary weaponry was US-supplied, with the AIM-7E Sparrow semi-active radar-homing missile associated with the AN/AWG-11 radar, and with AIM-9G Sidewinders for short-range engagements.

Numbers were gradually reduced until the Royal Navy accepted just 28 Phantoms, these serving with a single operational unit, No. 892 NAS, which served aboard HMS *Ark Royal* from June 1970 until December 1978.

## King of the seas

The Phantom served aboard *Ark Royal* alongside the Buccaneer S.Mk 2 and Gannet AEW.Mk 3, while from 1970 these were joined by the Westland Sea King HAS.Mk 1 to fulfil the ASW role. Based on the Sikorsky S-61D, the British-built Sea King HAS.Mk 1 was powered by Roll-Royce Gnome turboshafts and was equipped with locally specified search radar, sonar, Doppler and flight control system.

The first of 56 HAS.Mk 1s began flying trials with No. 700S NAS in August 1969, and had entered front-line use with four seagoing units by the mid-1970s. The Sea King HAS.Mk 2 and Mk 2A introduced in 1976 offered improved performance on account of its uprated engines and six-bladed tail rotor, while upgrade mission equipment included the sonar. A total of 21 new-build HAS.Mk 2 and Mk 2A helicopters were joined by 11 converted Mk 1s. In 1980 a much more significant advance was made by

### Specifications

Crew: 3
Powerplant: 2 x 1193kW (1600hp) H1400-1 Rolls-Royce Gnome turboshaft engines
Maximum speed: 265km/h (164mph)
Range: 1480km (919 miles)
Service ceiling: 3352m (11,000ft)
Dimensions: Rotor diameter 18.90m (62ft 01in); length 17.02m (55ft 10in); height 5.10m (16ft 9in)
Weight: 9750kg (21,495lb) loaded
Armament: Four torpedoes; one Whitehead A244S or Stingray, sea-skimming anti-ship missile, two anti-ship Sea Eagle or Exocet missiles

### ▼ Westland Sea King HAS.Mk 1

***No. 824 NAS, HMS* Ark Royal, *1976***

This helicopter was one of the original batch of 56 Sea King HAS.Mk 1s built at Yeovil in 1969–72 for Royal Navy anti-submarine warfare units. In 1976 it was embarked in *Ark Royal*. All Mk 1s were subsequently upgraded to HAS.Mk 2 standard from the mid-1970s.

### Specifications

Crew: 1
Powerplant: 1 x 95.6kN (21,500lbf) Rolls-Royce Pegasus Mk 104 vectored thrust turbofan
Maximum speed: 1110km/h (690mph)
Range: 740km (460 miles)
Service ceiling: 15,545m (51,000ft)
Dimensions: span 7.7m (25ft 3in); length 14.5m (47ft 7in); height 3.71m (12ft 2in)
Weight: 11,900kg (26,200lb) loaded
Armament: Two 30mm (1.2in) Aden cannons; provision for AIM-9 Sidewinder air-to-air missiles and two anti-shipping missiles, up to a total of 3629kg (8000lb)

### ▼ British Aerospace Sea Harrier FRS.Mk 1

***No. 800 NAS, HMS* Hermes, *1982***

Bearing three Falklands War kill markings, XZ457, the highest-scoring Sea Harrier of the conflict, is shown with undercarriage deployed and with the AIM-9L Sidewinder missiles that proved so effective in the South Atlantic. The aircraft was credited with two Argentine Navy A-4Qs and two Argentine Air Force Daggers.

the appearance of the Sea King HAS.Mk 5 with a new Sea Searcher radar, improved sonobuoy equipment and Orange Crop electronic support measures. As well as over 50 HAS.Mk 2s that were converted to this new standard, 30 King HAS.Mk 5s were newly built. The Sea King HC.Mk 4 was developed as a commando transport to replace the earlier Wessex HU.Mk 5. Orders were placed for 42 examples in 1979, these having accommodation for 28 troops in an enlarged cabin, together with floor armour and optional door-mounted machine-gun.

Since it was too small to operate the Phantom, *Hermes* was converted to become an assault carrier from 1970, while in 1971, HMS *Eagle* returned from its last cruise and into retirement. Although partially equipped for Phantom operations, fresh from refit, *Eagle* was disposed of in 1972, subsequently becoming a source of spares for *Ark Royal*, the Royal Navy's last Cold War conventional carrier.

For the twilight of its service, the 'Ark' operated in the Atlantic and Mediterranean, with an air group consisting of No. 892 NAS Phantoms, No. 809 NAS Buccaneers, Gannet AEW.Mk 3s from 'B' Flight of No. 849 NAS, and No. 824 NAS Sea Kings. After a final cruise, *Ark Royal* was paid off in December 1978.

The Harrier V/STOL fighter had been tested aboard Royal Navy carriers as early as 1969, but it was not until 1975 – inspired by US Marine Corps operations with the AV-8A – that the Admiralty ordered a navalized version. This new aircraft was to be operated from a new class of anti-submarine carrier (CVS), dubbed a 'through-deck cruiser', and equipped with a ski jump ramp to allow the Harriers to perform rolling take-offs. HMS *Hermes*, earlier 'demoted' to the role of assault carrier, latterly began to be used for ASW trials, and in 1979 embarked the new Sea Harrier for operational trials. In common with the three new CVS of the 'Invincible' class, *Hermes* was modified to receive a ski jump in 1980.

The BAe Sea Harrier FRS.Mk 1 was a minimum-change version of the Royal Air Force's land-based Harrier GR.Mk 1, but was optimized for air defence rather than ground attack. Thirty-one production aircraft were ordered, and these allied the proven V/STOL design with a Blue Fox pulse-modulated

### ▼ HMS *Hermes*

Flagship of the British forces in the Falklands campaign, *Hermes* steams through heavy weather with her defensive 'goalkeeper', a Royal Navy Type 22 frigate. Arranged on the deck, by now equipped with the 12° ski jump take-off ramp, is an air group of Sea Harrier FRS.Mk 1s and Sea King HC.Mk 4 helicopters.

radar, a revised cockpit for improved visibility, an improved Rolls-Royce Pegasus Mk 104 turbofan, a new head-up display and Doppler nav/attack system, and airframe modifications to suit operations at sea. After a first flight in August 1978 the first front-line unit was established as No. 800 NAS at RNAS Yeovilton in March 1980. As well as a training unit, the Sea Harrier populated three front-line squadrons, one of these being hastily established for the Falklands War.

## War in the South Atlantic

The primary role of the 'Invincible' class was to be ASW in support of NATO in the Atlantic, with Sea Kings the primary tool for this task, and with Sea Harriers providing air defence. However, when Argentina invaded South Georgia and the Falkland Islands on 2 April 1982, these new carriers were called upon to project British naval airpower much further afield. The Task Force sent to the South Atlantic included *Hermes* as flagship, together with HMS *Invincible*, and the carriers set sail on 5 April.

On 1 May the Task Force was in the operational zone, and a first strike was directed against Port Stanley airfield. Operated by No. 800 NAS (in *Hermes*) and No. 801 NAS (*Invincible*), the Sea Harriers flew both air defence and bombing missions, while Sea Kings provided a protective screen against

Argentine submarine activity. Combined with the infrared-guided AIM-9L Sidewinder missile, the Sea Harrier's prowess in air-to-air combat was soon made manifest, as it overcame Argentine Daggers and Mirage IIIs. While the Sea Harriers maintained combat air patrols, RAF Harrier GR.Mk 3s embarked in *Hermes* flew attack missions. By the end of 74 days of fighting, the Sea Harriers had scored 23 aerial victories, without any losses to Argentine aircraft. Ground defences claimed two Sea Harriers, and another four aircraft were lost through non-combat attrition. After the British landings began on 21 May, Sea Harriers operated from a landing strip at Port San Carlos. Following the end of the conflict, *Hermes* assumed training duties, while *Invincible* was relieved in the South Atlantic by the second vessel in the class, HMS *Illustrious*.

*Illustrious* benefited from a crash AEW programme embarked upon during the Falklands War, and for her first cruise was able to deploy the Sea King AEW.Mk 2A. In order to make good Falklands losses and other attrition, 23 more Sea Harriers were ordered following the war, for a total of 57, including three development machines. By the mid-1980s, the two carriers and their air groups had returned to their primary ASW mission, and were joined by the third and final vessel in the class, HMS *Ark Royal*, which was commissioned in 1985.

### ▼ Westland Sea King AEW.Mk 2A

**No. 849 NAS, 1985**

One of the key lessons of the Falklands War was the importance of returning to Royal Navy carriers an airborne early warning capability missing since the retirement of the Gannet AEW.Mk 3. The solution was provided in the form of the Sea King AEW.Mk 2A, with a Searchwater radar (as used in the Royal Air Force Nimrod) carried in an inflatable 'bag' installation on the starboard side. Developed under a crash programme from May 1982, the Sea King AEW.Mk 2A could detect a fighter-size target at a range of 201km (125 miles).

**Specifications**

Crew: 2–4

Powerplant: 2 x 1193kW (1600hp) H1400-1 Rolls-Royce Gnome turboshaft engines

Maximum speed: 265km/h (164mph)

Range: 1480km (919 miles)

Service ceiling: 3352m (11,000ft)

Dimensions: Rotor diameter 18.90m (62ft 01in); length 17.02m (55ft 10in); height 5.10m (16ft 9in)

Weight: 9750kg (21,495lb) loaded

Armament: N/A

# United States
## 1946–59

**The early 1950s saw the US Navy's carrier airpower heavily involved in the war in Korea, while at the same time pioneering jet operations and introducing ever more powerful aircraft carriers.**

THE US NAVY began the post-war era with the superlative F4U carrier fighter still in production, and indeed the AU-1 attack version did not make its first flight until late 1951. The last examples came off the production line in late 1952, and the Corsair remained in service with Navy and US Marine Corps land- and carrier-based units until 1955. The AU-1 was the preserve of the Marines, and saw Korean service from land bases. Meanwhile, the F4U-4 and F4U-4B served from carrier decks during the conflict in both Navy and Marine hands. The F4U-5 variant featured an uprated engine and was available as the F4U-5N night-fighter with radar in the wing.

Another backbone of the Navy's carrier-based airpower during World War II, the Avenger survived to see post-war service, most significantly in the anti-submarine warfare (ASW) and airborne early warning (AEW) roles that had come to prominence during the war. The TBM-3W2 and TBM-3S2 therefore operated as a 'hunter-killer' ASW team from escort and light carriers, while the TBM-3W version,

equipped with AN/APS-20 radar, was the first practical AEW platform available to the Navy carrier air wings. The last of the TBM-3Ws were retired in 1951, while the TBM-3W2 and -3S2 survived a little longer, remaining in front-line use until 1954.

### Definitive piston-engined fighter

Just too late to see wartime service was the Grumman F8F Bearcat, first flown in August 1944 and the ultimate expression of the company's single-seat piston-engined naval fighter line. Entering service with VF-19 in May 1945, the Bearcat did not see combat, but was the Navy's final front-line piston-engined fighter, and saw service until 1953, with active duty and reserve fighter, night-fighter and composite squadrons.

In terms of carrier attack aircraft, the conceptual successors to the wartime Dauntless and Avenger were the Martin AM Mauler and the Douglas

▲ **General Motors TBM-3W2 Avenger**

*VS-32, USS Palau, 1951*

An airborne early warning version of the TBM-3, the TBM-3W was equipped for surveillance, with the AN/APS-20 radar in a ventral radome. The TBM-3W2 was a further update intended for the anti-submarine role, in which it complemented the 'killer' TBM-3S2. This aircraft served in the ASW carrier USS *Palau* (CVE-122).

**Specifications**

| | |
|---|---|
| Crew: 3 | Service ceiling: 6523m (21,400ft) |
| Powerplant: 1 x 1417kW (1900hp) Wright | Dimensions: wingspan 16.51m (54ft 2in); |
| R2600-20 Cyclone 14 cylinder twin-row | length 12.42m (40ft 9in); height 4.19m (13ft |
| piston engine | 9in) |
| Maximum speed: 414km/h (217mph) | Weight: 7215kg (15,905lb) loaded |
| Range: 4321km (2685 miles) | Armament: None |

## Specifications

Crew: 1

Powerplant: 1 x 156kW (2100hp) Pratt & Whitney R-2800-34W Double Wasp radial piston engine

Maximum speed: 678km/h (421mph)

Range: 1778km (1105 miles)

Service ceiling: 11,796m (38,700ft)

Dimensions: span 10.92m (35ft 10in); length 8.61m (28ft 3in); height 4.21m (13ft 9in)

Weight: 5873kg (12,947lb) loaded

Armament: Four 12.7mm (.50in) M2 machine guns; up to 454kg (1000lb) of bombs or four 127mm (5in) rockets

### ▼ Grumman F8F-1 Bearcat

**VF-72, USS Leyte, 1949–50**

The major production version of the Bearcat added a dorsal fin and the R-2800-22W or 34W engine, 770 examples being completed. This aircraft, BuNo 95494, was almost the last F8F-1 built, and is shown here when assigned to Commander C. E. Clarke, commanding officer of VF-72. Replacing the Hellcat as the Navy's primary carrier fighter, the Bearcat was designed to operate from smaller carriers, like USS Leyte of the 'Essex' class.

## Specifications

Crew: 1

Powerplant: 1 x 2218kW (2975hp) Wright R-3350-4 Cyclone 18 radial piston engine

Maximum speed: 591km/h (376mph)

Range: 2885km (1800 miles)

Service ceiling: 9296m (30,500ft)

Dimensions: span 15.24m (50ft 0in); length 12.55m (41ft 2in); height 5.13m (16ft 10in)

Weight: 10,608kg (23,386lb) loaded

Armament: Four 20mm (.79in) cannon; up to 4488kg (10,698lb) of bombs

### ▼ Martin AM-1 Mauler

**US Navy Reserve, 1951**

Originally developed as the Martin BTM-1, the AM-1 Mauler saw only limited front-line service before being handed down to reserve formations when production ended. Although 132 examples were completed, another 651 were cancelled. Another 17 Maulers were completed as AM-1Qs for electronic countermeasures duties. The AM-1 version carried its weapons load on 15 external hardpoints.

AD Skyraider. The powerful Mauler was first flown in August 1944, and the AM-1 production version with a Wright Cyclone engine entered service with VA-17A in March 1948, but manufacture was restricted in favour of the more promising Skyraider and the aircraft were soon transferred to the Naval Air Reserve.

While the Mauler's service was destined to be brief, the Skyraider matured to become one of the greatest carrier aircraft of all time. In its initial form, known as the XBT2D-1 Destroyer II, the aircraft first flew in March 1945, and although conceived as a dive-bomber and torpedo-bomber, the Skyraider that entered service as the AD-1 in December 1946 was

more frequently used to carry bombs and rockets in the ground attack and close support roles. The adaptability of the design was proven by variants completed for the AEW and electronic warfare (EW) roles, while a redesign produced the AD-5 with side-by-side seating for two crewmembers. Despite its antiquated appearance, the Skyraider proved both rugged and versatile. By 1957 the El Segundo plant had turned out over 3000 examples of the Skyraider, and the type was the backbone of US Navy attack squadrons over both Korea and, in the early years of that conflict, Vietnam. The Skyraider also supplanted the Avenger in the AEW role, with the AD-3W and -4W representing successively improved versions

## Specifications

Crew: 1

Powerplant: 1 x 2013kW (2700hp) Pratt &
Whitney R-3350-26WA radial piston engine

Maximum speed: 520km/h (320mph)

Range: 2115km (1315 miles)

Service ceiling: 8660m (28,500ft)

Dimensions: span 15.25m (50ft 0in); length
11.84m (38ft 10in); height 4.78m (15ft 8in)

Weight: 11,340kg (25,000lb) loaded

Armament: Four 20mm (.79in) cannon; up to
3600kg (8000lb) of bombs, rockets, or other
stores

### ▼ Douglas AD-1 Skyraider

*VA-6B, USS* Coral Sea, *1948*

This example of the initial production version of the Skyraider was operated by the
'Black Lancers' of VA-6B when that unit was operating from the *Coral Sea* (CVB-
43) for that carrier's initial shakedown cruise. Also embarked were the AD-1s of
VA-6B, plus VF-6B with F4U-4s and VF-5B
with a mix of F4U-4s and photo-
reconnaissance F6F-5P Hellcats.

## Specifications

Crew: 1

Powerplant: 1 x 1715kW (2300hp) Pratt &
Whitney R-2800-32W radial engine

Maximum speed: 718km/h (446mph)

Range: 2425km (1507 miles)

Service ceiling: 11,308m (41,500ft)

Dimensions: span 10.16m (41ft 0in); length
10.27m (33ft 8in); height 4.5m (14.9ft)

Weight: 6654kg (13,846lb) loaded

Armament: Four 20mm (.79in) M3 cannon; ten
127mm (5in) rockets or up to 2390kg
(5200lb) of bombs

### ▼ Vought F4U-5N Corsair

*VC-3, USS* Princeton, *1953*

VC-3 was a composite squadron that operated from both carriers and land bases
during the Korean War. This particular aircraft was flown by Lieutenant Guy P.
Bordelon, the only Navy ace of the conflict. Flying the F4U-5N as part of a
detachment at Osan, Bordelon shot down five communist aircraft during missions
to counter 'Bed Check Charlie'
nocturnal nuisance raiders.

with AN/APS-20 radar in a 'guppy' radome, and with
two operators in a fuselage compartment. The AD-
5W was similar, but with side-by-side seating.

World War II had highlighted the importance of
carrier-based anti-submarine warfare aircraft, and a
successor to the Avenger in this role was the
Grumman AF Guardian. First flown in December
1945, the Guardian was fielded as a 'hunter-killer'
team: the two-seat AF-2S version for strike duties and
the four-seat AF-2W for surveillance. A Double Wasp
engine powered both types, which were the largest
single-engined piston aircraft to see service from a
carrier. Entering service in October 1950, the
Guardian was active aboard escort and light carriers
before being demoted to the Naval Reserve in 1955.

### Naval jet pioneer

The first all-jet carrier fighter to be ordered into
production was the McDonnell FH Phantom, first
flown in January 1945 under its original FD
designation. Powered by a pair of Westinghouse J30
engines, the FH was the first Navy jet to take off from
and land on a carrier, and the first jet to see service
with the Navy and Marine Corps. Operational
service began with VF-17A in July 1947, although
the type never undertook an operational cruise, and
was instead used to gain valuable experience in jet
operations at sea.

Another early jet entrant was the Ryan FR Fireball,
a conservative solution that allied a piston-engined
fighter with a Cyclone radial supplemented by a

General Electric J31 turbojet in the tail, and tricycle landing gear. The Fireball equipped just two squadrons, beginning with VF-66 that received production deliveries of the FR-1 from March 1945. Thereafter, the type was used for extensive trials work before being retired in 1947.

The North American FJ Fury was a straight-wing fighter that again saw only limited production, with just 30 examples completed. Development began as early as 1945, and the Fury made its initial flight in September 1946. Powered by an Allison J35 turbojet, the FJ-1 production aircraft began carrier operations aboard USS *Boxer* with VF-5A in March 1948. The FJ-1 saw out its service in the Naval Reserve, before being disposed of in the early 1950s.

Vought followed the Corsair with the F6U-1 Pirate fighter. Although it incorporated a patented aluminium/balsa skin, the Pirate was still a sluggish performer, on account of its underpowered Westinghouse J34 turbojet. Even when equipped with a primitive afterburner, the Pirate's performance was deficient, and although the type entered service in August 1949, just 30 examples were completed.

Far more radical than the company's F6U, the Vought F7U Cutlass was inspired by German wartime research, and featured a sharply swept wing and twin vertical tailfins mounted on the trailing edge, well outboard of a pair of engines. First flown in September 1948 as the XF7U-1, the Cutlass suffered from a troubled development, being

▲ **Vought F4U-4 Corsair**

F4U-4s returning from a combat mission over North Korea in September 1951 circle the USS *Boxer* (CV-21) as they wait for aircraft in the next strike to be launched from the flight deck – a plane-guard HO3S-1 hovers above the ship.

redesigned as the F7U-3 with J35, and later with afterburning J46 engines. The initial operational unit was VF-81 in May 1954, with the F7U-3. The Cutlass was the first US Navy fighter with missile armament, the F7U-3M version carrying four Sparrow I AAMs.

The Corsair played a prominent role in the Korean War, in which it was joined by the three most

▼ **Goodyear FG-1D Corsair**

*VMA-312, USS* Bataan, *1952*

In September 1952 Marine pilot Captain Jesse Folmar claimed the only MiG kill scored by a Corsair over Korea. Folmar shot down one MiG-15 jet with cannon fire before succumbing to the guns of another of the communist fighters. The FG-1D was a Goodyear-built version of the F4U-4. Marine Corsairs operated from the smaller escort carriers in Korea, including USS *Sicily* and *Bairoko*.

### Specifications

| | |
|---|---|
| Crew: 1 | Dimensions: span 12.49m (40ft 11.75in); |
| Powerplant: 1 x 1678kW (2250hp) Pratt & | length 10.27m (33ft 8.25in); height 4.50m |
| Whitney R-2800-18W Double Wasp 18- | (14ft 9in) |
| cylinder two-row radial engine | Weight: 8845kg (19,500lb) loaded |
| Maximum speed: 718km/h (446mph) | Armament: Six 12.7mm (.5in) machine guns, |
| Range: 2511km (1560 miles) | external bomb and rocket load of 907kg |
| Service ceiling: 12,650m (51,500ft) | (2000lb) |

Crew: 1

Powerplant: 1 x 26.5kN (5950lb) thrust Pratt &
Whitney J42-P-6/P-8 turbojet

Maximum speed: 925km/h (575mph)

Range: 2100km (1300 miles)

Service ceiling: 13,600m (44,600ft)

Dimensions: span 11.6m (38ft 0in); length
11.3m (37ft 5in); height 3.8m (11ft 4in)

Weight: 7462kg (16,450lb) loaded

Armament: Four 20mm (.79in) M2 cannon;
up to 910kg (2000lb) bombs, six 127mm
(5in) rockets

### ▼ Grumman F9F-2 Panther

**VF-781, USS Oriskany, 1952**

In a controversial incident in November 1952, F9F-2s from VF-781 were jumped by Soviet MiG-15s flying from near Vladivostok. Two MiGs were shot down and another damaged. One F9F was damaged but recovered safely. As a result of its political sensitivity, details of the incident were not revealed until years later.

successful first-generation US Navy jets: the Grumman F9F Panther, McDonnell F2H Banshee and Douglas F3D Skyknight.

First flown in November 1947 with a British Nene turbojet, the straight-wing F9F switched to the US-made Pratt & Whitney J42 derivative for the initial production aircraft, the F9F-2. First into service, however, was the F9F-3, with VF-51 in May 1949, this being powered by an Allison J33 engine. From July 1950 Panthers were in combat over Korea, claiming the Navy's first jet-versus-jet kill in November that year. A small number of aircraft were outfitted for photo-reconnaissance, and the initial production models were joined by the improved F9F-4 and -5, the last of which was delivered in early 1953. The final Panther was retired from front-line service in October 1958.

The F2H emerged as a refinement of McDonnell's FH Phantom, and made its first flight in January 1947, powered by a pair of J34 turbojets. The Banshee was produced in a number of variants, among which were the nuclear-capable F2H-2B, the F2H-2N night-fighter and the F2H-2P equipped for photo-reconnaissance. The first production aircraft went to VF-171 in March 1949 and Banshees saw considerable service over Korea, flying escort and reconnaissance missions from August 1951. After wartime service with the Navy and Marine Corps, later versions of the Banshee were superseded in fleet fighter and attack squadrons by F4Ds and F3Hs from the mid-1950s, although they still served in the night-fighter and nuclear-delivery roles until 1959.

The F3D was the US Navy's first jet night-fighter, with a crew of two seated side-by-side, twin J34 engines and an armament of four 20mm (.79in) cannon. First flown in March 1948, the Skyknight was equipped with AN/APQ-35 radar and entered service with a composite squadron, VC-3, in early 1951. During Korea the type made a handful of cruises aboard carriers, but saw its greatest success in a land-based role, scoring eight night kills in Marine Corps hands. The last Skyknights in service were EF-10Bs: equipped for electronic countermeasures, these saw action from land bases during the Vietnam War.

With its F9F-6 first flown in September 1951, Grumman introduced a swept wing, and the revised aircraft received the name Cougar. The F9F-6 and later models dispensed with the J42 and instead used

| Typical US Navy carrier air group, Korean War | |
|---|---|
| Carrier Air Group 3 | |
| CAG-3 | |
| USS Leyte (CV-32) | 'Essex' class |
| October 1950 to January 1951 | |
| VF-31 | F9F-2 Panther |
| VF-32 | F9F-2 Panther |
| VF-33 | F4U-4 Corsair |
| VF-34 | F4U-4 Corsair |
| VA-35 | AD-2 Skyraider |
| VC-61 | F2H-2P Banshee |
| VC-62 | F4U-5P Corsair |

the more powerful J48 (an American version of the British Tay) or the Allison J33. After entering service with VF-32 in November 1952, the Cougar became the most numerous carrier-based Navy fighter by the mid-1950s. The Atlantic Fleet withdrew the last fighter versions of the Cougar in 1959, although the F9F-8P photo-reconnaissance version continued in front-line service until early 1960.

## Sabre for the Navy

As early as 1951, North American began to improve its FJ Fury, incorporating features of the company's swept-wing F-86 Sabre land-based fighter. The resultant FJ-2 Fury was based on the USAF's F-86E and was first flown in December 1951. Powered by a Wright J65 engine, the FJ-2 featured cannon armament and later added Sidewinder AAMs to its weapons options. The subsequent FJ-3 added additional wing hardpoints for bombs or rockets, while the FJ-4B was the definitive production version, with uprated engine, increased fuel capacity and compatibility with both Sidewinder and Bullpup guided missiles. The swept-wing Fury went to sea aboard USS *Bennington* with VF-173 in 1955, and a total of 21 squadrons (including four of the Marine Corps) operated the FJ-3 variant. A further 12 units

### Specifications

| | |
|---|---|
| Crew: 1 | Service ceiling: 12,525m (41,100ft) |
| Powerplant: 2 x 7.1kN (1600lbf) Westinghouse | Dimensions: span 12.42m (40ft 9in); length |
| J30-WE-20 turbojets | 11.35m (37ft 3in); height 4.32m (14ft 2in) |
| Maximum speed: 771km/h (479mph) | Weight: 5459kg (12,035lb) loaded |
| Range: 1118km (695 miles) | Armament: Four 12.7mm (.50in) machine guns |

### ▼ McDonnell FH-1 Phantom
#### *VF-17A, 1949*

Appropriately renamed as the 'Phantom Fighters', VF-17A traded its F4U-4s for FH-1s in July 1947 and operated these from USS *Coral Sea* in summer 1948, before embarking in USS *Midway* for a cruise in early 1949. For its second carrier cruise, the squadron had been renamed as VF-171. When home-based, the squadron operated from NAS Quonset Point, Rhode Island.

### Specifications

| | |
|---|---|
| Crew: 1 | Service ceiling: 9754m (32,000ft) |
| Powerplant: 1 x 17.8kN (4000lbf) Allison J35- | Dimensions: span 9.8m (38ft 2in); length |
| A-2 turbojet | 10.5m (34ft 5in); height 4.5m (14ft 10in) |
| Maximum speed: 880km/h (547mph) | Weight: 7076kg (15,600lb) loaded |
| Range: 2414km (1500 miles) | Armament: Six 12.7mm (.50in) machine guns |

### ▼ North American FJ-1 Fury
#### *VF-5A, 1948*

After the FJ-1 began carrier operations in March 1948, VF-5 was redesignated VF-5A in November 1946, and was renamed as the 'Screaming Eagles'. The squadron made only a single carrier deployment aboard USS *Boxer* in March 1948. The unit was then redesignated again that August, as VF-51, and re-equipped with the F9F-2.

## Specifications

| | |
|---|---|
| Crew: 1 | Dimensions: span 12.73m (41ft 9in); length |
| Powerplant: 2 x 14.45kN (3250lbf) | 14.68m (48ft 2in); height 4.42m (14ft 6in) |
| Westinghouse J34-WE-34 | Weight: 11,437kg (25,214lb) loaded |
| Maximum speed: 933km/h (580mph) | Armament: Four 20mm (.79in) cannon; |
| Range: 1883km (1170 miles) | underwing racks with provision for two 227kg |
| Service ceiling: 9754m (32,000ft) | (500lb) or four 113kg (250lb) bombs |

### ▼ McDonnell F2H-2 Banshee

#### VF-62, USS Lake Champlain, 1953

The F2H was the first major production model of the Banshee, with a slightly lengthened fuselage containing additional fuel, wingtip tanks and uprated W34 turbojets. In excess of 300 were built, including this example operated by VF-62 'Gladiators', which was aboard USS Lake Champlain at the end of the Korean War.

(three of the Marine Corps) operated the FJ-4B from carriers, and this model also had a nuclear strike role. After 1962, surviving FJs were redesignated as F-1s.

## Troublesome Demon

McDonnell followed the Banshee with the more ambitious F3H Demon, a swept-wing fighter that was plagued by deficient powerplants. The Demon as first flown in August 1951 had dismal Westinghouse J40 engines and was a failure, and the F3H-1N initial production aircraft were rejected for service. Matters were addressed with the definitive F3H-2, powered by the Allison J71 and first flown in June 1955. The first operational Demons went to sea with VF-14 aboard USS Forrestal in January 1957. With the arrival of more capable equipment, the Demon was assured only a brief front-line career, although it did

see active service in three distinct variants: the F3H-2N with AIM-9 Sidewinder capability, the F3H-2M with Sparrow I missile armament, and the F3H-2 with provision for both types of missile. After 1962, survivors were redesignated in the F-3 series, and the type remained in front-line Navy service until 1964.

In the late 1940s the US Navy sought to establish a role for itself in the strategic nuclear strike business. As a stopgap solution, the Navy embarked Lockheed P2V Neptunes on larger carriers, the land-based patrol aircraft being configured for rocket-assisted take-off from carrier decks, and with provision for the carriage of nuclear weapons. Only embarked in the 'Midway' class, the P2V-3C was operated by two squadrons from September 1948 until September 1949. Effectively assigned one-way missions, the Neptunes were not equipped to recover on the

## Specifications

| | |
|---|---|
| Crew: 1 | Dimensions: span 12.7m (41ft 8in); length |
| Powerplant: 2 x 14.45kN (3250lbf) | 14.6m (48ft 2in); height 4.2m (13ft 11in) |
| Westinghouse J34-WE-34 turbojets | Weight: 12,927kg (28,500lb) loaded |
| Maximum speed: 847km/h (527mph) | Armament: None |
| Range: 1885km (1170 miles) | |
| Service ceiling: 14,175m (46,500ft) | |

### ▼ McDonnell F2H-2P Banshee

#### VMJ-1, 1952–53

The Marine Corps squadron VMJ-1 operated the reconnaissance version of the Banshee from carrier decks during the course of the Korean War, together with the Navy's VC-3 composite unit. First flown in October 1950, the F2H-2P replaced the Banshee's cannon armament with a camera nose.

The only Marine Banshee unit in Korea, Marine Photo Reconnaissance Squadron 1 (VMJ-1) was activated at Pohang in February 1952.

carriers after their sorties had been completed. North American was charged with developing a purpose-designed heavy carrier-based attack aircraft, creating the three-seat AJ Savage, powered by a pair of Pratt & Whitney Double Wasp radial engines, supplemented by a J33 turbojet in the tail. First flown in July 1948, the Savage saw active service from September 1949. While the US Navy was never able to assume the nuclear strike role from the USAF, the Savage proved to be a useful type, also undertaking tanker and photo-reconnaissance (AJ-2P) duties and being redesignated as the A-2 after 1962.

In order to supersede the Guardian and later members of the Avenger family, Grumman developed the S2F Tracker as an ASW aircraft that could combine hunter and killer roles in a common airframe. Powered by two Cyclone piston engines and carrying a crew of four, the Tracker was first flown in December 1952 and entered service in its S2F-1 initial production form with VS-26 in February 1954. Trackers, redesignated as S-2s after 1962, continued in front-line service until 1976. In addition to a number of conversions to US-2 utility transport standard, the Tracker formed the basis of a

### ▲ Sikorsky HRS-1

*HMR-161, 1952*

Established in January 1951, Marine Helicopter Transport Squadron One Sixty-One 'Grayhawks' operated the HRS-1, the Marine assault version of the HO4S. Seating eight troops, the first of 60 examples was delivered in April 1951, equipping nine HMR squadrons before the end of the conflict in Korea.

**Specifications**

| | |
|---|---|
| Crew: 2 | Dimensions: Rotor diameter 16.16m (53ft 0in); |
| Powerplant: 1 x 450kW (600hp) Pratt & | length 19.1m (62ft 7in); height 4.07m (13ft |
| Whitney R-1340-57 radial engine | 4in) |
| Maximum speed: 163km/h (101mph) | Weight: 3266kg (7200lb) loaded |
| Range: 652km (405 miles) | Armament: None |
| Service ceiling: 3200m (10,500ft) | |

### ▲ Sikorsky HO3S-1 Dragonfly

*HU-2, 1949*

A four-seat version of the HO2S, the HO3S-1 was the sole production of the S-51 Dragonfly for the US Navy, 88 examples being ordered. The HO3S-1 was standard plane-guard equipment on Navy carriers during Korea, and pioneered some of the first combat rescue missions, HU-2 'Fleet Angels' equipping with the type in 1948.

**Specifications**

| | |
|---|---|
| Crew: 1 | Dimensions: Rotor diameter 14.9m (49ft 0in); |
| Powerplant: 1 x 335kW (450hp) Pratt & | length 17.6m (57ft 8in); height 3.96m (12ft |
| Whitney R-985-AN-5 radial piston engine | 11in) |
| Maximum speed: 172km/h (107mph) | Weight: 2189kg (4825lb) loaded |
| Range: 579km (360 miles) | Armament: None |
| Service ceiling: 4510m (14,800ft) | |

## Specifications

Crew: 2

Powerplant: 2 x 15.1kN (3400lb) thrust
Westinghouse J34-WE-36 turbojets

Maximum speed: 852km/h (460mph)

Range: 2212km (1374 miles)

Service ceiling: 11,200m (36,700ft)

Dimensions: span 15.24m (50ft 0in); length
13.85m (45ft 5in); height 4.9m (16ft 1in)

Weight: 12,151kg (26,731lb) loaded

Armament: Four 20mm (.79in) Hispano-Suiza
M2 cannon; provision for bombs

### ▼ Douglas F3D-2 Skyknight

*VMF(N)-513, Kunsan, 1952–53*

The Skyknight conducted most of its operations from shore bases, although Navy composite squadrons took the night-fighter aboard carriers, and provided a detachment during the Korean War. More prominent were the Marine Corps-operated Skyknights that flew from land bases, scoring eight kills against communist aircraft. In Marine hands, the Skyknight also flew some Korean bombing sorties.

## Specifications

Crew: 3

Powerplant: 2 x 1864kW (2500hp) Pratt &
Whitney R-2800-48 piston engines and one
20.46kN (4600lbf) thrust Allison J33-A-19
turbojet

Maximum speed: 758km/h (471mph)

Range: 2623km (1630 miles)

Service ceiling: 12,192m (40,000ft)

Dimensions: span 22.91m (75ft 2in); length
19.22m (63ft 1in); height 6.52m (21ft 5in)

Weight: 23,973kg (52,852lb) loaded

Armament: Maximum offensive load 5443kg
(12,000lb), such as a 3447kg (7600lb) Mk 15
nuclear weapon, or six 726kg (1600lb)
conventional bombs and two wingtip fuel
tanks

### ▼ North American AJ-2 Savage

*VAH-6, USS* Lexington, *1956*

Wearing the grey and white livery introduced in the latter stages of its career, this AJ-2 (A-2B after 1962) was one of 70 production examples of this variant with uprated R-2800 engines, a taller fin and rudder, lengthened fuselage and increased fuel capacity. Heavy Attack Squadron Six 'Fleurs' served in USS *Lexington* (CVA-16) as part of Air Task Group 1 (ATG-1) in the Western Pacific in 1956.

dedicated carrier onboard delivery (COD) aircraft, the TF (later C-1) Trader. First flown in January 1955, the Trader served with fleet logistic support squadrons from 1955 until 1988.

The Trader provided the airframe for the Navy's first purpose-designed carrier AEW platform, the Grumman EF (later E-1B) Tracer. Recording its maiden flight in March 1958, the Tracer was based around the AN/APQ-82 radar system, and was operated by a crew of four. Operational service commenced with VAW-12 in January 1960 and a total of 10 active and Naval Reserve squadrons took

the type aboard fleet and anti-submarine warfare carriers until finally retired in November 1977.

## Supersonic fighters

Douglas' prolific designer Ed Heinemann followed the F3D with the F4D Skyray, a tailless single-seat fighter with a Pratt & Whitney J57 that propelled it to transonic speeds. Equipped with cannon armament and all-weather radar, the powerful Skyray was the first Navy fighter capable of supersonic speed in level flight and joined the fleet in April 1956, initially serving with VC-3. After 1962 the Skyray

## Specifications

Crew: 1

Powerplant: 1 x 28.25kN (6354lb) Allison J33
turbojet

Maximum speed: 1041km/h (647mph)

Range: 2111km (1312 miles)

Service ceiling: 12,800m (42,000ft)

Dimensions: span 10.5m (34ft 6in); length
12.9m (42ft 2in); height 3.7m (12ft 3in)

Weight: 9116kg (20,098lb) loaded

Armament: Four 20mm (.79in) M2 cannon;
six 127mm (5in) rockets; two 454kg
(1000lb) bombs

### ▼ Grumman F9F-7 Cougar

#### VF-21, NAS Oceana, 1954

While most members of the Panther/Cougar family were powered by the J48
engine, the F9F-7 was one of those that used the Allison J33. The F9F-7 was
otherwise similar to the F9F-6, the initial production
version of the Cougar. The aircraft was in
service at the time the Korean War was
coming to a close, but was too
late to see combat.

## Specifications

Crew: 1

Powerplant: 1 x 38kN (8500lb) Pratt & Whitney
J48-P-8A turbojet water injection engine

Maximum speed: 1041km/h (647mph)

Range: 1690km (1050 miles)

Service ceiling: 12,800m (42,000ft)

Dimensions: span 10.51m (34ft 6in); length
12.85m (42ft 1.5in); height 3.73m (12ft 3in)

Weight: 11,232kg (24,763lb) loaded

Armament: Four 20mm (.79in) M2 cannon; six
127mm (5in) rockets; two 454kg (1000lb)
bombs

### ▼ Grumman F9F-8 Cougar

#### VF-61, USS Intrepid, 1956

Seen here wearing the markings of the commander of the 'Jolly Rogers' squadron,
the F9F-8, first flown in January 1954, introduced a new wing of increased span,
carrying additional fuel. External stores options
included fuel tanks or Sidewinders. In 1956,
VF-61 was embarked in Intrepid in the
Mediterranean with CVG-8.

became the F-6A, by which time AIM-9 Sidewinder
AAM had been added to its armoury. Nine front-line
Navy squadrons operated the Skyray, together with
eight Marine squadrons.

A contemporary of the Skyray, the Grumman
F11F Tiger was a compact, swept-wing, single-seat
fighter, and was capable of supersonic speed in level
flight even without engaging the afterburner for its
Wright J65 (a US-built version of the British
Sapphire). Following a debut flight by the prototype
in July 1954, only a single variant, the F11F-1, saw
operational service, recording its service entry with
VA-156 in March 1957. From 1962, the Tiger was
designated as the F-11A, although the arrival of the
Crusader ensured that the last examples had been
retired from active service by April 1961. In total,

seven front-line Navy fighter squadrons operated the
Tiger, and it proved more long-lived in service with
land-based training units and the 'Blue Angels' team.

With the arrival in service of the larger carriers of
the 'Forrestal' class, the time came for the US Navy to
renew its carrier strike capabilities. The Ed
Heinemann-designed Douglas A3D Skywarrior was a
heavy swept-wing bomber and the successor to the AJ
Savage. Key features included accommodation for
three crew, a capacious internal bomb bay for the
carriage of free-fall nuclear weapons, and a pair of
20mm (.79in) cannon in a remotely operated rear
turret. First flown in October 1952 and ultimately
powered by two J57 engines, the first squadron of
A3D-1s was established in March 1956, as VAH-1.
The bomber version would see only limited combat

| Typical US Navy carrier air groups, late 1950s (Lebanon Crisis, 1958) | |
|---|---|
| Air Task Group 201 | |
| ATG-201 | |
| USS *Essex* (CVA-9) | 'Essex' class |
| VF-13 | F4D-1 Skyray |
| VF-62 | FJ-3M Fury |
| VA-83 | A4D-2 Skyhawk |
| VAH-7 | AJ-2 Savage |
| VAW-33 (Det) | AD-5Q Skyraider |
| VAW-12 | AD-5W Skyraider |
| | |
| USS *Saratoga* (CVA-60) | 'Forrestal' class |
| Carrier Air Group 3 | |
| CAG-3 | |
| VF-31 | F3H-2N Demon |
| VF-32 | F8U-1 Crusader |
| VA-34 | A4D-1 Skyhawk |
| VA-35 | AD-6 Skyraider |
| VAH-9 | A3D-2 Skywarrior |
| VFP-61 | F9F-6P Cougar |

Skyhawks were also found on carrier decks, beginning with the improved A4D-2 model. From 1962 the Skyhawk was redesignated in the A-4 series, and by the outbreak of the Vietnam War there were around 900 examples of the A-4B, C and E in service. In all, 32 Navy and two Marine Skyhawk squadrons operated from carrier decks during the conflict.

## Rotary-wing operations

Helicopter operations aboard Navy carriers began in earnest during the Korean War, with the Sikorsky HO3S the first type to be regularly embarked in carriers. Experimental operations with the Marine Corps HO3S-1 began in May 1948 aboard USS *Palau*, and a first operational US Navy helicopter squadron, HU-1, was established with the type in April that year. HU-1 and HU-2 provided detachments of HO3S aircraft for plane-guard duties aboard carriers, and the helicopters flew numerous rescue missions in Korea.

The Sikorsky HO4S-1 was the first Navy ASW helicopter, entering service in October 1951 with

### Specifications

Crew: 4

Powerplant: 2 x 1135kW (1525hp) Wright R-1820-82 radial piston engines

Maximum speed: 438km/h (272mph)

Range: 1558km (968 miles)

Service ceiling: 6949m (22,800ft)

Dimensions: span 21m (69ft 8in); length 12.8m (42ft 0in); height 4.9m (16ft 3in)

Weight: 11,069kg (24,408lb) loaded

Armament: Torpedoes, rockets, depth charges or one Mk 47 or Mk 101 nuclear depth charge

▼ **Grumman S2F-2 Tracker**

*VS-21, c. 1958*

This VS-21 Tracker is wearing the Midnight Blue scheme in which it began its career with the Navy in the mid-1950s. The S2F-2 featured an enlarged bomb bay to carry new types of homing torpedo, as well as a tailplane of increased span. VS-21 was redesignated as an anti-submarine squadron in April 1950, and after service in Korea began its transition to the S2F-1 in late 1954.

over Vietnam, but the Skywarrior was later adapted to fulfil carrier-borne tanker, strategic reconnaissance and electronic warfare duties. After 1962, the Skywarrior was designated as the A-3, and the last version in service, the EKA-3B tanker/electronic intelligence conversion, was retired by the Navy only in 1993.

The 'little brother' to the Skywarrior was the Douglas A4D Skyhawk, another Heinemann design, intended as a jet-powered successor to the AD Skyraider. Highly compact, although still nuclear-capable, the Skyhawk was in production from 1954 to 1979, and the initial production model, the A4D-1, entered service with a first operational squadron, VA-72, in October 1956. From 1959 Marine Corps

HS-1, and operating in hunter-killer teams, although with limited success. The similar HRS was the Marine Corps version of the same helicopter, and was delivered from April 1951. Marine-operated HRS operated from carriers in a rescue role, while Navy HO4S were deployed as plane-guard detachments.

The Piasecki HUP Retriever served with the Navy in the carrier plane-guard role for much of the 1950s, and survivors remained in service long enough to be designated in the UH-25 series after 1962. More successful in the ASW role was the Sikorsky HSS

Seabat, which entered service in August 1955. The Marine version was the HUS Seahorse, used as an assault transport. Again operating as hunter-killer teams, the HSS saw regular service from anti-submarine warfare carriers. The HUS-1, delivered from February 1957, saw use aboard amphibious assault ships from 1959, and in this capacity served in Vietnam from USS *Iwo Jima* and *Princeton*. By this time, the HUS-1 had been redesignated as the UH-34D under the new Tri-Service system of 1962.

## Specifications

| | |
|---|---|
| Crew: 1 | length 11.43m (37ft 6in); height 4.47m |
| Powerplant: 1 x 34.7kN (7800lbf) Wright J65- | (14ft 8.75) |
| W-2 turbojet | Weight: 9350kg (20,611lb) loaded |
| Maximum speed: 1091km/h (678mph) | Armament: Four 20mm (.79in) cannon; |
| Range: 1344km (835 miles) | underwing hardpoints for two tanks or two |
| Service ceiling: 16,640m (54,600ft) | stores of 454kg (1000lb) bombs or eight |
| Dimensions: span 11.3m (37ft 1in); | rockets |

### ▼ North American FJ-3M Fury

*VF-142, USS* Hornet, *1957*

The FJ-3M was a development of the FJ-3, which had added a deeper fuselage containing a more powerful Wright J65-W-2 or W-4 turbojet. The 'M' in the designation of this version signified the introduction of missile armament, in the form of AIM-9 Sidewinders. Eighty of this sub-variant were produced via conversion, being designated as MF-1Cs after 1962.

### ▼ Piasecki HUP-2 Retriever

*HU-1, 1956*

Ordered to fulfil the carrier plane-guard role, the Retriever was built as the HUP-1 between 1949 and 1952, with the first deliveries being made to HU-2 in February 1951. The follow-on HUP-2 had improved directional stability, allowing the endplate fins to be deleted, and featured a more powerful engine. HU-1 'Pacific Fleet Angels' flew the HUP-2 version between 1954 and 1961.

## Specifications

| | |
|---|---|
| Crew: 4 | Dimensions: Rotor diameter 10.6m (35ft 0in); |
| Powerplant: 1 x 404kW (550hp) Continental | length 9.7m (31ft 10in); height 3.8m (12ft |
| R-975-42 engine | 6in) |
| Maximum speed: 193km/h (120mph) | Weight: 2467kg (5440lb) loaded |
| Range: 574km (357 miles) | Armament: None |
| Service ceiling: 3799m (12,467ft) | |

# United States
## 1960–75

**The Vietnam War dominated the activities of the US Navy's carriers in the 1960s, air wings adapting in turn to face new mission demands while expanding their overall capabilities.**

AFTER THE TROUBLED development of many of its early jet fighters, the US Navy sought a fighter with genuine supersonic performance, with a request for proposals issued in 1952. The winning submission was the Vought F8U Crusader, later versions of which would be capable of speeds of almost Mach 2. Key design features included a high-mounted variable-incidence (folding) wing, enabling the fighter to land with its fuselage almost level, improving the pilot's view and permitting short-stroke undercarriage. The F8U saw combat success over Vietnam and a total of over 1200 examples were eventually completed over a production run spanning eight years, and including reconnaissance versions.

First flown in prototype form as the unarmed XF8U-1 in March 1955, the original primary role of the Crusader was a fleet defence and escort fighter. It was in this capacity that the first production F8U-1s were delivered to VF-32 in March 1957. Before the end of the year, the first examples had also begun to be delivered to the US Marine Corps, beginning with VMF-122. From the start of development to fleet

service had taken just under four years. The F8U-1 was designated F-8A after September 1962, and this version was primarily armed with AIM-9 Sidewinder missiles. The improved F8U-1E (Later F-8B) added a new all-weather interception radar and shared the armament of its predecessor: four 20mm (.79in) cannon, a pair of infrared-guided Sidewinders, and an optional rocket pack in the ventral position.

### Improved Crusaders

From the F8U-2 (F-8C) onwards, the Sidewinder capacity was doubled through the introduction of an extra missile rail on each side of the forward fuselage. The F8U-2 was also equipped with a more powerful version of the Pratt & Whitney J57 turbojet, and added fuselage strakes to improve stability. With a still more powerful engine, the F8U-2D (F-8D) saw relatively limited service, this version also introducing improved avionics and radar refinements. Production then switched to the definitive F8U-2NE (F-8E), with a strengthened wing tailored for use in the ground-attack role and capable of carrying free-fall

---

### Specifications

Crew: 1

Powerplant: 1 x 45kN (10,200lbf) Pratt & Whitney J57-P-8, -8A or -8B turbojet

Maximum speed: 1200km/h (722mph)

Range: 1100km (700 miles)

Service ceiling: 17,000m (55,000ft)

Dimensions: span 13.8m (33ft 6in); length 10.21m (45ft 3in); height 3.96m (13ft 0in)

Weight: 10,273kg (22,648lb) loaded

Armament: Four 20mm (.79in) Mk 12 cannon, stores for unguided rockets, air-to-air missiles and bombs

---

### ▼ Douglas F4D-1 Skyray
*VF-162, USS Intrepid, 1961–62*

VF-162 'Hunters' made just one deployment with the Skyray after commissioning on the fighter in September 1960. Operating in the Mediterranean, the squadron was assigned to CVG-6 aboard USS *Intrepid* between August 1961 and March 1962. In the course of this cruise, the F4D-1 became the F-6A. In April 1962 the unit began transition to the F-8A Crusader.

## Specifications

Crew: 1

Powerplant: 1 x 2000kW (2700hp) Wright
R-3350-26WA engine

Maximum speed: 518km/h (322mph)

Range: 2119km (1316 miles)

Service ceiling: 8686m (28,500ft)

Dimensions: span 15.2m (49ft 10in); length
11.8m (38ft 10in); height 4.7m (15ft 8in)

Weight: 11,337kg (25,000lb) loaded

Armament: Four 20mm (.79in) cannon; up to
3600kg (8000lb) of bombs, rockets, and other
stores

### ▼ Douglas A-1H Skyraider

*VA-145, USS* Constellation, *1965*

Seen as it appeared when serving in the Vietnam War from the USS *Constellation*, this Skyraider was built as a single-seat AD-6 model, becoming an A-1H in 1962. VA-145 'Swordsmen' played an important role in early US strikes against North Vietnamese targets, attacking the communists' torpedo boat force and supply depots.

## Specifications

Crew: 2

Powerplant: 2 x 48kN (10,900lbf) General
Electric J79-GE-8 afterburning turbojets

Maximum speed: 2123km/h (1320mph)

Range: 2075km (1289 miles)

Service ceiling: 15,880m (52,100ft)

Dimensions: span 16.16m (53ft 0in); length
23.32m (76ft 6in); height 5.91m (19ft 4.75in)

Weight: 21,605kg (47,530lb) loaded

Armament: One Mk 27 nuclear bomb, B28 or
B43 freefall nuclear bomb in internal
weapons bay; two B43, Mk 83, or Mk 84
bombs on two external hardpoints

### ▼ North American A3J-1 (A-5A) Vigilante

*VAH-7, USS* Enterprise, *1962*

As originally conceived, the Vigilante was a high-speed nuclear-armed strike aircraft, and as such was introduced to service (then still designated as the A3J-1) by VAH-7 in June 1961. The nuclear store (plus jettisonable fuel tanks) was carried in a tunnel between the engines and released by cartridge catapult. This particular aircraft was one of 37 A-5As later converted as an RA-5C.

### ▲ Grumman A-6 Intruder

A pair of Intruders in action during the Vietnam War. Serving with VA-196 'Main Battery', the aircraft were flying from USS *Constellation* in the Gulf of Tonkin in 1968.

## Specifications

Crew: 1

Powerplant: 1 x 42.3kN (14,250lbf) Allison J71-
A-2E (with afterburner)

Maximum speed: 1152km/h (716mph)

Range: 2900km (1800 miles)

Service ceiling: 13,000m (42,650ft)

Dimensions: span 10.77m (35ft 4in); length

17.98m (59ft 0in); height 4.45m (14ft 7in)

Weight: 17,700kg (39,000lb) loaded

Armament: Four 20mm (.79in) Colt Mk 12
cannon; four AIM-7 Sparrow air-to-air
missiles and two AIM-9 Sidewinder missiles;
2720kg (6000lb) bomb load

### ▼ McDonnell F3H-2 Demon

**VF-131, USS Constellation, 1962**

The F3H-2 (later F-3B) was the definitive production version of the Demon,
retaining the ability to launch either Sparrow or Sidewinder missiles (both of
which are seen on this example), while also being capable of carrying out strike
duties with free-fall bombs and unguided rockets. A total
of 239 was built.

bombs, rockets and the Bullpup command-guided
air-to-ground missile.

The Crusader was quickly configured as a
reconnaissance aircraft, initially as the F8U-1P (later
RF-8A) with the cannon of the original fighter

### ▼ Grumman F11F-1 Tiger

Assigned to the 'Astronauts' of VF-33, this F11F-1 prepares to depart the wooden
deck of USS Intrepid. The squadron was assigned to Carrier Air Group Six (CVG-6)
for a deployment to the Mediterranean between February and August 1959.

replaced by cameras. After entering service with VFP-
61, the initial operating unit for the variant, F8U-1P
aircraft from VFP-62 took part in the Cuban Missile
Crisis in 1962, flying vital low-level reconnaissance
sorties from land bases in the US. Over Southeast
Asia, the carrier-based Crusader was in action from
the start, in fighter escort, ground attack and
reconnaissance capacities. In aerial combat over
Vietnam, Crusaders claimed 18 MiGs destroyed,
while VFP-63 bore the brunt of the type's

reconnaissance missions in theatre. Surviving RF-8As were later remanufactured to RF-8G standard, extending their service lives and retrofitting them with ventral fins and an uprated J57 engine.

Early in the war, the F-8C and F-8D were the most important Crusader fighters, supported by the RF-8A for reconnaissance. In the later years of the conflict, the F-8D was the dominant fighter version, with the RF-8G assuming responsibility for the reconnaissance mission. Even after the arrival of the Phantom II, the Crusader continued to operate in the conflict, flying from the smaller 'Essex'-class carriers that could not accommodate the larger F-4. In order to extend their service lives, the F-8D and F-8E were rebuilt as the F-8H and F-8J, respectively, these also featuring blown flaps. The final cruise by fighter Crusaders was made aboard the USS *Oriskany* in 1975. The unarmed reconnaissance version remained in fleet service somewhat longer, finally being retired in 1982. Thereafter, service was limited to squadrons of the Naval Air Reserve, which made periodic visits to carrier decks until October 1986. During the course of an illustrious career, the Crusader had served with around 70 squadrons of the US Navy and Marine Corps.

## Phantom supreme

From the McDonnell stable, the troubled F3H was followed by the legendary F4H Phantom II, which was soon incorporated as a McDonnell Douglas product, running to an eventual production total of around 1500 for the naval variants. Based around the AN/APG-72 radar and a pair of powerful General Electric J79 engines, the Phantom II recorded its first flight in prototype XF4H-1 form in May 1958. The initial production version was a fleet interceptor and attack aircraft, the F-4B (previously F4H-1), although early duties focused exclusively on air defence, using radar-guided AIM-7B Sparrow and infrared-guided AIM-9B Sidewinder AAMs.

After initial carrier trials aboard USS *Independence* in 1960, the production F-4B began to be delivered to replacement air groups for initial crew training, the first of these units being VF-121 established in June of the same year. The first operational squadron, meanwhile, was VF-74 of the Atlantic Fleet. The Phantom II was involved in the war in Vietnam from the outset, and first saw combat in August 1964 when F-4Bs assigned to VF-142 and VF-143 and flying from USS *Constellation* provided cover for Navy air strikes in response to the Gulf of Tonkin incident. The following year, a Navy Phantom II scored the first of many MiG kills that would be registered during the campaign in Southeast Asia.

The F-4G flown in March 1963 saw only limited production and service, but completed one Vietnam combat cruise aboard USS *Kitty Hawk*. The primary change on the G model was the introduction of a digital datalink to permit automated interception and carrier operations. The initial service operator of the F-4G was VF-96 in 1963, followed by VF-213, which took the aircraft to Southeast Asia in 1965.

In March 1965 a reconnaissance development of the Phantom II, the RF-4B, took to the air, equipped

| Specifications | |
|---|---|
| Crew: 1 | 16.5m (54ft 3in); height 4.8m (15ft 9in) |
| Powerplant: 1 x 43.2kN (10,000lbf) Pratt & | Weight: 15,464kg (34,100lb) loaded |
| Whitney J57-P12 turbojet | Armament: Four 20mm (.79in) Colt-Browning |
| Maximum speed: 1630km/h (1013mph) | Mk 12 cannon, two AIM-9 Sidewinders on |
| Range: 2294km (1425 miles) | fuselage cheek rails, and a rocket pack |
| Service ceiling: 15,956m (52,350ft) | carrying 32 70mm (2.75in) Mighty Mouse |
| Dimensions: span 10.8m (35ft 8in); length | folding-fin rockets under the fuselage |

▼ **Vought F8U-1 Crusader**

*VF-211, USS* Lexington, *1960*

Later the top-scoring US Navy squadron in Vietnam (seven kills), VF-211 began Crusader operations with the F8U-1 (later F-8A). The 'Fighting Checkmates' first took the F8U-1 to sea aboard USS *Lexington* in October 1960, before making two further Pacific cruises in USS *Hancock* by December 1963. Thereafter the unit re-equipped with the F-8E.

**Specifications**

Crew: 1

Powerplant: 1 x 78kN (17,500lbf) Pratt & Whitney J57-P-20 turbojet

Maximum speed: 1975km/h (1225mph)

Range: 2294km (1425 miles)

Service ceiling: 15,956m (52,350ft)

Dimensions: span 10.8m (35ft 8in); length

16.5m (54ft 3in); height 4.8m (15ft 9in)

Weight: 15,464kg (34,100lb) loaded

Armament: Four 20mm (.79in) Colt-Browning Mk 12 cannon, and four AIM-9 Sidewinders on twin fuselage cheek rails

▼ **Vought F8U-2N (F-8D) Crusader**

*VMF(AW)-451, NAS Atsugi, 1962–63*

Built as a ship-based F8U-2N, this Crusader is shown during land-based service with a Marine all-weather fighter squadron. The aircraft displays the twin Sidewinder launch rails that were introduced on the F8U-2 series, while the previous rocket packs were deleted.

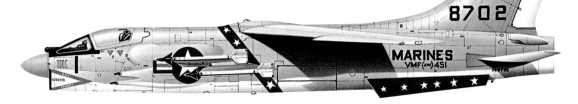

with side-looking and forward-looking radar and other sensors. The RF-4B saw exclusive service with the Marines, and land-based operations over Vietnam began out of Da Nang in 1965.

First flown in May 1966, the F-4J arrived on station for Vietnam service in 1968, with the initial operators being VF-33 and VF-102 on board USS *America*. The F-4J differed from its predecessors in having a new AN/AWG-10 pulse-Doppler fire control radar, structural refinements and more robust undercarriage. The F-4J was responsible for the Phantom II's most successful air-to-air combat, when on 10 May 1972 no fewer than 11 MiGs were claimed destroyed. A Marine F-4J also achieved that service's only MiG kill during the conflict.

The F-4N flown in June 1972 was produced via conversion of existing F-4B airframes, adding various updated systems. The final naval derivative of the Phantom II was the F-4S, first flown in July 1977 and produced as an update of the F-4J fleet, and including wing slats for enhanced manoeuvrability. It was an F-4S that made the Phantom II's final carrier deployment, when an aircraft of reserve unit VF-202 landed on USS *America* in October 1986.

The Phantom became a signature weapon of the air war in Vietnam, but was ably supported by earlier carrier-based types. At the start of US combat operations in 1964, there were some 200 A-1 Skyraiders still in US Navy service, these operating primarily from the smaller 'Midway'-class carriers as well as from the USS *Constellation*, *Independence*, *Kitty Hawk*, *Ranger* and, in an electronic countermeasures capacity, *Enterprise*. As well as attack

and close support missions, A-1s flew rescue support and even gained success in air-to-air combat, downing MiG-15s in incidents in 1965 and 1966. The last versions to see combat service with the Navy were the two-seat A-1E (formerly AD-5) and the single-seat A-1J (AD-7). The last attack-configured A-1s flew their final sorties with VA-25 from USS *Coral Sea* in February 1968, although EA-1Fs continued to fly combat support missions until the end of that year.

## Vietnam attack assets

Skywarriors saw only limited service as bombers over Vietnam in 1965–66, but the type remained a constant on carrier decks until the end of US involvement in 1973. Until then, the Skywarrior was primarily engaged on photo-reconnaissance (RA-3B), electronic reconnaissance/countermeasures and tanking duties, with detachments provided by VAH, VAQ and VAP squadrons. From early on in the conflict, most Skywarriors had been converted for use as tankers, either as KA-3Bs or as EKA-3B combined electronic warfare/tanker platforms, and as such these provided the Navy with its most capable aerial refuelling assets throughout the war. After deploying aboard carriers regularly from the late 1960s, the final EKA-3B detachment (provided by VAQ-130) stood down in mid-1974, in order to transition to the EA-6B Prowler.

Replacing the A-1 within light attack squadrons, the A-4 was first committed to action in Vietnam in August 1964, during the initial Navy strikes. The initial A-4B, C and E models that saw action early in

## Specifications

Crew: 1

Powerplant: 1 x 34.7kN (7800lbf) Wright
J65-W-16A turbojet

Maximum speed: 1078km/h (670mph)

Range: 1480km (920 miles)

Service ceiling: 14,935m (49,000ft)

Dimensions: span 8.38m (27ft 6in); length
12.22m (40ft 1.5in); height 4.66m (15ft 3in)

Weight: 12,437kg (27,420lb) loaded

Armament: Two 20mm (.79in) Mk 12 cannon;
provision for 2268kg (5000lb) of stores,
including air-to-surface missiles, bombs,
clusters bombs, dispenser weapons, rocket-
launcher pods, cannon pods, drop tanks and
ECM pods

### ▼ Douglas A-4C Skyhawk

#### *VA-144, USS* Kitty Hawk, *1966–67*

The A-4C (previously A4D-2N) of 1959 was the first Skyhawk to introduce a
lengthened nose, which contained improved avionics, including a terrain avoidance
radar, autopilot and Low-Altitude Bombing System (LABS).

This was the most prolific version, with 638 being
completed. VA-144 'Roadrunners' operated its
A-4Cs from USS *Kitty Hawk* between
November 1966 and June 1967, flying
missions over Vietnam.

## Specifications

Crew: 1

Powerplant: 1 x 37kN (8400lbf) Pratt & Whitney
J52-P-6A turbojet

Maximum speed: 1083km/h (673mph)

Range: 1867km (1160 miles)

Service ceiling: 12.3km (40,050ft)

Dimensions: span 8.3m (27ft 6in); length

12.2m (40ft 1in); height 4.6m (15ft 2in)

Weight: 11,111kg (24,500lb) loaded

Armament: Two 20mm (.79in) Mk 12 cannon;
provision for 3719kg (8200lb) of stores,
including air-to-surface missiles, bombs,
clusters bombs, dispenser weapons, rocket-
launcher pods, drop tanks and ECM pods

### ▼ Douglas A-4E Skyhawk

#### *VA-72, USS* Independence, *1965*

VA-72 'Blue Hawks' served aboard USS *Independence* when that carrier was
sailing in the South China Sea during air operations over Vietnam in May 1965.
The unit was the Navy's first operational Skyhawk
squadron, receiving A4D-1s in September
1956, becoming operational a month
later. The unit transitioned to the
A-7B in 1970.

the conflict were later joined by the A-4F with a
distinctive avionics 'hump' on the spine, this model
appearing in service in 1967. In total, 32 Navy and
two Marine Corps A-4 squadrons completed 62
combat cruises over Vietnam, while others saw action
from land bases. Reflecting its importance in the
fighting, a total of 195 Skyhawks was lost in combat,
the highest loss rate of the war. In addition to its
primary attack and close support roles, the A-4
conducted tanker, air defence and defence
suppressions missions during the war, the latter
including missions launching AGM-45 Shrike
missiles against radar sites. Despite replacement by
the A-6 and A-7, the Skyhawk was in action until the
end, with examples on board USS *Hancock* for its
final Southeast Asia cruise in 1973–74.

A replacement for the venerable Skywarrior in the
heavy attack category was sought, and North
American designed the A3J Vigilante in response.
The Vigilante was originally schemed as a high-
performance strike aircraft that would carry a single
nuclear store in a fuselage compartment between the

## Specifications

Crew: 3

Powerplant: 2 x 46.7kN (10,500lbf) Pratt &
Whitney J57-P-10 turbojets

Maximum speed: 982km/h (610mph)

Range: 3380km (2100 miles)

Service ceiling: 12,495m (41,000ft)

Dimensions: span 22.10m (72ft 6in); length
23.27m (76ft 4in); height 6.95m (22ft 9.5in)

Weight: 37,195kg (82,000lb) loaded

Armament: Two 20mm (.79in) M3L cannon;
5800kg (12,800lb) of free fall bombs, mines
or nuclear weapons

### ▼ Douglas A-3B Skywarrior

*VAH-2, USS* Coral Sea, *1965*

Built as an A3D-2, this Skywarrior is shown as it appeared when operating in the
Gulf of Tonkin off the coast of Vietnam, by now redesignated
as an A-3B. VAH-2 was the first squadron to introduce
the A-3 to combat in Vietnam, commencing
bombing missions in March 1965. Note the
hose-and-drogue refuelling unit
below the fuselage.

twin J79 engines. A first YA3J-1 prototype flew in
August 1958, followed by a short production run of
A3J-2 (subsequently A-5B) attack aircraft from 1962.
The A-5A/B relied on an inertial navigation system
and digital attack computer for bombing accuracy,
and could carry a free-fall nuclear weapon that was
ejected from an internal bay that also accommodated
additional fuel tanks. Other stores could be carried
underwing, on either two (A-5A) or four (A-5B)
external hardpoints. However, the Vigilante's mission
profile soon shifted, and as early as June 1962 a long-
range reconnaissance version entered flight test, as the
A3J-3 (later RA-5C).

After carrier trials in USS *Saratoga* in summer
1960, the first operational unit was VAH-7, equipped
with the A3J-1 in June 1961. The attack variants saw
only limited operational service before the RA-5C
was introduced, with RVAH-5 being the first
squadron equipped with the reconnaissance version,
aboard USS *Ranger*. The RA-5C saw extensive service
with nine different squadrons over Vietnam, making
use of its extensive sensor suite that was housed in a
'canoe' fairing below the fuselage. The sensors
included optical equipment as well as side-looking
radar, an infrared line-scanner and ECM systems.
RA-5Cs were active over Southeast Asia until 1973,
after which the Vigilante was gradually removed from
the inventory, the last examples being retired by
RVAH-7 in November 1979.

The next carrier strike aircraft was a Grumman
product, the A-6 Intruder first being flown in April
1960. Significantly more compact than the
Skywarrior, the long-range A-6 also offered a true all-

weather capability and became standard equipment
among all US Navy and Marine Corps heavy attack
squadrons, replacing the Skyraider on carrier decks.
The Intruder was powered by two Pratt & Whitney
J52 turbojets and had accommodation for a crew of
two seated side-by-side. Key to its capabilities was a
powerful Norden bombing and navigation radar that
was part of the digital integrated attack navigation
equipment (DIANE).

The initial production version of the Intruder was
the A-6A (briefly designated A2F-1 under the pre-

### ▲ USS *Kitty Hawk* (CV-63)

A Vietnam-era scene aboard the carrier USS *Kitty Hawk* in 1965–66, as an F-4G of
VF-213 prepares to launch, with an RA-5C of RVAH-13 in the foreground.

1962 system), which was delivered to VA-42 from February 1963. The first operational unit was VA-75, which stood up the following year and made an initial deployment aboard USS *Independence* in May 1965, before heading into combat in Vietnam in July.

In late 1967 VA-75 introduced the A-6B version, tailored for defence suppression missions and suitably equipped with provision to carry the AGM-78 Standard anti-radar missile. The A-6C was fielded from early 1970, initially with VA-165. This version featured the trails-roads interdiction multi-sensor (TRIM) with forward-looking infrared and low-light level television (LLTV) sensors for use against the Ho Chi Minh trail and other communist supply routes. Both A-6B and C models were converted from A-6A airframes. Another conversion was the KA-6D tanker, which retained its bombing capability but could deliver fuel and had provision for up to five external tanks to increase overall capacity.

## Ultimate Intruder

The ultimate Intruder strike version, the A-6E, entered service in September 1971, and was first deployed by VA-85 a year later, aboard USS *Forrestal*. The A-6E featured entirely revised avionics, with a new digital computer, new multi-mode radar and other improvements. In all, no fewer than 17 operational squadrons flew variants of the Intruder, together with two fleet replacement and two reserve units.

When it came to replacing the A-4 Skyhawk, the Navy settled on the Vought A-7 Corsair II, a light

| Typical US Navy carrier air wing, Vietnam War (early) | |
|---|---|
| Carrier Air Wing 21 | |
| CVW-21 | |
| USS *Hancock* (CVA-19) | 'Essex' class |
| December 1965 to August 1966 | |
| VF-24 | F-8C Crusader |
| VF-211 | F-8E Crusader |
| VA-212 | A-4E Skyhawk |
| VA-215 | A-1H/J Skyraider |
| VA-216 | A-4C Skyhawk |
| VAH-4 | KA-3B Skywarrior |
| VAQW-13 | EA-1F Skyraider |
| VFP-63 | RF-8G Crusader |
| VAW-111 | E-1B Tracer |

| Typical US Navy carrier air wing, Vietnam War (late) | |
|---|---|
| Carrier Air Wing 14 | |
| CVW-14 | |
| USS *Constellation* (CVA-64) | 'Kitty Hawk' class |
| October 1969 to May 1970 | |
| VF-142 | F-4J Phantom II |
| VF-143 | F-4J Phantom II |
| VA-27 | A-7A Corsair II |
| VA-85 | A-6A/B Intruder |
| VA-97 | A-7A Corsair II |
| RVAH-7 | RA-5C Vigilante |
| VAQ-133 | EKA-3B Skywarrior |
| VAW-113 | E-2A Hawkeye |

## Specifications

Crew: 2

Powerplant: 2 x 48kN (10,800lbf) General Electric J79-GE-8 turbojets

Maximum speed: 2391km/h (1485mph)

Range: 2592km (1610 miles)

Service ceiling: 18,897m (62,000ft)

Dimensions: span 11.6m (38ft 4in); length 17.7m (58ft 3in); height 4.9m (16ft 3in)

Weight: 24,761kg (54,600lb) loaded

Armament: Four semi-recessed AIM-7 Sparrow air-to-air missiles and provision for up to 7257kg (16,000lb) of missiles, rockets and bombs carried on centreline pylon below the fuselage and on four underwing hardpoints

▼ **McDonnell Douglas F-4B Phantom II**

**VF-142 *USS* Constellation, *1965***

VF-142 'Ghostriders' deployed its F-4Bs to the Gulf of Tonkin on four occasions between 1964 and 1969, three times on board USS *Constellation*.

attack aircraft that was developed from the general concept established by the F-8 Crusader. The requirement for a Skyhawk replacement was formulated in 1963, and a first pre-production A-7A flew in September 1965. The first series-production examples had been delivered to two fleet training squadrons, VA-122 and VA-174, by 1966. The operational squadron VA-147 was the first to deploy the Corsair II in combat over Southeast Asia, when embarked in USS *Ranger* in late 1967.

By the time of the 1973 ceasefire, the A-7 had replaced the A-4 on all but one deployed carrier. From the early 1970s the A-7 saw considerable action over Vietnam, delivering both free-fall and guided weaponry, as well as rockets. Typical missions flown included raids over North Vietnam in 1972, together

### ▼ McDonnell Douglas F-4G Phantom II

*VF-213, USS* **Kitty Hawk**, *1965–66*

Only a dozen examples of the F-4G were completed, these adding AN/ASW-21 digital datalink to the F-4B airframe. This example wears an experimental camouflage scheme adopted for operations in Vietnam, and is armed with 227kg (500lb) free-fall bombs on multiple ejector racks, plus Sidewinder missiles.

### ▲ McDonnell Douglas F-4B Phantom II

Although originally fielded in the fleet air defence role, the Navy's F-4B soon established itself as an air-to-ground platform, as evidenced by this example from VF-96 aboard USS *Enterprise*, unleashing unguided Zuni rockets.

with aerial minelaying during the final phase of US participation in the conflict.

The initial A-7A was soon joined by the improved A-7B with an uprated Allison TF41 turbofan engine. Next in line was the A-7C, intended to overcome

### Specifications

Crew: 2

Powerplant: 2 x 54.2kN (17,000lbf) General Electric J79-GE-8A afterburning turbojets

Maximum speed: 2390km/h (1485mph)

Range: 958km (595 miles)

Service ceiling: over 18,975m (62,250ft)

Dimensions: span 11.7m (38ft 5in); length 19.2m (63ft 0in); height 5.02m (16ft 5.5in)

Weight: 28,300kg (62,390lb) loaded

Armament: Four semi-recessed AIM-7 Sparrow air-to-air missiles; provision for up to 7257kg (16,000lb) of missiles, rockets and bombs carried on centreline pylon below the fuselage and on four underwing hardpoints

## Specifications

| | |
|---|---|
| Crew: 4 | Dimensions: span 22.12m (72ft 7in); length |
| Powerplant: 2 x 1525hp (1121kW) Wright R- | 13.26m (43ft 6in); height 5.33m (17ft 6in) |
| 1820-82WA radial engines | Weight: 10,630kg (23,435lb) loaded |
| Maximum speed: 450km/h (280mph) | Armament: 2200kg (4800lb) bomb payload in |
| Range: 2170km (1350 miles) | the internal bomb bay, external hardpoints |
| Service ceiling: 6700m (22,000ft) | for torpedoes and depth charges |

### ▼ Grumman S-2E Tracker
#### *VS-21, USS* Kearsarge, *1970*

Depicted armed with Mk 44 ASW torpedoes under the wing, this S-2E of VS-21 'Fighting Redtails' represents the final production version of the Tracker. This aircraft was home-based at NAS North Island, Virginia, but is depicted detached to USS *Kearsarge*, a modernized 'Essex'-class ASW carrier that served until 1970.

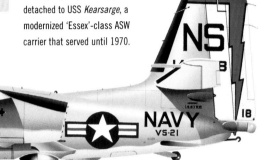

## Specifications

| | |
|---|---|
| Crew: 1 | Service ceiling: 17,983m (59,000ft) |
| Powerplant: 1 x 80.1kN (18,000lbf) thrust Pratt | Dimensions: span 10.72m (35ft 2in); length |
| & Whitney J57-P-22 afterburning turbojet | 16.61m (54ft 6in); height 4.8m (15ft 9in) |
| Maximum speed: 1975km/h (1227mph) | Weight: 15,422kg (34,000lb) loaded |
| Range: 966km (600 miles) | Armament: None |

### ▼ Vought RF-8G Crusader
#### *VFP-63, USS* Oriskany, *1972*

As the ultimate reconnaissance Crusader, the RF-8G was produced via upgrade of the original RF-8A, adding a J57-P-22 engine in a strengthened airframe, ventral fins, and updated equipment. Assigned to VFP-63's Det 43, this particular aircraft was lost in a landing accident aboard USS *Oriskany* in December 1972.

some of the deficiencies encountered with the powerplant of the interim A-7B.

A third variant of the Corsair II was available in time to fly missions during the closing stages of the war in Southeast Asia. This was the A-7E, which became the definitive production version, remaining in service into the early 1990s with various improvements. The basic A-7E introduced revised avionics and a more reliable powerplant. By the time the Navy retired the Corsair II in the wake of the 1991 Gulf War, the type had equipped no fewer than 38 squadrons, including two training units six squadrons of the Naval Air Reserve, plus a handful of trials and special duties formations.

## AEW replacement

As a replacement for the E-1B Tracer, Grumman developed an all-new design to fulfil the carrier-borne AEW role. Originally styled as the W2F Hawkeye, the aircraft was powered by twin Allison T56 turboprops and featured a pressurized cabin with stations for three mission systems operators, in addition to the two-man flight deck. The primary sensor was the AN/APS-96 radar mounted above the rear fuselage. Other notable recognition features were the four vertical tailfins to increase keel area, and wings that folded back to lie parallel against the rear fuselage for carrier stowage. The first production variant was the E-2A (formerly W2F-1), which

## Specifications

Crew: 2

Powerplant: 2 x 79.4kN (17,860lbf) General
   Electric J79-GE-10 afterburning turbojets

Maximum speed: 2230km/h (1385mph)

Range: (with drop tanks) 5150km (3200 miles)

Service ceiling: 20,400m (67,000ft)

Dimensions: span 16.15m (53ft 0in); length
   23.11m (75ft 10in); height 5.92m (19ft 5in)

Weight: 36,285kg (80,000lb) loaded

Armament: None

### ▼ North American RA-5C Vigilante

**RVAH-5, USS Constellation, 1968**

This Vigilante operated from USS *Constellation* stationed off the coast of Vietnam. Clearly visible is the ventral 'canoe' fairing that accommodated optical and electronic equipment. RVAH-5 was the first squadron to be equipped with the RA-5C, in June 1964, and initially sailed aboard the USS *Ranger*. Vigilantes proved almost immune to North Vietnamese air defences.

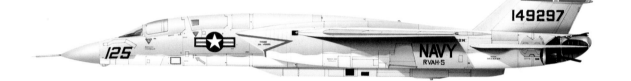

### ▼ McDonnell Douglas RF-4B Phantom II

**VMFP-3, MCAS El Toro, 1975**

A total of 46 RF-4B tactical reconnaissance aircraft was completed for the Marine Corps, these serving with VMCJ-1, VMCJ-2, VMCJ-3 and, as here, VMFP-3 'Eyes of the Corps'. Marine Phantom II units were carrier-capable, and made occasional deployments aboard carriers. VMFP-3 took detachments of RF-4Bs aboard USS *Midway* at regular intervals between October 1975 and December 1983, operating as part of CVW-11. Otherwise, the unit was home-based at El Toro, California.

## Specifications

Crew: 2

Powerplant: 2 x 75.5kN (17,000lbf) General
   Electric J79-GE-8 turbojets

Maximum speed: 2390km/h (1485mph)

Range: 3701km (2300 miles)

Service ceiling: 18,898m (62,000ft)

Dimensions: span 11.7m (38ft 5in); length
   17.77m (58ft 3in); height 4.95m (16ft 3in)

Weight: 20,231kg (44,600lb) loaded

Armament: None

entered service with VAW-11 in 1964. The following year the Hawkeye began its participation in the Vietnam War, with a four-aircraft detachment from VAW-11 sailing aboard USS *Kitty Hawk* in October. By the end of the decade the improved E-2B had appeared, this adding a digital mission computer among other equipment upgrades. The E-2B model made its first combat cruise to Southeast Asia in 1969.

## Defence suppression

With the growing importance of the defence suppression and electronic warfare missions clearly demonstrated during the Vietnam War, the move was made to adapt the Intruder for such duties. The first

effort in this direction was a Marine Corps project, the EA-6A being a quick-change derivative of the A-6A. Only operated by the USMC, the EA-6A was a tactical electronic jamming aircraft and saw limited use from Navy carrier decks in the early 1970s.

The definitive EA-6B Prowler was a four-seat development of the A-6, and became the standard electronic warfare support aircraft aboard US Navy carriers, serving with both Navy and Marine Corps units. The first prototype Prowler was adapted from an A-6A and first flew in May 1968, before a first operational squadron, VAQ-129, stood up in July 1971. The EA-6B added two additional seats to the Intruder airframe together with the AN/ALQ-99 tactical jamming system. The ALQ-99 consisted of radar receivers in the top of the tailfin, plus up to five external jamming pods. A communications jammer was also installed internally, and between them the Prowler's electronic warfare aids could disable hostile radars across four different frequency bands. Over Vietnam the EA-6B replaced the EKA-3B for electronic warfare missions, the first sorties being flown by VAQ-132 in July 1972.

In the ASW role, the S-2 soldiered on in service throughout the 1960s, and was subject to a number of upgrades. From 1960, the type was assigned to carrier anti-submarine air groups (CVSG), while from 1971 the Tracker was adopted aboard multi-purpose carriers as part of a new-look air wing.

The production total of 1120 aircraft encompassed the original S-2A (formerly S2F-1) that was manufactured until 1961, with surveillance radar, magnetic anomaly detector (MAD) and electronic countermeasures (ECM) equipment. The addition of the Julie/Jezebel active/passive detection system produced the S-2B (S2F-1S), while the S-2F

## Specifications

Crew: 2

Powerplant: 2 x 79kN (17,900lb) General Electric J79-GE-10 thrust with afterburning turbojets

Maximum speed: 2299km/h (1428mph)

Range: 2222km (1380 miles)

Service ceiling: 16,672m (54,700ft)

Dimensions: span 11.6m (38ft 4in); length 17.7m (58ft 3in); height 4.7m (15ft 8in)

Weight: 25,396kg (56,000lb) loaded

Armament: Four air-to-air missiles and provision for up to 7257kg (16,000lb) of missiles, rockets and bombs

### ▼ McDonnell Douglas F-4J Phantom II

#### *VF-96, USS* Constellation, *1972*

Each Carrier Air Wing stationed off Vietnam operated two fighter squadrons. In the case of USS *Constellation* during its 1972 spring cruise, these were VF-92 and VF-96, equipped with F-4Js. This particular aircraft was flown by Lieutenants Randall Cunningham and William P. Driscoll when they shot down three MiG-17s on 10 May 1972.

### ▼ Sikorsky SH-3A

#### *HC-1, USS* Constellation, *1972*

The SH-3A Sea King was the initial ASW version of the Sea King, having been developed under the HSS-2 designation. In addition to its primary role, the SH-3A also equipped a number of utility squadrons, providing transport and rescue duties for carrier battle groups. When serving in the plane-guard role, the Sea King would be launched during flight operations, and would assume a position in the hover to the port of the carrier.

## Specifications

Crew: 4

Powerplant: 2 x 1044kW (1400hp) General Electric T58-GE-10 turboshaft engines

Maximum speed: 267km/h (166mph)

Range: 1005km (624 miles)

Service ceiling: 4480m (14,700ft)

Dimensions: Rotor diameter 18.9m (62ft 0in); length 22.15m (72ft 8in); height 5.13m (16ft 9in)

Weight: 9525kg (21,000lb) loaded

Armament: Four Mk 46/44 anti-submarine torpedoes or nuclear depth charge

## Specifications

Crew: 2

Powerplant: 2 x 41kN (9300lbf) Pratt & Whitney
J52-P-8A turbojets

Maximum speed: 1040km/h (646mph)

Range: 2173km (1350 miles)

Service ceiling: 12,268m (40,250ft)

Dimensions: span 16.1m (53ft 0in); length
16.6m (54ft 9in); height 4.9m (16ft 2in)

Weight: 24,353kg (53,699lb) loaded

Armament: A maximum load of 6804kg
(15,000lb) of offensive weapons carried on
four underwing hardpoints and one centreline
hardpoint

### ▼ Grumman A-6A Intruder

**VA-165, USS Constellation, 1971–72**

Carrying a load of 500lb (227kg) Mk 82 conventional bombs underwing, this A-6A
was in service with VA-165, part of the Pacific Fleet Intruder community, home-
based at NAS Whidbey Island, Washington. VA-165 operated from USS
*Constellation* on Vietnam combat duty between October 1971
and December 1974, with its A-6As supported by
KA-6D tankers, and latterly joined by A-6Bs.

## Specifications

Crew: 2

Powerplant: 2 x 41.4kN (9300lbf) Pratt &
Whitney J52-P-8A turbojets

Maximum speed: 1043km/h (648mph)

Range: 1627km (1011 miles)

Service ceiling: 14,480m (47,500ft)

Dimensions: span 16.15m (53ft 0in); length
16.69m (59ft 10in); height 4.95m (16ft 3in)

Weight: 26,581kg (58,600lb) loaded

Armament: A maximum load of 6804kg
(15,000lb) of offensive weapons carried on
four underwing hardpoints and one centreline
hardpoint

### ▼ Grumman EA-6A Intruder

**VMAQ-2, USS Midway, 1977–8**

The Marines pioneered the adaptation of the Intruder airframe for the defence
suppression role, with the EA-6A modification. Equipped with internal electronics
and external jamming pods, the two-seat EA-6A provided occasional four-aircraft
detachments to carrier decks. Some 21 production
EA-6As were completed, these serving over
Vietnam with VMCJ-1 and VMCJ-2.

(S2F-1S1) marked an effort to improve all aspects of
the ASW sensor suite. The S-2C (S2F-2) represented
the first major change on the production line, and
featured an enlarged weapons bay and revised tail
surfaces. The S-2D (S2F-3) heralded the final
significant modification, with changes to the wing,
fuselage and engine nacelles, as well as new radar,
MAD and ECM equipment. The S-2D was
manufactured until 1962, when production switched
to the definitive S-2E (S2F-3S) with the tactical
navigation (TACAN) system and additional
sonobuoys. The last of the line were completed in
1967, after which the S-2G was produced via
upgrade, adding Bullpup air-to-ground missile
capability to the 'Echo' version.

As well as a service career with over 20 anti-
submarine squadrons, the Tracker served with utility
and composite squadrons, often being flown by the
former in unarmed US-2 configuration. A final
deployment by VS-37 and VS-38 aboard USS
*Kitty Hawk* in 1975 marked the end of the Tracker's
frontline service, and the type was finally retired in
August 1976.

In the COD role, the ageing Trader gave way to a
development of the E-2A, in the shape of the
Grumman C-2 Greyhound. The wing of the
Hawkeye was allied to a new, larger fuselage with a
cargo ramp. First flown in November 1964, the C-2A
entered service with VRC-50 in December 1966 and
immediately saw service in support of carriers

operating off the coast of Vietnam. The first batch of 17 production aircraft was completed by 1967, and these saw service at bases in Italy and Japan, as well as in the US.

## Matchless interceptor

After the failure of the General Dynamics F-111B carrier interceptor, Grumman developed the F-14 Tomcat as a powerful, missile-armed carrier fighter. From 1962 Grumman had been prime contractor for the weapons system of the F-111B, and the resulting AN/AWG-9 fire control system was shoehorned into the Tomcat. First flown in December 1970, the Tomcat suffered from some teething troubles before

emerging as the finest interceptor of its generation. As the successor to the Phantom II in the fleet air defence role, the two-seat Tomcat employed variable-geometry wings, allied with Pratt & Whitney TF30 engines inherited from the F-111B. The weapons system included the long-range AIM-54 Phoenix AAM – a weapon unique to the Tomcat – together with the medium-range AIM-7 Sparrow and short-range AIM-9 Sidewinder, and an on-board 20mm (.79in) multi-barrel cannon. The AWG-9 allowed the Tomcat to track 24 targets simultaneously at ranges of around 160km (100 miles). Once prioritized, six targets could be engaged simultaneously. Other sensors included an infrared

### Specifications

Crew: 1

Powerplant: 1 x 50.5kN (11,350lbf) Pratt & Whitney TF30-P-6 turbojet

Maximum speed: 1112km/h (691mph)

Range: 3669km (2280 miles)

Dimensions: span 11.8m (38ft 9in); length

14.0m (46ft 1in); height 4.9m (16ft 0in)

Weight: 17,223kg (38,000lb) loaded

Armament: Two 20mm (.79in) Colt Mk 12 cannon; up to 6804kg (15,000lb) of bombs, air-to-surface missiles or other stores

### ▼ Vought A-7A Corsair II

*VA-93, USS* Midway, *1969*

The original A-7A as introduced to operational service over Vietnam in 1967 soon established itself as the mainstay of the Navy's light attack mission, displacing the A-4. The 'Blue Blazers' of VA-93 were home-based at NAS Atsugi in Japan, this aircraft being assigned to CVW-5. Noteworthy is the Sidewinder launch rail below the wing, aft of the cockpit.

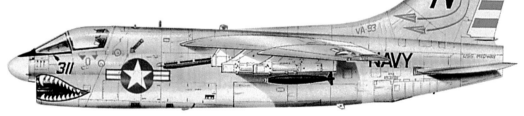

### Specifications

Crew: 1

Powerplant: 1 x 54.2kN (12,190lbf) thrust Pratt & Whitney TF30-P-8 turbofan engine

Maximum speed: 1123km/h (698mph)

Range: 1150km (4100 miles)

Dimensions: span 11.8m (38ft 9in); length

14.06m (46ft 1.5in); height 4.9m (16ft 0.75in)

Weight: 19,050kg (42,000lb) loaded

Armament: Two 20mm (.79in) Colt Mk 12 cannon; up to 6804kg (15,000lb) of bombs, air-to-surface missiles or other stores

### ▼ Vought A-7B Corsair II

*VA-46, USS* John F. Kennedy, *1975*

Between September 1970 and August 1977, USS *John F. Kennedy* was home to A-7Bs from VA-46 'Clansmen' (note the tartan trim on the tailfin), assigned to Carrier Air Wing 1 (CVW-1). Essentially similar to the A-7A initial-production model, the A-7B differed in its use of a TF30-P-8 engine, and a total of 196 was built, some being re-engined with the TF30-P-408.

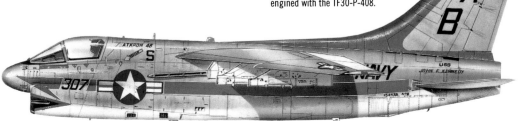

## Specifications

Crew: 2

Powerplant: 2 x 79kN (17,900lbf) General
Electric J79-GE-8B turbojets

Maximum speed: 2415km/h (1500mph)

Range: 1770km (1100 miles)

Service ceiling: 15,239m (50,000ft)

Dimensions: span 11.6m (38ft 4in); length
17.7m (58ft 3in); height 4.9m (16ft 3in)

Weight: 26,303kg (58,000lb) loaded

Armament: One 20mm (.79in) M61A1 rotary
cannon; four AIM-7 Sparrow missiles; up to
5888kg (12,980lb) of munitions mounted on
underwing pylons

### ▼ McDonnell Douglas F-4N Phantom II

**VF-111, USS Coral Sea, 1974–75**

Resplendent in the 1970s-era markings of the famous 'Sundowners', this Phantom
II is an example of the F-4N, created through the remanufacture of existing F-4B
airframes from 1972, and broadly equivalent to the F-4J model. VF-111 operated
the F-4N between 1974 and 1977, before switching to the F-14A.

search and track system carried in a housing under
the nose.

Powered by the less-than-perfect TF30, the
original F-14A production model was in production
for 15 years, with 545 examples completed.
Throughout its service, the F-14A was systematically
improved through modifications to its engines,
increasing power output and reliability.

The F-14A entered service with a first training unit,
VF-124, in October 1972, before VF-1 and VF-2 took
the new fighter aboard USS *Enterprise* for an initial
operational cruise in the Western Pacific in September
1974. There followed the first two squadrons within
the Atlantic Fleet, VF-14 and VF-32 going aboard USS
*John F. Kennedy* in June 1975, and operating in the
Mediterranean. Ultimately, Tomcat deployment peaked
at a strength of 22 front-line squadrons, together with
replacement training squadrons, and assorted Naval Air
Reserve and test and evaluation units.

During the 1960s the Kaman HU2K (later H-2)
Seasprite assumed the role of carrier search and rescue
platform, and HU2K-1 (UH-2A) and HU2K-1U
(UH-2B) models served with rescue detachments,
together with a number of HH-2Cs configured for
combat rescue. The first operator of the initial UH-
2A variant was HU-2, established in December 1962.
Between them, HU-1 and HU-2 provided Seasprite
utility helicopter detachments to carriers of the
Pacific and Atlantic Fleets, respectively.

US Navy rotary-wing operations were entirely
overhauled with the arrival of the Sikorsky SH-3 Sea

King, first flown in March 1959 as the YHSS-2.
Despite its designation suggestive of the fact that it
was a development of the earlier HSS-1 (SH-34)
Seabat, the HSS-2 Sea King was an all-new design.
Equipped with an amphibious hull and powered by a
pair of General Electric T58 turboshafts, the Sea King
was primarily designed a replacement for the Seabat
in the ASW role, before adopting an expanded
mission profile that included search and rescue,
utility transport and mine countermeasures.

### Ruling the waves

While the Seabat had operated in the established
formula of hunter-killer pairs, the HSS-2 combined
both functions in a single airframe, and as such
provided carriers with a inner-zone ASW screen,
ultimately complementing the fixed-wing S-3 Viking
in this role. In addition, the Sea King saw widespread
service as an ASW platform from other larger US
Navy warships. The mission equipment of the HSS-2
included an AN/AQS-13 dipping sonar, auto-hover
system, AN/APN-130 Doppler radar and radar
altimeter and up to four homing torpedoes. In order
to be better accommodated on warships, the Sea King
was provided with powered blade-folding, while the
complete tail could also be manually folded to reduce
dimensions further. The HSS-2 entered service with
HS-3 in September 1961 and was redesignated as the
SH-3A in the same month. The SH-3D was an
improvement of the basic ASW version, adding more
powerful engines and a modified tailplane, but

## Specifications

Crew: 4

Powerplant: 2 x 41.26kN (9275lbf) General
Electric TF34-GE-2 turbofans

Maximum speed: 795 km/h
(493mph)

Range: 5121km (3182 miles)

Service ceiling: 12,465m (40,900ft)

Dimensions: span 20.93m (68ft 8in); length
16.26m (53ft 4in); height 6.93m (22ft 9in)

Weight: 23,831kg (52,539lb) loaded

Armament: Up to 2220kg (4900lb) on four
internal and two external hardpoints capable
of carrying bombs, torpedoes, mines, depth
charges, missiles and nuclear weapons

### ▼ Lockheed S-3A Viking

*VS-32, USS* John F. Kennedy, *1977*

During the latter years of the Cold War, the Vikings of VS-32 'Norsemen' were
shore-based at NAS Cecil Field, Florida, and operated
under the command of Air Anti-Submarine Warfare
Wing One. The squadron formed a component of
Carrier Air Wing 1 (CVW-1), operating from
carriers of the Atlantic Fleet, including the
*JFK* between 1976 and 1989.

## Specifications

Crew: 2

Powerplant: 2 x 1137kW (1525hp) Wright R-
1820-82WA Cyclone 9-cylinder radial piston
engine

Maximum speed: 462km/h (287mph)

Range: 2092km (1300 miles)

Dimensions: span 21.2m (69ft 6in); length
12.9m (42ft 2in); height 4.9m (16ft 3in)

Weight: 13,222kg (29,150lb) loaded

Armament: None

### ▼ Grumman C-1A Trader

*USS* Nimitz, *1980*

Nicknamed *Salt One*, C-1A BuNo 146044 was assigned to CVW-8 aboard USS
*Nimitz* during Exercise Teamwork '80. It was one of 87
examples of the C-1A (originally TF-1) that were
procured for COD duties in support of US Navy
carriers. The enlarged fuselage compared to
the Tracker provided accommodation for up
to seven passengers or capacity for up to
1588kg (3500lb) of cargo.

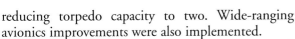

reducing torpedo capacity to two. Wide-ranging avionics improvements were also implemented.

Removing the ASW equipment from the SH-3A produced the SH-3G, converted between 1969 and 1972. This was used aboard carriers as a utility transport and plane-guard, with provision for additional fuel for long-range rescue missions. Meanwhile, the definitive ASW version of the Sea King was the SH-3H, again with additional fuel capacity. Following the adoption of the multi-role carrier concept, and prior to the arrival of the SH-60 Seahawk, the six-aircraft squadrons of SH-3D/H

helicopters were responsible for the inner-zone ASW protection of the carrier battle group.

The 'Hotel' version was produced via conversion of existing SH-3A, D and G airframes from 1971. An important new capability was the detection of anti-ship missiles, using a new radar carried beneath the mid-fuselage, and a towed MAD 'bird' stowed under the starboard sponson. Other changes included a 24-round launcher for marine marker smoke bombs, a chaff dispenser, and improved active/passive sonar systems relating to the sonobuoys and dipping gear, respectively.

# United States
## 1976–89

**The latter years of the Cold War saw the emergence of the multi-role carrier air wing, as carriers were configured to launch the full spectrum of offensive and defensive air missions.**

THE SUCCESSOR TO the S-2 Tracker in the carrier-based, fixed-wing ASW role was the Lockheed S-3 Viking, the last major new type to join US Navy carrier air wings before the end of the 1970s. Designed to meet the VSX (Aircraft, ASW, Experimental) requirement issued in 1967, and powered by two fuel-efficient TF34 turbofans, the initial S-3A was equipped with an extensive avionics suite that included the AN/APS-116 surveillance radar, AN/ASQ-81 MAD gear, a forward-looking infrared sensor and an acoustic processing system provided with 60 sonobuoys. Combined, these sensors were capable of detecting and tracking a new generation of quiet, deep-diving Soviet submarines. Weapons consisting of conventional bombs, depth bombs, mines or torpedoes were accommodated within an internal bay or on underwing pylons.

After a first flight in April 1972, the S-3A entered service with VS-41 in February 1974, with a first operational deployment made by VS-29 in late 1975. By the time manufacture concluded in mid-1978, a total of 187 Vikings had rolled off the production line. Operating alongside ASW-configured Sea Kings, the Viking provided the carrier battle group with its outer-zone anti-submarine warfare capability.

Both tanker (KS-3A) and utility transport/COD (US-3A) versions were planned and flight-tested, although neither entered quantity production. At peak strength, Vikings served with 14 US Navy squadrons.

### Night Intruder

Improvements to the A-6E Intruder produced the TRAM (Target Recognition Attack Multi-sensor) modification, identified by a sensor turret below the nose, which carried the AN/ALQ-33 forward-looking infrared system. Allied with a laser rangefinder and designator, this permitted the delivery of laser-guided precision-guided munitions. Also included was an AN/ASN-92 Carrier Airborne Inertial Navigation System (CAINS). The first TRAM-equipped A-6E flew in March 1974, and the complete system was being test-flown before the end of that year. The last of the definitive A-6E versions were delivered in 1992 and the TRAM version became standard across the fleet, with surviving earlier models (the A-6A, B, C and KA-6D) being upgraded accordingly.

The Prowler fleet was also subject to a step-by-step programme of upgrades, introduced to the EA-6B through the successive EXCAP and ICAP projects.

### Specifications

| | |
|---|---|
| Crew: 2 | 16.69m (54ft 76in); height 4.93m (16ft 17in) |
| Powerplant: 2 x 41.3kN (9300lb) Pratt & Whitney J52-P-8A turbojets | Weight: 26,581kg (58,600lb) loaded |
| Maximum speed: 1043km/h (648mph) | Armament: Five external hardpoints with provision for up to 8165kg (18,000lb) of stores, including nuclear weapons, bombs, missiles, and drop tanks |
| Range: 1627km (1011 miles) | |
| Service ceiling: 14,480m (47,500ft) | |
| Dimensions: span 16.15m (53ft 0in); length | |

▼ **Grumman A-6E Intruder**

*VA-65, USS Independence, mid-1970s*

This VA-65 'Tigers' A-6E served as part of Carrier Air Wing 7 (CVW-7) aboard USS *Independence* for a series of Mediterranean cruises between June 1973 and October 1977, and wears the colourful markings that were commonplace in that period. As was typical for Intruder units, the squadron included four KA-6D tankers, the air wing's primary refuelling asset.

## Specifications

**Crew:** 4

**Powerplant:** 2 x 49.8kN (11,200lbf) Pratt & Whitney J52-P-408 turbojets

**Maximum speed:** 982km/h (610mph)

**Range:** 1769km (1099 miles)

**Service ceiling:** 11,580m (38,000ft)

**Dimensions:** span 16.15m (53ft 0in); length 18.24m (59ft 10in); height 4.95m (16ft 3in)

**Weight:** 29,484kg (65,000lb) loaded

**Armament:** None on early models, retrofitted with external hardpoints for four AGM-88 HARM air-to-surface anti-radar missiles

### ▼ Grumman EA-6B Prowler

*VAQ-134, USS* Enterprise, *1976–78*

VAQ-134 received the Prowler in 1971, and took the type into combat over Vietnam. This aircraft is seen carrying a full complement of AN/ALQ-99 jamming pods. The 'Garudas' were home-based at NAS Whidbey Island, Washington, but operated from the deck of USS *Enterprise* as part of CVW-14 between July 1976 and October 1978. Established in 1969, VAQ-134 was a former KA-3B/EKA-3B operator.

The Extended Capability (EXCAP) joined the fleet in the mid-1970s, just too late to see combat service in Southeast Asia, and allowed jamming across eight, rather than four, frequency bands, and with increased computer memory capacity. Further improvements to the EA-6B were represented by the Improved Capability I and II (ICAP) programmes, which provided for improved jamming capabilities, ICAP I focusing on communications jamming, while ICAP II (introduced as a rolling programme from 1980 onwards) concentrated on improvements to the external jamming pods, as well as the on-board computers and communications systems. ICAP also added compatibility with the AGM-88 High-speed Anti-Radiation Missile (HARM) for lethal suppression of enemy air defences missions. The first of the ICAP I Prowlers made a first operational cruise aboard USS *Nimitz* with VAQ-135 in late 1977, while the ICAP II joined the front-line fleet with an initial deployment with VAQ-137 in 1985. In the early 1980s the Prowler was called to action in the suppression of Syrian radars over Lebanon in 1982; by this time, 12 squadrons were equipped with the Prowler, including one Marine unit.

After initial flight trials beginning in January 1971, the much-improved E-2C Hawkeye was introduced to the fleet in 1973, the new aircraft featuring the new AN/APS-120 radar, a lengthened nose containing elements of the AN/ALR-59 passive detection system, and with a new air scoop above the cabin. Internally, the E-2C received new mission computers and an inertial navigation system. The first operational deployment by the E-2C was recorded by VAW-123 aboard USS *Saratoga* in September 1974. The E-2C received another new

### ◀ US Navy A-7E Corsair II operators, mid-1980s

By the mid-1980s, surviving Navy A-7Es had traded their previous flamboyant colours for these more subdued markings and overall grey camouflage. From top to bottom, the units depicted here comprise VA-72, home-based at NAS Cecil Field, Florida, and assigned to CVW-1; VA-97 home-based at NAS Lemoore, California, assigned to CVW-15; VA-174 home-based at NAS Cecil Field, and serving as the Atlantic Fleet replacement training squadron; and VA-195 home-based at NAS Lemoore and assigned to CVW-19. By this stage, the respective Atlantic and Pacific A-7E communities operated under Light Attack Wing One and Light Attack Wing Pacific.

radar in 1976, with the AN/APS-125 adding improved overland capabilities through the introduction of the Advanced Radar Processing System (ARPS), while in 1980 the E-2C was outfitted with the AN/APS-138 with an increased detection range. From 1988 the AN/APS-139 radar was fitted as standard on the E-2C Group 1, together with new engines and mission computer system. The Group I was built as new and provided AEW and control for 1980s missions over Lebanon and Libya.

During the 1970s the Navy planned to introduce a lightweight counterpart to the 'heavy' F-14 Tomcat fleet interceptor, and eventually selected the McDonnell Douglas F/A-18 Hornet as a flexible multi-role fighter that would replace the A-7 Corsair II in the attack role, as well as surviving F-4 Phantom IIs in the fleet defence role. The original design of the Hornet was derived from that of the land-based Northrop YF-17, before undergoing changes making it suitable for carrier operations, and permitting both air defence and attack missions to be carried out using a common airframe. Based around the AN/APG-65 radar, the aircraft was capable of engaging multiple aerial targets as well as attacking ground targets with a high degree of precision.

In November 1978 a first flight was achieved by one of an initial 11 development aircraft. The first F/A-18A unit was the fleet replacement squadron, VFA-125, which equipped with the new type in November 1980. An initial Marine squadron followed, and in January 1983 VMFA-314 became the first Hornet unit to attain operational capability.

The first operational Navy squadron was VFA-25, which had begun to receive the new fighter in August 1983. In 1985 the Hornet made its first operational cruise, when VFA-25 and VFA-113 embarked in USS *Constellation*. By mid-1987, a total of 371 single-seat F/A-18As had been completed, together with 39 two-seat F/A-18B trainers, although the latter did not see use from carriers.

## Tomcat developments

Joining the Hornet were improved versions of the F-14A Tomcat, which replaced the original infrared search and track sensor with the Television Camera Set (TCS) from 1983. Other modifications to the Tomcat during the 1980s included the Tactical Air Reconnaissance Pod System (TARPS) located under the rear fuselage, while the F-14A+ was the first version with the General Electric F110 turbofan. The F110 finally gave the Tomcat the engine it deserved, with improved reliability as well as increased power.

The F-14A+ (later redesignated F-14B) entered service in the late 1980s, and other changes included improved cockpit displays, a new radar warning receiver, and revisions to the fire control and radar systems. Over Lebanon in the early 1980s, the Tomcat was used to fly both reconnaissance and combat air patrol sorties. Equipped with TARPS, the Tomcat served as a replacement for the RA-5C and RF-8G reconnaissance aircraft within the carrier air wing. Unlike its predecessors in the role, the TARPS-equipped F-14 could fly the reconnaissance mission while also carrying a full load of air-to-air missiles.

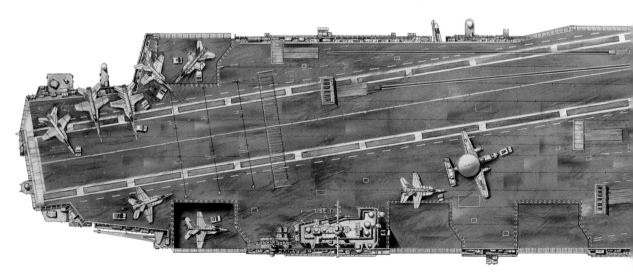

## Specifications

Crew: 2

Powerplant: 2 x 92.9kN (20,900lbf) Pratt & Whitney TF30-P-412A turbofans

Maximum speed: 2517km/h (1564mph)

Range: 3220km (2000 miles)

Service ceiling: 17,070m (56,000ft)

Dimensions: span 19.55m (64ft 1.5in); length 19.1m (62ft 8in); height 4.88m (16ft)

Weight: 33,724kg (74,349lb) loaded

Armament: One 20mm (.79in) M61A1 Vulcan rotary cannon; external pylons for a combination of AIM-7 Sparrow medium range air-to-air missiles, AIM-9 medium range air-to-air, and AIM-54 Phoenix long range air-to-air missiles

### ▼ Grumman F-14A Tomcat

#### *VF-32, USS* John F. Kennedy, *1977*

When VF-32 'Swordsmen' introduced the F-14A, colourful markings and a grey and white colour scheme were the order of the day, these giving way to toned-down markings and an overall grey scheme from the late 1970s. Home-based at NAS Oceana, Virginia, this aircraft is seen while deployed with Carrier Air Wing 1 (CVW-1) aboard USS *John F. Kennedy*, and carries an AIM-7 Sparrow missile semi-recessed under the fuselage. 'Swordsmen' Tomcats operated from *JFK* with CVW-1 between June 1975 and August 1977.

Three examples of this version were typically assigned to each carrier.

Despite the introduction of the Hornet, the A-7 Corsair II remained in front-line service into the early 1990s. Prior to the full introduction of the Hornet, the A-7E remained the most important carrier-based light attack aircraft, with almost 300 examples in operation in the early 1980s, serving with 24 active squadrons. Flying from the USS *Independence*, the A-7E saw combat during Operation Urgent Fury, the US assault on Grenada in October 1983, before flying further strikes against targets in Lebanon later that year. In 1987–88, the A-7E was employed against Iranian objectives in the Persian Gulf.

The US Navy's carriers were heavily involved in the crises surrounding Libya in the mid-1980s. In 1981 a pair of F-14As from VF-41, flying from USS *Nimitz* during a series of 6th Fleet exercises, downed a pair of Libyan Su-22s using Sidewinder missiles, after they reportedly came under fire. The Hornet saw its combat debut during Operations Prairie Fire and El Dorado Canyon against Libya in March and April 1986, with both Navy and Marine squadrons flying strikes from the deck of USS *Coral Sea*. Among the missions flown by the F/A-18As was defence suppression, using AGM-88 HARM missiles against Libyan air defence radars – this was also the first occasion that the HARM had been employed in

### ◄ USS *Nimitz* (CVN-68)

Lead vessel in the first class of nuclear-powered 'super-carrier' to be built in quantity, the USS *Nimitz* was the largest warship ever built at the time of its appearance. Commissioned into service in May 1975, the carrier is depicted with a typical late 1980s air group that comprised 14 F-14s, 36 F/A-18s (arranged on deck and launching from waist and no. 1 catapults), eight S-3s, four EA-6Bs, four E-2s (one example seen on deck), four SH-60Fs, two HH-60Hs (one seen flying plane-guard) and two C-2s. The 'Nimitz' class eventually yielded 10 vessels.

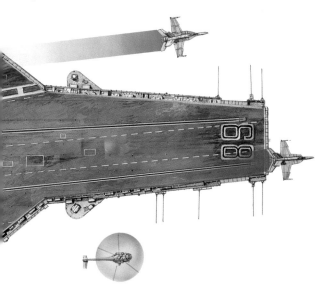

## Specifications

Displacement: 97,000 tons (full load)

Length: 332.85m (1092ft)

Beam: 40.84m (134ft)

Draught: 11.3m (37.7ft)

Speed: 30+ kts

Aircraft: Approximately 85

Armament: Three Mk 25 Sea Sparrow launchers, four 20mm (.79in) Phalanx close-in weapon systems

Complement: Ship: 3200 Air Wing: 2480

## ▼ US Navy Carrier Air Wing, 1979

In terms of the variety of different types operated, and the breadth of its (multi-role) capabilities, the US Navy carrier air wing arguably reached its apogee in the late 1970s and early 1980s. As the carrier fleet transitioned to the powerful 'Nimitz' class of nuclear-powered carrier (CVN), the typical air wing expanded to include

**1st Squadron (12 x F14A)**

**2nd Squadron (12 x F14A)**

**1st Squadron (12 x A-7A)**

**2nd Squadron (12 x A-7B)**

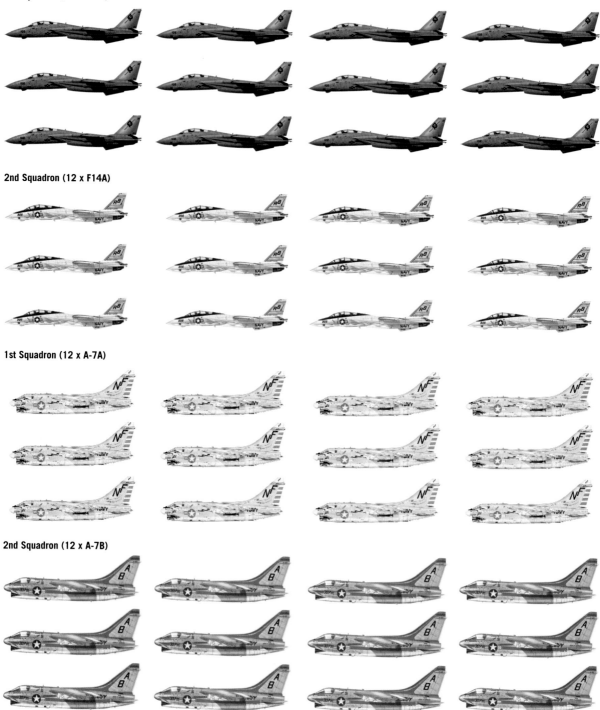

approximately 86 aircraft, comprising two squadrons each of 12 F-14A Tomcat interceptors, two light attack squadrons each of 12 A-7 Corsair IIs, a medium attack squadron of 10 A-6E Intruders and four KA-6D tankers, a squadron of four EA-6B Prowler electronic warfare aircraft, a fixed-wing anti-submarine warfare unit with 10 S-3 Vikings, a helicopter squadron with six SH-3 Sea Kings and a squadron of four E-2 Hawkeyes for airborne early warning. C-2 Greyhounds were routinely embarked for COD duties.

**14 x A-6**

**10 x S-3**

**4 x EA-6B**

**4 x E-2A**

**6 x SH-3H**

**1 x C-2A**

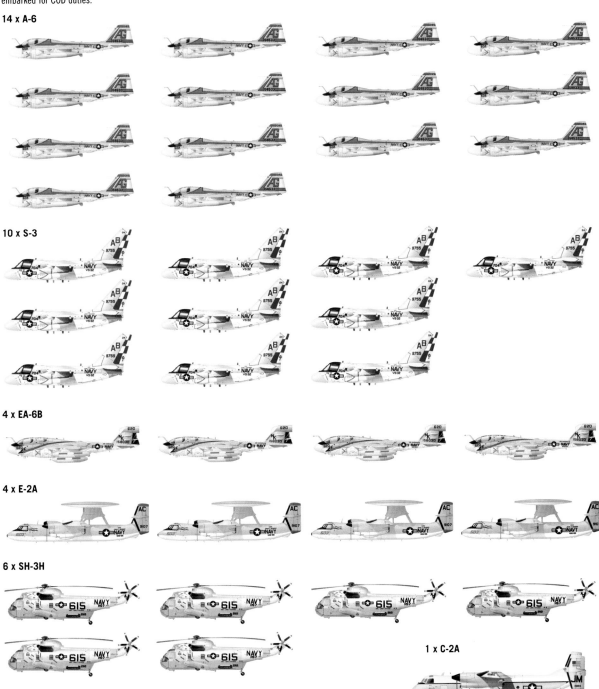

| Typical US Navy carrier air wing, mid-1970s | |
|---|---|
| Carrier Air Wing 14 | |
| CVW-14 | |
| USS *Enterprise* (CVAN-65) | 'Enterprise' class |
| 1974–5 | |
| VF-1 | F-14A Tomcat |
| VF-2 | F-14A Tomcat |
| VA-196 | A-6A/KA-6D Intruder |
| VA-27 | A-7E Corsair II |
| VA-97 | A-7E Corsair II |
| RVAH-12 | RA-5C Vigilante |
| VAQ-137 | EA-6B Prowler |
| VAW-113 | E-2B Hawkeye |
| VQ-1 (Det 65) | EA-3B Skywarrior |
| HS-2 | SH-3D Sea King |
| HC-7 (Det) | HH-3A/SH-3G Sea King |

combat. Also involved in the Libyan raids were EA-6Bs, flying defence suppression missions, F-14s tasked with combat air patrols, and A-7Es, the latter flying attack sorties against Libyan objectives. In 1989 tensions in the Mediterranean flared again, and a pair of Tomcats from VF-32 flying from USS *John F. Kennedy* shot down two Libyan MiG-23s after these had flown a number of aggressive manoeuvres. One MiG was downed using a Sparrow missile, the second at closer range with a Sidewinder.

## Marine modernization

The arrival of a new class of vessel in 1976 marked a major advance in capabilities for the US Marine Corps. The five-strong 'Tarawa' class of LHA (amphibious assault ships – general purpose) offered a considerably increased aviation component compared to the previous 'Iwo Jima'-class LPH (landing platform helicopters).

The seven 'Iwo Jima'-class vessels were introduced as replacement for the three 'Essex'-class conversions (USS *Boxer*, *Princeton* and *Valley Forge*) that had served in the 1960s as helicopter-carrying amphibious assault ships. The 'Iwo Jimas' had deck space for seven CH-46 or four CH-53 helicopters, while a total of up to 20 rotary-wing assets could be embarked. The vessels were also capable of embarking AV-8 Harriers.

The 'Tarawa' design boosted aviation capacity such that up to 19 CH-46s or 11 CH-53s could be

▼ **Grumman A-6E Intruder**

Seen during the swansong of its career, this VA-65 TRAM-equipped A-6E prepares to launch from the USS *Theodore Roosevelt* (CVN-71) while on station in the Mediterranean to support Operation Provide Comfort over Iraq in 1991.

## Specifications

Crew: 2

Powerplant: 2 x 41.3kN (9300lbf) Pratt &
 Whitney J52-P-8 turbojets

Maximum speed: 1043km/h (648mph)

Range: 1627km (1011 miles)

Service ceiling: 14,480m (47,500ft)

Dimensions: span 16.15m (53ft 0in); length

16.69m (54ft 8in); height 4.93m (16ft 2in)

Weight: 26,581kg (58,600lb) loaded

Armament: Five external hardpoints with
 provision for up to 8165kg (18,000lb) of
 stores, including nuclear weapons, bombs,
 missiles and drop tanks

### ▼ Grumman A-6E Intruder

#### VA-85, *USS* John F. Kennedy, *1983*

The ultimate Intruder was the TRAM (Target Recognition Attack Multi-sensor)
modification, which added an AN/ALQ-33 forward-looking infrared turret under the
nose, together with a laser rangefinder and designator, allowing the delivery of
precision-guided weapons. Part of the Atlantic Fleet, VA-85 'Black Buckeyes' was
shore-based at NAS Oceana, Virginia.

## Specifications

Crew: 2

Powerplant: 2 x 3803kW (5100hp) Allison
 T56-A-427 turboprop engines

Maximum speed: 626km/h (389mph)

Range: Unrefuelled time at 320km/h (200mph)
 from base – 4 hours

Service ceiling: 11,275m (37,000ft)

Dimensions: span 24.56m (80ft 7in); length
 17.54m (57ft 7in); height 5.58m (18ft 3in)

Weight: 18,363kg (54,426lb) loaded

Armament: None

### ▼ Northrop E-2C Hawkeye

#### VAW-126, *USS* John F. Kennedy, *1983*

An E-2C from the 'Seahawks' of VAW-126 that served aboard USS *John F. Kennedy*
in 1983 as part of Carrier Air Wing Three (CVW-3). Operating in conjunction with
the F-14 Tomcat, the E-2C provided a very effective air defence umbrella for the
carrier group, serving as a 'mini-AWACS' to direct the interceptors to hostile
aircraft and anti-ship missiles.

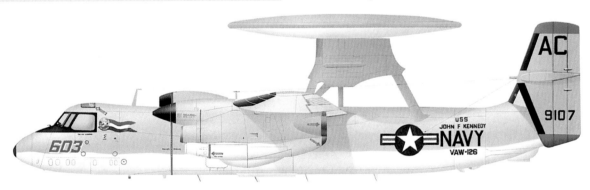

embarked in the hangar, while up to 12 CH-46s or
nine CH-53s could be parked on deck. AV-8s could
be routinely embarked, and the air group also
included AH-1 and UH-1 helicopters. All
five 'Tarawa'-class LHAs had been commissioned
by 1980.

The 'Tarawa' design was followed by an improved
LHD (amphibious assault ships – multi-purpose),
the 'Wasp' class, the first of which was commissioned
in 1989. With these new vessels, total CH-46
capacity was increased to 42 in the assault role,
although a more common air group comprised 12

CH-46s, four CH-53s, three or four UH-1Ns, four
AH-1Ws and six AV-8Bs.

US interest in the British Aerospace Harrier began
in the early 1960s, and the Marine Corps evaluated
the aircraft in 1968, with orders following shortly
after. The Marines required a V/STOL close support
aircraft that could operate from amphibious assault
ships (as well as from hastily prepared airstrips), and
as such the service pioneered the use of the Harrier in
a maritime context. By 1974 orders for 110 examples
had been placed, and these were manufactured in the
UK, while the aircraft were marketed by McDonnell

Douglas as the AV-8A. Essentially similar to the RAF Harrier GR.Mk 1, the aircraft were modified to become compatible with AIM-9 Sidewinder missiles and incorporated some US-specific avionics. Eight examples of a two-seat training version were supplied as the TAV-8A as part of the final batch of deliveries.

The initial recipient of the AV-8A was VMA-513 in March 1971, and despite an alarming attrition rate, the aircraft saw useful service aboard the 'Iwo Jima' class of LHAs, and later from the 'Tarawa'-class LHAs. Surviving AV-8As were put through a service

life extension programme to emerge as AV-8Cs, which also differed in their use of under-fuselage strakes for improved aerodynamic performance, and a radar warning receiver. Just three front-line Marine squadrons operated the single-seat AV-8A/C and the type was soon withdrawn from service when the first of the much-improved Harrier IIs arrived in service in the early 1980s.

Inspired by the AV-8A, the Marines sought a new and more capable Harrier, and this emerged as the AV-8B, a joint development by McDonnell Douglas

---

▼ **US Navy E-2C Hawkeye units, mid-1980s**

By the early 1980s Hawkeyes were in service with six West Coast and six East fleet units (11 of which are featured here and opposite), and with two Fleet Readiness Squadrons.

◀ **VAW-127**

Assigned to Carrier Air Wing 13 (CVW-13) in the mid-1980s, this squadron was shore-based at NAS Norfolk, Virginia. The 'Seabats' saw action against Libya in 1986, operating from USS *Coral Sea*.

◀ **VAW-123**

Shore-based at NAS Norfolk, Virginia, VAW-123 was assigned to CVW-1. The squadron made the first Hawkeye deployment, when it joined USS *Saratoga* for a Mediterranean cruise in September 1974.

◀ **VAW-126**

Shore-based at NAS Norfolk, Virginia, VAW-126 'Seahawks' was assigned to CVW-3 in the mid-1980s, although it was also assigned to CVW-8 earlier in the decade.

◀ **VAW-124**

VAW-124 was also shore-based at NAS Norfolk, Virginia, and was assigned to CVW-8 in the mid-1980s.

◀ **VAW-125**

VAW-125 was shore-based at NAS Norfolk, Virginia, and the squadron's assignment was CVW-11.

and British Aerospace, which began to enter service with the Marines in 1983. The AV-8B Harrier II introduced a new, long-span wing with supercritical aerofoil, the British-developed leading-edge root extension (LERX) to increase manoeuvrability, and extensive use of composite materials. The new wing

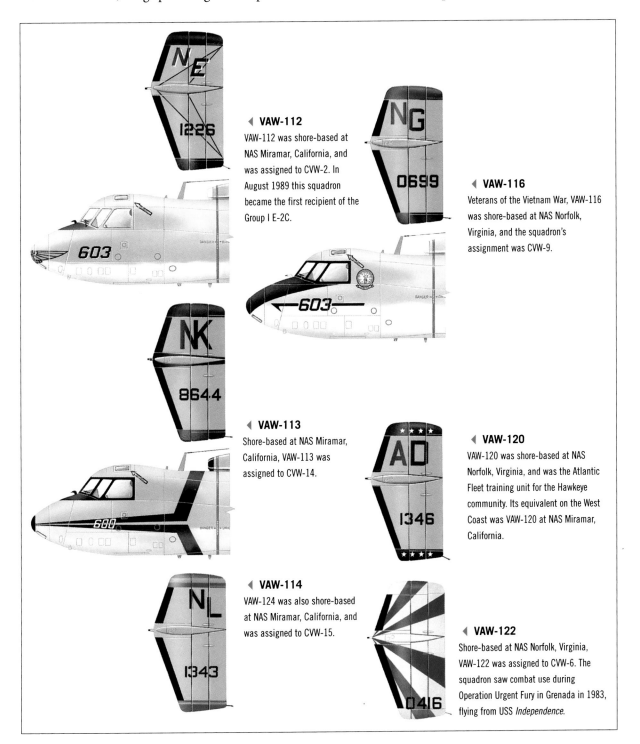

◀ **VAW-112**
VAW-112 was shore-based at NAS Miramar, California, and was assigned to CVW-2. In August 1989 this squadron became the first recipient of the Group I E-2C.

◀ **VAW-116**
Veterans of the Vietnam War, VAW-116 was shore-based at NAS Norfolk, Virginia, and the squadron's assignment was CVW-9.

◀ **VAW-113**
Shore-based at NAS Miramar, California, VAW-113 was assigned to CVW-14.

◀ **VAW-120**
VAW-120 was shore-based at NAS Norfolk, Virginia, and was the Atlantic Fleet training unit for the Hawkeye community. Its equivalent on the West Coast was VAW-120 at NAS Miramar, California.

◀ **VAW-114**
VAW-124 was also shore-based at NAS Miramar, California, and was assigned to CVW-15.

◀ **VAW-122**
Shore-based at NAS Norfolk, Virginia, VAW-122 was assigned to CVW-6. The squadron saw combat use during Operation Urgent Fury in Grenada in 1983, flying from USS *Independence*.

also provided for an increased fuel capacity and payload, which could now be carried on six pylons. Key to improved performance was a new Rolls-Royce F402 engine of increased power, with successively more powerful sub-variants of this engine introduced during production. The pilot was seated within a revised, digital cockpit, inspired by that of the F/A-18, and with a new canopy providing better visibility. Avionics included the Angle-Rate Bombing System, incorporating a television tracker in the nose. A two-seat version was developed as the TAV-8B and fielded from 1987, although this was used only for training at shore bases. The single-seat AV-8B Harrier II equipped eight front-line Marine Corps squadrons.

## Dependable Sea Knight

The backbone of the Marines' air assault capacity was for a long time the Boeing CH-46 Sea Knight, a tandem-rotor design that entered service in June 1964 with HMM-265. A true workhorse, the Sea Knight expanded upon its primary assault role to undertake search and rescue, medical evacuation, special operations, humanitarian and other support roles. The basic model first introduced by the Marines was the CH-46A (originally procured under the designation HRB-1), which soon replaced the HUS-1 as a standard assault transport within medium-lift squadrons. Typically carrying 12–18 troops, although with a maximum capacity of 25, the US Navy also

▲ **Grumman C-2A Greyhound**

*VR-24, NAS Sigonella*

Seen while based at Sigonella in Sicily, this C-2A was operated by VR-24 'The World's Biggest Little Airline', and was responsible for providing COD facilities for 6th Fleet carriers operating in the Mediterranean. The C-2A can accommodate up to 28 passengers or a cargo load of 4536kg (10,000lb).

### Specifications

| | |
|---|---|
| Crew: 4 | Service ceiling: 10,210m (33,500ft) |
| Powerplant: 2 x 3400kW (4600hp) Allison T56-A-425 turboprop engines | Dimensions: span 24.6m (80ft 7in); length 17.3m (56ft 10in); height 4.85m (14ft 11in) |
| Maximum speed: 553km/h (343mph) | Weight: 49,394kg (22,405lb) loaded |
| Range: 2400km (1496 miles) | Armament: None |

▲ **McDonnell Douglas/BAe AV-8A Harrier**

*VMA-231, USS Franklin D. Roosevelt, 1977*

This AV-8A is depicted carrying underwing rocket launchers and fuel tanks, together with the British 30mm (1.18in) ADEN cannon carried under the fuselage. As well as assault ships, VMA-231 'Ace of Spades' deployed its AV-8As on board the carrier USS *Franklin D. Roosevelt* in 1976–77.

### Specifications

| | |
|---|---|
| Crew: 1 | Dimensions: span 7.7m (25ft 3in); length 13.87m (45ft 6in); height 3.45m (11ft 4in) |
| Powerplant: 1 x 91.2kN (20,500lbf) Rolls-Royce Pegasus 10 vectored-thrust turbofan engine | Weight: 11,340kg (25,000lb) loaded |
| Maximum speed: 1186km/h (737mph) | Armament: One 30mm (1.18in) Aden cannon or similar gun; maximum of 2268kg (5000lb) of stores on under-fuselage and underwing points for rockets and bombs |
| Range: range with one in flight refuelling 5560km (3455 miles) | |
| Service ceiling: 15,240m (50,000ft) | |

### ▲ Bell AH-1T SeaCobra

A pair of AH-1T SeaCobras idles on the flight deck of the amphibious assault ship USS *Guadalcanal* (LPH-7). Note the TOW launchers on the nearest aircraft.

### Specifications

Crew: 4

Powerplant: 2 x 1044kW (1400hp) General Electric T58-GE-10 turboshaft engines

Maximum speed: 267km/h (166mph)

Range: 1005km (624 miles)

Service ceiling: 4480m (14,700ft)

Dimensions: Rotor diameter 18.9m (62ft 0in); length 22.15m (72ft 8in); height 5.13m (16ft 9in)

Weight: 9525kg (21,000lb) loaded

Armament: Two Mk 46/44 anti-submarine torpedoes or nuclear depth charge

### ▼ Sikorsky SH-3H Sea King

*HS-7, USS* John F. Kennedy, *1983*

This Sea King from HS-7 'Shamrocks' is one of the definitive SH-3H ASW models, which incorporated the Canadian Marconi LN66 radar beneath the fuselage, and which were produced via conversion of 112 earlier SH-3A, D and G airframes. Alongside inner-zone ASW, the SH-3H provided carrier plane-guard duties.

### Typical US Navy carrier air wing, mid-1980s (Operation *Eldorado Canyon*)

| Carrier Air Wing 13 | (Nominal strength) |
| --- | --- |
| CVW-13 | |
| USS *America* (CV-66) | 'Kitty Hawk' class |
| 1986 | |
| VF-33 | F-14A Tomcat (12) |
| VF-102 | F-14A Tomcat (12) |
| VA-34 | A-6E Intruder (14) |
| VA-46 | A-7E Corsair II (12) |
| VA-72 | A-7E Corsair II (12) |
| VAQ-135 | EA-6B Prowler (4) |
| VAW-125 | E-2C Hawkeye (4) |
| HS-11 | SH-3H Sea King (6) |

## Specifications

Crew: 1

Powerplant: 2 x 71.1kN (16,000lbf) General
Electric F404-GE-400 turbofans

Maximum speed: 1912km/h (1183mph)

Range: 1065km (662 miles)

Service ceiling: 15,240m (50,000ft)

Dimensions: span 11.43m (37ft 6in); length

17.07m (56ft 0in); height 4.66m (15ft 3.5)

Weight: 25,401kg (56,000lb) loaded

Armament: One 20mm (.79in) M61A1 Vulcan
rotary cannon; nine external hardpoints with
provision for up to 7711kg (17,000kg) of
stores

### ▼ McDonnell Douglas F/A-18A Hornet

*VFA-113, USS* Constellation, *1985*

VFA-113 'Stingers' were one of the first two front-line Hornet units to make an operational cruise aboard USS *Constellation* as part of CVW-14, between February and August 1985; the other was VFA-25. The Hornet soon established itself as a reliable performer, requiring less maintenance than the F-14As and A-6E/KA-6Ds also embarked.

adopted the CH-46A, with their UH-46A version serving with helicopter combat support squadrons.

The next major version of the Sea Knight for the Marines was the CH-46D, with uprated General Electric T58 turboshafts, while the CH-46F was the last major production model in this series, introducing revised avionics and in production from 1968 to 1971, alongside an equivalent UH-46F for use by the Navy. The CH-46E was produced only via upgrade of earlier airframes, but emerged as the definitive Marine assault version, with a further uprated powerplant, new rotor blades and improved crash protection. The CH-46F was produced via

conversion from 1977. In order to keep them viable into the 1990s and beyond, the Marine Sea Knight fleet was further upgraded in the late 1980s, with a service life extension programme that added additional fuel capacity, an emergency flotation system and an improved self-protection suite including countermeasures dispensers.

## Heavyweight lifter

While the Sea Knight handled the Marines' medium-lift requirements, the Sikorsky CH-53 provided a heavyweight lift capability. Developed to meet an original Marine Corps requirement specified in the

### ▼ Bell AH-1J SeaCobra

*US Marine Corps, 1977*

After an enthusiastic evaluation of the US Army's AH-1G HueyCobra, the first of the dedicated Marine Cobras was the AH-1J, which brought with it the added reliability of a twin-engined powerplant, in this case a military version of the civilian Pratt & Whitney Canada Turbo Twin-Pac. The first batch of 49 AH-1Js was ordered in May 1968, with a further 20 aircraft being delivered during 1974–75.

## Specifications

Crew: 2

Powerplant: 1 x 1342kW (1800hp) Pratt &
Whitney Canada T400-CP-400 twin-turbine

Maximum speed: 352km/h (218mph)

Range: 571km (355 miles)

Service ceiling: 3475m (11,398ft)

Dimensions: Rotor diameter 13.4m (43ft 11in);

length 13.5m (44ft 3in); height 4.1m (13ft
5in)

Weight: 4525kg (9979lb) loaded

Armament: One 20mm (.79in) M197 cannon;
14 70mm (2.75in) Mk 40 rockets; eight
127mm (5in) Zuni rockets; two AIM-9 air-to-
air missiles

early 1960s, the prototype YCH-53A first flew in October 1964 and was followed by the initial production CH-53A Sea Stallion, which began to be fielded by HMH-463 in late 1966. The unit was in action in Vietnam with its new helicopters the following year. Alongside the CH-53A for Marine troop and cargo lift, the Navy adopted the RH-53A version for minesweeping, also putting this version to use during the closing stages of the war in Vietnam.

The next major production model for the Marines was the CH-53D, with increased power through the use of more powerful General Electric T64 turboshafts coupled with an uprated transmission.

The CH-53E Super Stallion was created by adding a third engine mounted on the centreline behind the rotor head and driving a seven-blade main rotor.

### ▼ Bell AH-1T SeaCobra

*US Marine Corps*

Seen here armed with pods for unguided 2.75in (70mm) rockets, this AH-1T reveals some of the changes made to the Improved SeaCobra, including a fuselage and tail boom stretch of 3ft 7in (1.09m) allowing for additional fuel capacity. Other changes included the improved main and tail rotor systems of the Bell Model 214, and the uprated T400-WV-402 powerplant. Most of the 57 AH-1Ts later received modifications permitting TOW missile capability.

### Specifications

| | |
|---|---|
| Crew: 2 | length 17.68m (58ft); height 4.32m (12ft 2in) |
| Powerplant: 1 x 1469kW (1970hp) Pratt & | Weight: 6350kg (14,000lb) loaded |
| Whitney Canada T400-WV-402 twin-turbine | Armament: Chin housing 1 x 20mm (.79in) |
| Maximum speed: 277km/h (1789mph) | M197 three-barrel cannon; underwing |
| Range: 420km (260 miles) | attachments for 69.85mm (2.75in) rocket |
| Service ceiling: 2255m (7400ft) | pods, flare dispensers, grenade dispensers, |
| Dimensions: Rotor diameter 14.6m (48ft 0in); | and Minigun pods |

### Specifications

| | |
|---|---|
| Crew: 2 | length 25.4m (83ft 4in); height 5.09m (16ft |
| Powerplant: 2 x 1394kW (1869hp) General | 9in) |
| Electric T58-GE-16 turboshaft engines | Weight: 9707kg (21,400lb) loaded |
| Maximum speed: 256km/h (159mph) | Armament: Normally none, but provision for |
| Range: 996km (206 miles) | two door-mounted 12.7mm (.5in) MGs and |
| Service ceiling: 4300m (14,000ft) | one ramp-mounted 7.62mm (.3in) MG |
| Dimensions: Rotor diameter 15.24m (50ft 0in); | |

### ▼ Boeing CH-46E Sea Knight

*US Marine Corps*

Built in 1969 as a CH-46F for the US Marine Corps, this particular helicopter saw operational service with both HMM-162 and HMM-261 before being converted to CH-46E standard and being written off in 1983. The definitive CH-46E standard was produced via conversion of 273 CH-46A and D models, which received General Electric T58-GE-16 turboshafts providing additional power.

Other changes included a stretched fuselage, an enlarged tailplane, increased fuel capacity and a refuelling probe fitted as standard. The Super Stallion was also adopted for mine countermeasures operations by the Navy, as the MH-53E Sea Dragon, a three-engined minesweeper version with enlarged sponsons carrying additional fuel for long-range operations as well as mine warfare equipment.

The first of the Bell AH-1 Cobras to serve with the Marines were AH-1G models requisitioned from the US Army during the Vietnam War, but in 1971 a dedicated maritime version was fielded, as the AH-1J SeaCobra. This differed from land-based Cobras in its Pratt & Whitney Canada T400 twin-turboshaft powerplant and more potent armament based around a three-barrel 20mm (.79in) cannon in an under-nose turret. The AH-1T Improved SeaCobra was a version with a lengthened fuselage carrying additional fuel, and more powerful engines, and adopted the dynamic system of the Bell Model 214. This model was ultimately refined to create the AH-1W SuperCobra (see Chapter 4).

## Specifications

Crew: 2

Powerplant: 2 x 2927kW (3925hp) General Electric T64-GE-413 turboshaft engines

Maximum speed: 315km/h (196mph)

Range: 1000km (621 miles)

Service ceiling: 5106m (16,750ft)

Dimensions: Rotor diameter 22.01m (72ft 2.8in); length 26.97m (88ft 6in); height 7.6m (24ft 11in)

Weight: 19,100kg (42,000lb) loaded

Armament: Provision for two window-mounted 12.7mm (.5in) machine guns and one ramp-mounted 12.7mm (.5in) machine gun

### ▼ Sikorsky CH-53D Sea Stallion
#### *HMH-462, MCAS Tustin, 1989*

Wearing the 'YF' tailcode of the 'Heavy Haulers' of HMH-462 at Tustin, California, this CH-53D is typical of the type during its early period of Marine Corps service, before the switch from olive drab to overall grey camouflage. HMH-462 still operated its CH-53Ds during the 1991 Iraq War, but soon after began the process of conversion to the more powerful CH-53E Super Stallion.

## Specifications

Crew: 2

Powerplant: 3 x 2756kW (3695hp) General Electric T64-GE-416 engines

Maximum speed: 315km/h (196mph)

Range: 2075km (1289 miles)

Service ceiling: 5640m (18,504ft)

Dimensions: Rotor diameter 24.08m (79ft 0in); length 30.19m (99ft 0in); height 8.97m (29ft 5in)

Weight: 31,640kg (69,754lb) loaded

Armament: Provision for window-mounted 7.62mm (.3in) or 12.7mm (.5in) machine guns

### ▼ Sikorsky MH-53E Sea Dragon
#### *US Navy, 1987*

The MH-53E mine countermeasures version of the Super Stallion was provided to four Navy squadrons: HM-14, 15, 18 and 19. The first MH-53E took to the air in December 1981 and is equipped to sweep waterways for mines by flying above the surface, towing electronic or magnetic sweeping gear, as well as carrying equipment to neutralize moored mines. The Sea Dragon has a secondary role of Navy Vertical Onboard Delivery.

**▲ Sikorsky CH-53D Sea Stallions**

Although the CH-53E Super Stallion now dominates the Heavy Marine Helicopter Squadrons, the twin-engined CH-53D Sea Stallion remains in use. These examples, assigned to HMH-362, are preparing to launch from the flight deck of the amphibious assault ship USS *Bonhomme Richard* (LHD-6) during an exercise in 2008.

## Utility 'Hueys'

Alongside the attack-configured AH-1, the Marine aviation component typically included a handful of Bell UH-1s, operating alongside the gunships. Marine experience with the 'Huey' had been assembled during the Vietnam War, when the service operated UH-1Es, these being navalized versions of the US Army's standard UH-1B. In order to provide its amphibious assault ships with a utility helicopter,

the Marines fielded the UH-1N Twin Huey, the first of which was received by HMA-269 in April 1971. Combining a lengthened airframe with twin Pratt & Whitney Canada PT6 turboshafts, the UH-1N could also be used for special forces operations or even as a light gunship. During the US intervention in Grenada, UH-1Ns flew command and control missions to direct operations by AH-1Ts and an assault force of CH-46Es and CH-53Ds.

### Specifications

Crew: 2

Powerplant: 3 x 2756kW (3695hp) General Electric T64-GE-416 engines

Maximum speed: 315km/h (196mph)

Range: 2075km (1289 miles)

Service ceiling: 5640m (18,504ft)

Dimensions: Rotor diameter 24.08m (79ft 0in); length 30.19m (99ft 0in); height 8.97m (29ft 5in)

Weight: 33,300kg (73,504lb) loaded

Armament: Provision for two window-mounted 12.7mm (.5in) machine guns and one ramp-mounted 12.7mm (.5in) machine gun

**▼ Sikorsky CH-53E Super Stallion**

*HC-1, NAS North Island, 1991*

A first Marine CH-53E squadron, HMH-464, was activated in February 1981. The three-engined Super Stallion has also seen service with the Navy, as in the case of this example flown by HC-1 'Fleet Angels', based at North Island, California, and one of three US Navy Helicopter Combat Support Squadrons to operate the Super Stallion. After sending CH-53E and SH-3G detachments to the Gulf during the 1991 Gulf War, HC-1 disbanded in April 1994.

# Chapter 4

# The Modern Era

Following the end of the superpower standoff that had characterized the Cold War years, the operators of aircraft carriers began to adapt their vessels and their carrier air components to become more flexible in order to meet the demands of an increasingly uncertain world. While the numbers of carriers fielded across the globe has reduced since their Cold War heyday, the roles in which these vessels serve has increased, and carrier airpower is invariably a feature of large-scale, multinational military operations, whatever their objective. At the same time, while the variety of different carrier aircraft may have reduced, the missions they are called upon to perform are as diverse as at any time before.

◀ **USS *Dwight D. Eisenhower* (CVN-69)**

A powerful signifier of US military dominance at the end of the Cold War, USS *Dwight D. Eisenhower* (CVN-69), second of the 'Nimitz' class of super-carriers, passes through the Suez Canal in 1990, en route to the Gulf for Desert Shield. By this stage, the air wing (CVW 7) comprised two squadrons each of F-14B Tomcats and F/A-18A Hornets, and one each of A-6E/KA-6Ds, E-2Cs, EA-6Bs, S-3Bs and SH-3Hs.

# Argentina
## 1984–PRESENT

**After a period of limited availability, the ageing carrier *25 de Mayo* was finally withdrawn from service in the late 1990s, although carrier aviation continued aboard foreign warships.**

AT THE END of the Falklands War, the Argentine Navy's carrier ARA *25 de Mayo* was subject to refurbishment that finally rendered it capable of embarking the Super Étendard. However, the carrier's limited dimensions and equipment meant that the A-4Q Skyhawk remained the primary combat type. Post-war, the Sea King fleet expanded through the arrival of four additional Agusta-built AS-61D-4s, these joining five Sikorsky S-61D-4s.

The last of the Skyhawks saw out their final years of service primarily in the advanced training role, and for a time it was expected that they would be replaced by more advanced A-4Es. These never materialized, and eventually just three operational Skyhawks remained by 1986. The last two survivors were withdrawn by the Navy in early 1988, having been transferred to the 2a Escuadrilla de Caza y Ataque.

March 1988 also saw a final deployment by Argentine Navy S-2 Trackers aboard the *25 de Mayo*. The Argentine Navy upgraded part of its Tracker fleet to S-2UP standard, with new TPE331 turboprops. Funds were allocated to an upgrade programme to be completed by Israel Aircraft Industries, and an initial conversion was flown in January 1993, with five more upgrade kits being provided. Three additional

| Argentine Navy carrier air units | |
|---|---|
| Carrier-deployable units, 1982–83 | |
| Grupo Aeronaval Embarcado | Base Aeronaval Comandante Espora |
| **Escuadra Aeronaval 2** | |
| Escuadrilla Aeronaval Antisubmarina | S-2A/E and US-2A Tracker |
| 2a Escuadrilla Aeronaval de Helicópteros | S-61D-4 |
| **Escuadra Aeronaval 3** | |
| 1a Escuadrilla Aeronaval de Helicópteros | Alouette III |
| 2a Escuadrilla de Caza y Ataque | Super Étendard |
| 3a Escuadrilla de Caza y Ataque | A-4Q Skyhawk |

S-2Gs were taken on hand to maintain a front-line fleet of six turboprop-powered Trackers.

## Carrier withdrawal

Despite its refit, by 1985, *25 de Mayo* was in poor shape, and no longer considered fully operational, troubled as it was by problems with its outdated machinery. By 1988 it had been decided that the carrier would receive a more comprehensive overhaul,

### Specifications

Crew: 1

Powerplant: 1 x 49kN (11,023lbf) SNECMA Atar 8K-50 turbojet

Maximum speed: 1180km/h (733mph)

Range: 1820km (1130 miles)

Service ceiling: 13,700m (44,950ft)

Dimensions: span 9.6m (31ft 6in); length 14.31m (46ft 11.2in); height 3.86m (12ft 8in)

Weight: 12,000kg (26,445lb) loaded

Armament: Two 30mm (1.18in) cannon, provision for up to 2100kg (4630lb) of ordnance, including Exocet air-to-surface missiles

▼ **Dassault Super Étendard**

*2a Escuadrilla de Caza y Ataque, 1982*

At the time of the Falklands War, Argentina had received five Super Étendards and several AM.39 Exocet anti-ship missiles. The remaining aircraft stayed in France while the initial pilots completed their training. During the conflict, only four aircraft were involved in combat operations, which were flown from Rio Grande, while the fifth aircraft remained at BA Comandante Espora for use as a spares source. All 14 aircraft were delivered by 1983.

#### ▼ 2a Escuadrilla de Caza y Ataque

The Argentine Navy's operating unit for the Super Étendard was established at BA Comandante Espora in 1981.

#### ◀ Super Étendard markings

2a Escuadrilla de Caza y Ataque received a total of 14 Super Étendards, which received the serials 3-A-201 to 3-A-214. The unit converted to the new type at BA Comandante Espora, Puerto Belgrano, in March 1981, with pilot conversion in France from 1980.

#### ▲ Dassault Super Étendard

Despite the withdrawal of the *25 de Mayo*, the Argentine Super Étendard fleet retains its carrier qualifications, and has operated from both Brazilian and US Navy carrier decks. Here, a Super Étendard performs a touch-and-go on the deck of USS *Abraham Lincoln* (CVN-72) off the coast of South America.

including new machinery, but this project was suspended. For most of the 1990s the carrier thus remained in dock at Puerto Belgrano. Finally, in 1997, the *25 de Mayo* was officially retired.

Although lacking a carrier of its own, the Argentine Navy continues to put aircraft to sea, with both S-2s and Super Étendards making periodic deployments aboard the Brazilian Navy carriers NAeL *Minas Gerais* and *São Paolo*. These operations allow the Navy to retain a core of carrier-qualified pilots, and these also take part in occasional training exercises aboard US Navy carriers.

Due to limitations on aircraft numbers and budget constraints, the Argentine Navy maintains a core fleet of around six operational Super Étendards at any one time, and these are home-based at Base Aeronaval Comandante Espora from where they are operated by 2a Escuadrilla de Caza y Ataque.

# Brazil
## 1999–PRESENT

**France's former carrier *Foch* provided a replacement for the previous Brazilian Navy carrier *Minas Gerais*, and now embarks an air group based around A-4 Skyhawk jet fighters.**

THE FORMER FRENCH carrier *Foch* was acquired by Brazil in the second half of 1999 and renamed NAE *São Paolo*, replacing the *Minas Gerais* in service in early 2001. The new carrier would also resume operations with conventional aircraft, according to a government law passed in 1998 that permitted the Força Aéronaval da Marinha do Brasil (Brazilian Naval Air Arm) to re-establish its fixed-wing element.

The primary equipment for the new carrier was the McDonnell Douglas A-4KU Skyhawk, with 20 former Kuwaiti Air Force aircraft being purchased in late 1997, and delivered to 1° Esquadrão de Aviões de Interceptação e Ataque (VF-1) 'Falcões' in the course of late 1999. These are supported by three former Kuwaiti TA-4KU two-seat trainers. The aircraft received the local designation AF-1 and AF-1A, respectively. After making its initial flight in Brazil in 1999, the Skyhawk made its first landing aboard

*Minas Gerais* in September 2000 and VF-1 began its service aboard the carrier the following January. The arrival of the new carrier *São Paolo* in February 2001 saw the *Minas Gerais* paid off in the second half of that year.

The new-look Brazilian Navy carrier air group is based around the A-4KU, tasked with air defence armed with Sidewinder missiles, and anti-ship attack missions using unguided rockets and bombs. The A-4KU version originally developed for land-based

### ▼ Douglas A-4KU (AF-1) Skyhawk

Known locally as the AF-1, an A-4KU Skyhawk embarked on the Brazilian aircraft carrier *São Paulo* performs a 'touch-and-go' landing aboard the aircraft carrier USS *Ronald Reagan* (CVN-76) in the South Atlantic in 2004. Noteworthy in this view of the aircraft is its in-flight refuelling probe, and array of weapons pylons. Together with twin 20mm (.79in) internal cannon, the AF-1 can be armed with AIM-9 Sidewinders for air defence duties, or with bombs and rockets.

## Brazilian Navy Carrier Air Units

Carrier-deployable units, 2011

| Comando da Força Aeronaval | ComForAerNav | | |
|---|---|---|---|
| | | Local designation | Base |
| 1° Esquadrão de Helicópteros Anti-Submarinos (1st Squadron of Anti-submarine Helicopters, HS-1) | AS-61D-3/S-61D-3 | SH-3A/B | São Pedro da Aldeia |
| 1° Esquadrão de Helicópteros de Instrução (1st Helicopter Training Squadron, HI-1) | Bell 206B | IH-6B | São Pedro da Aldeia |
| 1° Esquadrão de Helicópteros de Emprego Geral (1st Utility Helicopter Squadron, HU-1) | HB350/HB355 Esquilo | UH-12/UH-13 | São Pedro da Aldeia |
| 2° Esquadrão de Helicópteros de Emprego Geral (1st Utility Helicopter Squadron, HU-2) | AS332/AS532 Super Puma/Cougar | UH-14 | São Pedro da Aldeia |
| 3° Esquadrão de Helicópteros de Emprego Geral (1st Utility Helicopter Squadron, HU-3) | HB350 Esquilo | UH-12 | Manaus-Ponta Pelada |
| 4° Esquadrão de Helicópteros de Emprego Geral (1st Utility Helicopter Squadron, HU-4) | Bell 206B | IH-6B | Ladário-Base Fluvial |
| 5° Esquadrão de Helicópteros de Emprego Geral (1st Utility Helicopter Squadron, HU-5) | HB350 Esquilo | UH-12 | Ilha do Terrapleno de Leste |
| 1° Esquadrão de Aviões de Interceptação e Ataque (1st Interceptor and Attack Squadron, VF-1) | A-4KU/TA-4KU Skyhawk | AF-1/AF-1A | São Pedro da Aldeia |

service with Kuwait is similar to the US Marine Corps A-4M Skyhawk II version, with an uprated J52-P-408 engine common to both the single- and two-seat versions and with a distinctive squared-off tailfin. Although a successor to the A-4 has yet to be seriously considered, the Navy has suffered some problems with its Skyhawks, the combined result of budget cuts, expensive spares and problems with maintenance contracts relating to the J52 engines.

The rotary-wing component of the carrier air group consists of assets drawn from seven helicopter squadrons tasked with different duties, and which are mainly land-based at São Pedro da Aldeia.

### Anti-submarine backbone

The ASW mission is handled by the Sea King fleet of 1° Esquadrão de Helicópteros Anti-Submarinos, its SH-3A/B aircraft also capable of employing the AM.39 Exocet missile for anti-shipping strike, this latter capability being introduced during an upgrade undertaken in Italy in the mid-1980s. Other weapons options include Mk 46 torpedoes and Mk 9 depth bombs. Although consisting of both US-built Sikorsky S-61D-3 and Italian-manufactured Agusta AS-61D-3 models, the Sea King fleet is uniformly designated as the SH-3. The original fleet was joined by three ex-US Navy SH-3Hs in 1996, these being

equipped with more modern sonar equipment and designated as the SH-3B. At the time of writing, the three SH-3Bs were supported by four SH-3As.

Delivered from 1987, the Eurocopter AS332 Super Puma and AS532 Cougar are flown by 2° Esquadrão de Helicópteros de Emprego Geral and are primarily used for transport and assault tasks. As such, they can be found embarked in both the *São Paolo* and in Brazilian Navy assault ships. The aircraft are to be eventually replaced by 16 locally built Helibras UH-15 Super Cougars (based on the Eurocopter EC725), with Turbomeca Makila 2A turbine engines and forward-looking infrared sensors. Built locally by Helibras, the Eurocopter Ecureuil has been adopted in both the single-engined HB350 (based on the AS350) and twin-engined HB355 (AS355) forms. Known locally as the Esquilo, these helicopters are used for utility purposes and are assigned to three squadrons. In addition to its primary utility duties, the Esquilo can be armed with gun pods and unguided rockets for use as a light attack platform during either coastal patrol or amphibious assault operations. The Bell 206B JetRanger III is operated by both training and general-purpose squadrons. The JetRangers are periodically operated from the carrier for general purpose transport and liaison duties.

# China

## 1998–PRESENT

**China's ambitious carrier-building plans call for the fielding of an indigenous nuclear-powered carrier by 2020, with a former Soviet carrier now being refurbished to gain initial experience.**

CHINA'S AIRCRAFT CARRIER ambitions began to take shape in the late 1990s, with the acquisition of the former Soviet Navy aircraft carrier *Varyag*. This vessel was originally laid down as the *Riga* in the late 1990s as a sister vessel to the Project 1143.5 *Tbilisi* (now *Admiral Kuznetsov*), but was never completed and work on it ended in 1992, after the break-up of the USSR. Acquired by China in 1998, the *Varyag* arrived at China's Dalian shipyard in March 2002. Refurbishment began soon after, and the vessel is now projected to enter service as a training asset, prior to the People's Liberation Army Navy (PLAN) fielding its first indigenously designed carrier. While the *Varyag* utilizes a ski jump take-off ramp, future Chinese carriers may adopt a catapult launch arrangement, as used on US Navy super-carriers.

After several years of limited activity, as of early 2011 the ex-*Varyag* was nearing completion at Dalian, having received both radar installations and defensive armament. At the same time, China officially admitted for the first time that it has embarked on an aircraft carrier construction programme. An official report confirmed that construction of an indigenous carrier was approved in 2009. The plan envisages a conventionally powered carrier with a displacement of between 50,000 and 60,000 tons that will be launched in 2014–15. The conventional carrier will be followed by a nuclear-powered carrier to be launched around 2020. In the meantime, the former *Varyag* might enter service as a training vessel as early as 2012, according to estimates by the US Office of Naval Intelligence. Land-based training facilities for the future naval air wing are being prepared at Xingcheng and Xian. Furthermore, a land-based facility has been constructed at Wuhan in order to test features of the carrier and its aircraft, and to train aircrew and deck crew, this incorporating a full-scale mock-up of the ski jump ramp and a simulated hangar deck.

### Future air wings

The prospective air wing for the PLAN's future carriers will almost certainly be based around a version of the Soviet-designed Sukhoi Su-27 fighter. China's Shenyang produces locally built versions of the Su-27 as the J-11, and has also developed the J-15, a carrier-borne version equivalent to the Su-33 operated by the Russian Navy. At one time it was

### Specifications*

Crew: 1

Powerplant: 2 x 74.5kN (16,750lbf) AL-31F
   afterburning turbofans

Maximum speed: 2300km/h (1430mph)

Range: 3000km (1860 miles)

Service ceiling: 17,000m (55,800ft)

Dimensions: span 14.7m (48ft 3in); length
   21.94m (72ft 0in); height 5.93m (19ft 5in)

Weight: 29,940kg (66,010lb) loaded

Armament: One 30mm (1.18in) GSH-30-1
   cannon; up to 6500kg (14,300lb) munitions
   including four R-27 and R-73 air-to-air
   missiles

(*Specifications for Russian Su-33 – J-15 data
   not available)

▼ **Shenyang J-15**

*Unit unknown, 2011*

The prototype J-15 is seen in its primer finish, as worn during its initial flight-test campaign. The aircraft draws heavily upon the Su-33 carrier fighter, with canard foreplanes, a shortened tail 'sting' and an arrester hook. Internally, however, the Chinese fighter is expected to use indigenous avionics and powerplant.

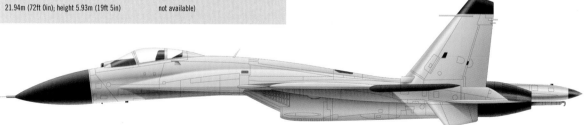

**▲ Ex-Varyag**

By spring 2011, the former *Varyag* was nearing readiness to embark on its maiden voyage. Purchased from Ukraine in the early 1990s, the aircraft carrier will reportedly be named *Shi Ling* in People's Liberation Army Navy service. The vessel is seen here undergoing modernization in the port of Dalian.

expected that China would purchase a quantity of Russian-built Su-33s, but instead elected to develop a type based on the structural configuration of the Russian fighter, including folding wings, canards and a shortened tailcone, with avionics and weapons systems from the locally built J-11B land-based fighter. Dubbed Flying Shark, the J-15 was informed by extensive studies of a single Su-33 prototype acquired via Ukraine around 2001.

Final assembly of the first prototype J-15 probably began in 2008, and a first flight reportedly took place in August 2009. If, as expected, the production version of the J-15 draws upon J-11B technologies, the fighter may be expected to incorporate a Chinese multi-mode pulse-Doppler radar and an updated 'glass' cockpit with new multifunction displays and wide-angle head-up display. Another feature of the J-11B that could be adopted for the J-15 is the indigenous WS-10 powerplant, replacing the original AL-31F turbofan.

The J-15 appears to be a low-cost, interim solution to the PLAN's carrier fighter requirement, and future developments may see the appearance of a fully indigenous carrier-capable fighter developed by the No 601 Institute, or perhaps even a carrier-based development of the Chengdu J-10 fighter.

The first helicopter confirmed to form part of the PLAN's forthcoming carrier air wing is an airborne early warning platform. This is based on the Changhe Z-8, itself a Chinese-built version of the French Sud Aviation Super Frelon. The Z-8 AEW version incorporates an external radar array that can be stowed within the rear fuselage when not in use. The array is likely lowered to permit 360° coverage. Mock-ups of both the J-15 and Z-8 AEW have been observed on the dummy carrier deck at Wuhan.

Another helicopter type very likely to feature on the deck of a future PLAN carrier is the Harbin Z-9, a Chinese-built version of the Aérospatiale AS365N Dauphin 2. The Z-9 is already in PLAN service in a utility transport role, as the Z-9C, and this would be a prime candidate for search and rescue and plane-guard duties from a PLAN aircraft carrier.

In order to train the required aircrew for the PLAN carrier aviation component, a variant of the Guizhou JL-9 advanced trainer has apparently been developed, with strengthened landing gear, arrester hook and other modifications required for operations from carriers, or from land-based training facilities equipped with dummy decks.

# France

## 1990–PRESENT

**The only European power to possess a nuclear-powered carrier, France maintains a single vessel with a powerful and versatile air wing, proven in combat on a number of occasions.**

THE FRENCH NAVY carriers began the 1990s involved in peacekeeping operations over the Balkans, beginning in 1993. The combat operations that followed over Kosovo saw the involvement of *Foch*, and its air wing of Super Étendards, Étendard IVPs, Alizés and helicopters. Missions flown included air strikes, reconnaissance and refuelling. In 1998 the withdrawal of *Clémenceau* left *Foch* as the only French carrier in service, before the introduction to operational service of an all-new nuclear-powered carrier, the *Charles de Gaulle,* in 2001.

The new carrier features a revised air wing of up to 40 Dassault Rafale M fighters, Super Étendard Modernisés, Northrop Grumman E-2C Hawkeyes and helicopters. While *Clémenceau* was paid off in 1998, *Foch* was transferred to Brazil in 2000, after action during Operation Allied Force over Kosovo.

Arrival of the new carrier saw the successive retirement of the Crusader, Étendard IVP and Alizé. The introduction of the E-2C marked an entirely new carrier-based airborne early warning capability, with four aircraft arriving in 1998. The spearhead of the current air wing is the Rafale M, the first of which were delivered to Landivisiau in December 2000.

This state-of-the-art fighter is capable of performing a wide range of missions, including air defence (with Mica missiles), nuclear strike (using the ASMP-A missile), conventional precision attack (including with the SCALP cruise missile and the GPS/infrared-aided AASM precision-guided missile, allied with the Damoclès laser designation pod), reconnaissance (Reco NG pod), and buddy tanking using a centreline store. Eventually the Rafale M will assume full responsibility for offensive missions, but until that time it is capably supported by the upgraded Super Étendard Modernisé.

### Étendard modernized

Like the Rafale M, the Super Étendard Modernisé has been introduced to service in a succession of capability enhancements, or Standards, each of which brings new technologies and capabilities. The ultimate Standard 5 for the Super Étendard remains in service with Flottilles 11F and 17F, and includes new radios and the Rover system to exchange data with troops on the ground, and has seen action in Afghanistan and Libya. New weapons include the 113kg (250lb) GBU-58 laser-guided bomb.

### Specifications

Crew: 1

Powerplant: 2 x 73kN (16,424lbf) SNECMA M88-2 turbofans

Maximum speed: 2130km/h (1324mph)

Range: 1853km (1152 miles)

Service ceiling: 16,800m (55,000ft)

Dimensions: span 10.9m (35ft 9.175in); length 15.3m (50ft 2.5in); height 5.34m (17ft 6.25in)

Weight: 19,500kg (42,990lb) loaded

Armament: One 30mm (1.18in) DEFA 791B cannon, 14 external hardpoints with provision for up to 6000kg (13,228lb) of stores

▼ **Dassault Rafale M**

*Flottille 12F, 2002*

This is Rafale M1, the first production example, which was delivered to the French Navy in July 1999. The aircraft is seen carrying a typical 'omni-role' armament fit, with wingtip MICA air-to-air missiles (fitted with radar-homing seeker heads) and underwing 227kg (500lb) GBU-12 laser-guided bombs and external fuel tanks.

| French Navy carrier air units | | |
|---|---|---|
| Carrier-deployable units, 2011 | | |
| Aéronautique Navale | | |
| Flottille 4F | E-2C Hawkeye | Lann-Bihoué |
| Flottille 11F | Super Étendard Modernisé | Landivisiau |
| Flottille 12F | Rafale M | Landivisiau |
| Flottille 17F | Super Étendard Modernisé | Landivisiau |
| * Flottille 31F | NH90 | Hyères |
| Flottille 32F | EC225 SECMAR | Lanvéoc-Poulmic |
| Flottille 34F | Lynx | Lanvéoc-Poulmic |
| Flottille 35F | Dauphin, Alouette III | Hyères |
| Flottille 36F | Panther | Hyères |
| CEPA/Escadrille 10S | various | Hyères |
| ESHE/Escadrille 22S | Alouette III | Lanvéoc-Poulmic |
| * former Lynx unit disbanded June 2010 in preparation of NH90 deliveries | | |

At the time of the French intervention in Libya in 2011, the *Charles de Gaulle* air wing exhibited a typical composition, with 12 Rafale Ms, six Super Étendard Modernisés, two E-2Cs, two Dauphins, two Caracals, one Alouette III and one Puma. The

### ▼ *Charles de Gaulle* (R91)

At one time expected to be the lead ship in a class of two, the 40,000-ton *Charles de Gaulle* is today the French Navy's sole carrier. France has plans to construct a second carrier, but this will be of a different design, and perhaps with some commonality with the forthcoming British 'Queen Elizabeth' class.

Aérospatiale (now Eurocopter) SA356F Dauphin was introduced in 1990 and serves as the primary search and rescue and plane-guard platform aboard the carrier, supported by the veteran SA319 Alouette III, the latter only being used for daylight operations. Dauphins and Alouettes are also used for force-protection missions, with pintle-mounted machine-guns or an embarked Marine sniper. For logistic and support missions, the carrier embarks the French Army Aviation Aérospatiale SA330 Puma, used for vertical replenishment and logistics missions. The Eurocopter EC225 Caracal fulfils the SECMAR (secours maritime) role, and is appropriately equipped for rescue missions at sea, replacing the Super Frelon in this role.

▲ **Northrop Grumman E-2C Hawkeye**

Seen during 'cross-decking' with the USS *John C. Stennis*, the E-2C is the largest aircraft to have ever served from a French carrier. The four aircraft deploy to the carrier as two-aircraft detachments, and use their AN/APS-145 radar to detect air and surface targets, transmitting real-time data to other aircraft and ships using the Link 16 system.

▼ **French Navy Super Étendard units**

The French Navy's Super Étendard was provided to three front-line units, plus a carrier training unit, Escadrille 59S.

◀ **Flottille 11F**

This unit was re-established at Landivisiau in September 1978, becoming operational with the Super Étendard in February 1979. Flottille 11F will start converting to the Rafale in mid-2011.

◀ **Flottille 14F**

Landivisiau-based Flottille 14F converted to the type from April 1979, being a former F-8E(FN) operator. The unit was later disbanded as part of budget cuts, together with Escadrille 59S.

◀ **Flottille 17F**

The last of the three front-line formations to adopt the Super Étendard, Flottille 17F did so in September 1980, converting to the type at Hyères. In 2011, Flottille 17F was equipped with the latest Standard 5 aircraft, compatible with the Rover video-transmission terminal.

# India
## 1988–PRESENT

**With an indigenous carrier in development, and a Russian-built carrier soon to joint the fleet, the Indian Navy is well on the way to establishing a robust carrier arm.**

THE INDIAN NAVY carrier arm began a major period of modernization with the introduction of the BAe Sea Harrier in 1984. Acquisition of the new fighter was followed by induction of a second carrier, the former HMS *Hermes* entering service as the INS *Viraat* (R22) in 1987. Since the carrier had already been adapted for V/STOL operations with a 12° ski jump, it was tailor-made to support the Sea Harrier FRS.Mk 51, of which an eventual 23 examples were acquired, supported by six two-seaters for land-based training. The Sea Harrier first saw service from INS *Vikrant*, which had been fitted with a ski jump to allow a first launch by the new fighter in 1990. The ageing carrier made its final cruise in 1994, after which *Viraat* remained India's sole carrier.

The *Viraat* can theoretically support an air group comprising up to 30 Sea Harriers, although limited serviceability and availability meant that by 2011, only around 10 examples were left in service. These are supported by the Sea King Mk 42B that operates in the ASW role, and which is sometimes supported by the Kamov Ka-28 in the same role, although the latter are generally operated from smaller surface combatants. Other rotary-wing equipment includes the Sea King Mk 42C for commando assault and vertical replenishment, the Ka-31 for airborne early warning, and the HAL Chetak for utility transport and search and rescue/plane-guard duties.

### Russian carrier plans

In 1998 India signed a memorandum of understanding with Russia concerning the transfer of the former *Admiral Gorshkov* (ex-*Baku*). Previously operated as a V/STOL carrier, the carrier is being adapted for Indian service with equipment for short take-off but arrested recovery operations, including a ski jump and arrester gear. As such, the centrepiece of the new air group will be the Mikoyan MiG-29K fighter. India ordered 12 single-seat MiG-29Ks and four two-seat MiG-29KUBs in January 2004. The first four examples were subsequently delivered in early 2009. A further 30 aircraft are on option and could be delivered by 2015. The contract for the *Admiral Gorshkov* also includes additional Ka-28 and Ka-31 helicopters. Up to 24 MiG-29Ks will be embarked, together with six helicopters, or a combination of fixed- and rotary-wing types up to a total of 24 aircraft. Once commissioned into service,

### Specifications

Crew: 1

Powerplant: 1 x 95.6kN (21,500lbf) Rolls-Royce Pegasus vectored thrust turbofan

Maximum speed: 1110km/h (609mph)

Range: 1000km (620 miles)

Service ceiling: 15,545m (51,000ft)

Dimensions: span 7.7m (25ft 3in); length 14.5m (47ft 7in); height 3.71m (12ft 2in)

Weight: 11,900kg (26,200lb) loaded

Armament: Two 30mm (1.18in) cannons, provisions for AIM-9 Sidewinder or Matra Magic air-to-air missiles, and two Harpoon or Sea Eagle anti-shipping missiles; up to a total of 3629kg (8000lb) bombs

▼ **BAe Sea Harrier FRS.Mk 51**

*INAS 300 'White Tigers', 1980s*

Home-based at INS Hansa in Goa, the Indian Navy Sea Harrier fleet has recently suffered from a lack of serviceability. Efforts have been made to improve capabilities, however, with long-running plans to re-equip the fleet with new Israeli-supplied Elta EL/M-2032 multi-mode fire-control radar and Rafael Derby air-to-air missiles. Indian Navy Sea Harriers are capable of launching BAe Sea Eagle anti-ship missiles.

## Indian Navy carrier air units

| Carrier-deployable units, 2011 | | |
|---|---|---|
| **Western Fleet Command** | | |
| INAS 300 'White Tigers' | Sea Harrier FRS.Mk 51 | INS Hansa, Dabolim |
| INAS 303 'Black Panthers' | MiG-29K/KUB | INS Hansa, Dabolim |
| INAS 552 'Braves' | Sea Harrier FRS.Mk 51/T.Mk 60 | INS Hansa, Dabolim |
| INAS 321 'Angels' | Chetak | INS Shikra, Mumbai, and dets |
| INAS 330 'Harpoons' | Sea King Mk 42A/B | INS Shikra, Mumbai |
| Marine Commando Flight 'Zappers' | Sea King Mk 42C | INS Shikra, Mumbai |
| **Eastern Fleet Command** | | |
| INAS 339 'Falcons' | Ka-28/31 | INS Dega, Vizag |
| INAS 350 | UH-3H Sea King | INS Dega, Vizag |
| INAS 561 'Rotors' | Chetak | INS Rajali, Arokanam |
| **Southern Fleet Command** | | |
| INAS 336 'Flaming Arrows' | Sea King Mk 42A/B | INS Garuda, Kochi |

▲ **BAe Sea Harrier FRS.Mk 51**

A Sea Harrier is refuelled aboard *Viraat* in 2007. Noteworthy is the latest overall grey paint scheme to reduce visibility, the fixed in-flight refuelling probe and the Israeli-made electronic countermeasures pod carried under the starboard wing. Operator INAS 300 was the former Indian Navy Sea Hawk squadron.

the carrier will be named INS *Vikramaditya*. With the *Vikramaditya* subject to delays and cost increases, the Indian Navy intends to retain *Viraat* in service until 2020, although this will be dependent upon continued availability of the Sea Harrier. Looking further ahead, a first indigenous carrier, to be named INS *Vikrant*, will likely be completed around 2014–15. In common with its two predecessors, the 40,000-ton carrier will feature a ski jump for fixed-wing aviation operations, and its air group is planned to include a navalized version of the HAL Tejas lightweight indigenous fighter.

# Italy
## 1985–PRESENT

**A relative latecomer to the field of carrier aviation, Italy re-established a Navy Air Corps in 1956 and introduced its first carrier, *Giuseppe Garibaldi*, in 1985, initially as an assault carrier.**

ITALY'S FIRST CARRIER began operations in the assault carrier role, with SH-3s and Agusta AB212s in the air group. The Agusta-built SH-3D had been introduced in the ASW role in 1969, while the first of 68 AB212s was fielded in 1976. In 1989 a new law was passed that permitted the Italian Navy (Marina Militare) to operate fixed-wing carrier aircraft, and in 1991 the first two Harriers landed on the *Garibaldi*.

### Italian Harriers
Italy's McDonnell Douglas AV-8Bs were received from September 1991, in Harrier II+ form, with AN/APG-65 multi-mode radar conferring a multi-role capability. Sixteen single-seat AV-8Bs were complemented by two TAV-8Bs for shore-based training at Grottaglie, near Taranto. In order to embark the new jets, the *Garibaldi* had been completed with a ski jump. By 1994, Harriers were routinely operating from the carrier. The Harriers have been employed from *Garibaldi* in several operations, seeing action over Somalia in 1995, Operation Allied Force over the former Yugoslavia in

| Forze Aeree della Marina Militare | |
|---|---|
| Carrier-deployable units, 2011 | |
| **MARISTAELI Luni** | La Spezia |
| 1° Gruppo Elicotteri | EH101 |
| 5° Gruppo Elicotteri | AB212, NH90 |
| | |
| **MARISTAELI Catania** | Sicily |
| 2° Gruppo Elicotteri | AB212 |
| 3° Gruppo Elicotteri | EH101 |
| | |
| **MARISAER Grottaglie** | Taranto |
| 4° Gruppo Elicotteri | SH-3D Sea King, AB212 |
| Gruppo Aereo | AV-8B/TAV-8B Harrier II+ |

1999, Enduring Freedom in Afghanistan in 2001, and in Lebanon in 2006.

Alongside the Harrier operator, Gruppo Aereo, the Italian Navy's aviation component includes five helicopter squadrons shore-based at three facilities,

### Specifications
Crew: 4

Powerplant: 1 x 1398kW (1873hp) Pratt & Whitney Canada PT6T-6 turboshaft engine

Maximum speed: 240km/h (149mph)

Range: 615km (382 miles)

Service ceiling: 3200m (10,498ft)

Dimensions: Rotor diameter 14.63m (48ft 0in); length 17.39m (57ft 0in); height 4.01m (13ft 16in)

Weight: 5070kg (11,177lb) loaded

Armament: 2 x Mk 46 torpedoes

▼ **Agusta-Bell AB212ASW**

*5° Gruppo Elicotteri*

The workhorse of the Italian Navy, the AB212 was primarily employed as an ASW platform, although in recent years it has assumed responsibility for search and rescue, electronic warfare, special operations and assault transport duties. The AB212ASW entered Italian Navy service in 1976, with MM/APS-705 search radar above the cabin, dipping sonar and Mk 46 torpedoes.

## Specifications

Crew: 1

Powerplant: 1 x 105kN (23,500lbf) Rolls-Royce
F402-RR-408 vectored thrust turbofan

Maximum speed: 1070km/h (662mph)

Range: 556km (300 miles)

Dimensions: span 9.25m (30ft 4in); length
14.12m (46ft 4in); height 3.55m (11ft 8in)

Weight: 10,410kg (22,950lb) loaded

Armament: One 25mm (.98in) General
Dynamics GAU-12 Equalizer 5-barreled

Gatling cannon mounted under-fuselage; six
under-wing pylon stations holding up to
5988kg (13,200lb) payload; four LAU-5003
rocket pods (each with 19 CRV7 70mm
[2.75in] rockets); four AIM-9 Sidewinder or six
AIM-120 AMRAAM air-to-air missiles; six
AGM-65 Maverick air-to-surface missiles;
Paveway laser-guided bombs or CBU-100
Cluster Bombs or Mark 77 napalm canisters

### ▼ Boeing (McDonnell Douglas) AV-8B Harrier II+
*Gruppo Aereo (GRUPAER), 2000*

Italy's pair of two-seat Harriers and the first three single-seaters were built by McDonnell Douglas and shipped to Taranto in *Garibaldi*, while Alenia assembled the remaining 13 single-seaters. Delivery of the final aircraft took place in 1998. This example is seen with laser-guided bombs, Sidewinders and external fuel tanks carried underwing.

and responsible for just under 60 aircraft. Units at Luni are mainly concerned with providing operational and logistics support, while those at Catania are assigned both operational and training roles. Finally, a single unit at Grottaglie is dedicated to the support of marine assault and special forces operations.

Since 2005, Italian Navy helicopters have been contributing to the NATO-led mission in Afghanistan, employing AB212s and SH-3Ds from bases at Kabul and Herat, while the first EH101 deployment was made in 2011.

## Helicopter modernization

The Italian Navy is currently in the process of modernization, with the NH Industries NH90 helicopter replacing the AB212 fleet. Meanwhile, by 2012 the Sea King will have been entirely replaced by the AgustaWestland EH101. Aircraft will soon embark in a second carrier, with the *Cavour* shortly to join the fleet. While the *Garibaldi* was developed as a helicopter carrier, the *Cavour* has been designed as a genuine carrier, to operate a fixed-wing air group. In fact, the new vessel was utilised in relief operations after the Haitian earthquake in 2010.

Ultimately, the *Cavour* will replace the embarked Harrier with the Lockheed Martin F-35 Joint Strike Fighter. Since *Cavour* is twice the size of *Garibaldi* it will carry twice the number of aircraft. The total

embarked air group will consist of up to 20 aircraft including 14 JSFs and six heavy helicopters. The Italian Navy is currently the only export customer for the F-35B short take-off and vertical landing (STOVL) version of the JSF. The first two JSFs will be delivered to the Italian Navy in 2014 and will initially be used for training in the US, before the first operational examples arrive in Italy from 2015, with a total of 22 aircraft on order.

Operational capability with the embarked JSF is planned to be achieved no later than 2017–18, allowing the Harrier to be retired.

The introduction of the *Cavour* to routine operations will allow the *Garibaldi* to return to its previous helicopter carrier role, with an emphasis on amphibious operations. With the full retirement of the Sea King by 2012, the carrier's air group will be based around the EH101 and NH90. However, additional rotary-wing capability can be added in the form of Italian Army A129 Mangusta attack helicopters and CH-47 Chinook transport helicopters. The last of the Sea King fleet, which once numbered 36 examples, are SH-3D versions operated solely in the assault configuration in support of amphibious and special forces.

A total of 56 NH90s are on order, 46 in the NFH version for surveillance, anti-surface and anti-submarine warfare, and 10 in the TTH version, the latter equipped for assault operations.

# Russia

## 1990–PRESENT

**With the fall of the Soviet empire, the fleet of helicopter and V/STOL cruisers diminished, and today a single carrier remains in use, this conducting conventional fixed-wing operations.**

THE FIRST OF the new generation of Soviet carriers capable of embarking conventional fixed-wing aircraft, the Project 1143.5 was intended to embark Yak-41 VTOL fighters, together with conventional take-off and landing Sukhoi Su-25Ks and Su-27Ks. Compared to the previous Project 1143 vessels, the new carrier adopted a more conventional configuration, with a full-length flight deck. In 1980 the design was revised, with the carrier's catapults being removed and the air group now being based upon the Yak-41, supported by Su-27Ks and Mikoyan MiG-29Ks that would be launched with the aid of a ski jump. In order to test the new Su-27K and MiG-29K a dummy deck with ski jump was constructed at Saki in the Crimea, with tests for both types commencing in 1982.

Construction work on the Project 1143.5 began in 1982, and the carrier was initially to be named *Riga*, and later *Leonid Brezhnyev*, and latterly *Tbilisi*. In November 1989 fixed-wing operations commenced aboard the new carrier, with experimental work conducted by prototypes of the Su-27K, MiG-29K and the two-seat Su-25UTG shipborne trainer.

Since 1990, the Project 1143.5 has operated under the name *Admiral Kuznetsov*, and at the time of the collapse of the USSR, the carrier was still undergoing trials. Thereafter, budgetary constraints saw development of the MiG-29K abandoned, and the Su-27K was left as the centrepiece of the air group. Whereas the MiG-29K was a true multirole type, capable of both air defence and attack missions, the Su-27K was a dedicated fleet interceptor. Also abandoned was the Yak-41, which was cancelled in 1992. Plans to field a sister carrier, *Riga* (subsequently named *Varyag*), were scrapped in a similar timeframe, with the vessel left incomplete. The first of a larger class of carrier had also been laid down, but this vessel, the nuclear-powered, 70,000-ton *Ulyanovsk*, was broken up in dock in late 1991.

### *Kuznetsov* into service

With the *Admiral Kuznetsov* in service, the Russian Navy began to dispose of its earlier carriers. When the USSR broke up, there were two 'Moskva'-class helicopter carriers in commission, together with the four 'Kiev'-class ships. By the mid-1990s both

## Specifications

| | |
|---|---|
| Crew: 1 | 10.25in) |
| Powerplant: 2 x 122.5kN (27,557lbf) Lyul'ka AL-31M turbofans | Weight: 30,000kg (66,138lb) loaded |
| Maximum speed: 2500km/h (1500mph) | Armament: One 30mm (1.18in) GSH-3101 cannon with 149 rounds; 10 external |
| Range: 1500km (930 miles) | hardpoints with provisions for 6000kg |
| Service ceiling: 18,000m (59,055ft) | (13,228kg) of stores, including the AA-10 |
| Dimensions: span 14.7m (48ft 2.75in); length 21.94m (71ft 11.5in); height 6.36m (20ft | 'Alamo' and R-73 (AA-11 'Archer') air-to-air missiles |

### ▼ Sukhoi Su-33

*1st Squadron, 279th KIAP*

This Su-33 is seen wearing the markings of the 1st Squadron of the 279th KIAP (aircraft of the 2nd Squadron display tiger insignia on the tailfin). The aircraft carries a weapons load of live R-27 (AA-10 'Alamo') and short-range R-73 (AA-11 'Archer') air-to-air missiles. Note also the retractable refuelling probe, shortened tail 'sting', arrester hook and canard foreplanes of this version.

'Moskvas' had been disposed of, and problems with the propulsion systems of the 'Kievs' saw their operations limited, and they were similarly scrapped or decommissioned, the most modern of these, *Admiral Gorshkov*, being sold to India.

After completing trials work in the Black Sea, the *Admiral Kuznetsov* was transferred to the Northern Fleet in 1991, although the first Su-27K fighters for the air group did not arrive until 1993. The carrier completed its first cruise between December 1995 and March 1996, sailing in the Mediterranean. On officially entering service in 1998, the Su-27K fighter received the revised designation Su-33. The *Admiral Kuznetsov* remained in dock during 1996 and 1997, before returning to sea in 2000. The carrier returned to dock for maintenance between 2001 and 2004, and then resumed operational service in the North Atlantic in late 2004. The Atlantic was once again the theatre of operations for a 2005 cruise, and in 2006 the carrier was under way in the Barents Sea. In 2008 and 2009, successive exercises were conducted in the Mediterranean.

For the time being, the *Admiral Kuznetsov* remains the sole carrier in Russian service. Theoretically capable of embarking an air group of up to 40 aircraft, in practice the carrier goes to sea with a much smaller air component. During its first cruise, for example, the carrier embarked 15 Su-27Ks, a single Su-25UTG and 11 Ka-27 series helicopters. The rotary-wing component includes Ka-27PLs for ASW missions, the Ka-27PS for SAR and plane-guard, and the Ka-31 for airborne early warning. On occasions, the carrier has embarked the Ka-29, an assault transport development of the Ka-27, although these are more usually associated with amphibious vessels.

## Carrier 'Flanker'

As the navalized version of the Su-27, the Su-33 features several modifications for ship-borne use, including folding wings and tailplanes, and canard foreplanes to increase lift. The undercarriage is reinforced, and an arrester hook is carried below a shortened tail 'sting'. A retractable in-flight refuelling probe is fitted. In order to train prospective Su-33 pilots and to help existing pilots retain currency for carrier operations, the two-seat Su-25UTG is an unarmed version of the Su-25 ground-attack aircraft, strengthened for carrier operations and with an arrester hook. As well as going to sea aboard *Admiral Kuznetsov*, these aircraft operate from the dummy deck training facility at Saki. Although located in Ukraine, the latter base remains in use with the

| Specifications | |
|---|---|
| Crew: 2 | height 5.40m (17ft 8in) |
| Powerplant: 2 x 1660kW (2225hp) Klimov TV3- | Weight: 12,600kg (27,778lb) loaded |
| 117VMA turboshaft engines | Armament: Four-barrel Gatling-type GShG-7.62 |
| Maximum speed: 250km/h (155mph) | 7.62mm (.3in) machine gun; pylons for two |
| Range: 460km (285 miles) | four-round packs of 9M114 Shturm (AT-6 |
| Service ceiling: 5000m (16,404ft) | 'Spiral') ASMs and two UV-32-57 or B-8V20 |
| Dimensions: Rotor diameter 15.9m (52ft 2in); | 80mm (3.1in) rocket pods |
| length 11.6m (38ft 6in); | |

### ▼ Kamov Ka-29
#### *Russian Navy, early 1990s*

An irregular visitor to the deck of the *Admiral Kuznetsov* is the Ka-29 assault transport helicopter, this example being depicted with B-8 rocket pods on the outrigger pylons. Dubbed 'Helix-B' by NATO, this heavily armed helicopter is more usually associated with the 'Ivan Rogov' class of amphibious transport ship. Unlike the Ka-27, the Ka-29 carries no radar or ASW equipment. Instead, it incorporates the Shturm guided air-to-ground missile system from the Mil Mi-24V land-based assault helicopter.

▲ **Sukhoi Su-33**
At this time still operated under the original Su-27K designation, a carrier 'Flanker' lands on the deck of the *Admiral Kuznetsov*. While the landing aircraft is an in-service machine, the example in the foreground is T10K-9, the last of the pre-production batch of aircraft that were used for carrier trials.

Russian Navy, which makes regular deployments with its Su-33s and Su-25UTGs.

The operating unit for both the Su-33 and Su-25UTG is the 279th Independent Carrier-borne Fighter Aviation Regiment (279th KIAP), based at Severomorsk-3, near Murmansk. The regiment consists of three squadrons, two of which are equipped with around 20 Su-33s, while the third operates as a training unit, with seven Su-25UTGs and eight (non-carrier-capable) Su-27UB two-seaters.

In future, Russia intends to field new carriers, with plans announced in 2011 for the construction of a nuclear-powered aircraft carrier by 2012. Eventually, Russia aims to build at least three carriers for service with the Northern and Pacific Fleets. In terms of future carrier aircraft, a multi-role side-by-side two-seat version of the Su-33 has been developed, the Su-33UB recording its first flight in 1999, and undergoing carrier trials in 2000. More likely equipment for any new carrier is the reborn

MiG-29K, however. Although originally discarded by the Russian Navy, recent orders from the Indian Navy suggest that the multi-role fighter may also have a future in Russian service. The latest MiG-29K standard includes a multi-mode Zhuk radar, uprated RD-33 engines and an increased-area folding wing.

| *Admiral Kuznetsov* air wing | | |
|---|---|---|
| Carrier-deployable units, 2011 | | |
| Northern Fleet | | |
| Mixed Shipborne Air Division | HQ Severomorsk | |
| 279th KIAP | Severomorsk-3 | |
| 1st and 2nd Squadrons | Su-33 | 20 |
| 3rd Squadron | Su-25UTG | 7 |
| | Su-27UB | 8 (land-based only) |
| 830th OKPLVP | Ka-27PL/PS | Severomorsk-1 |

# Spain
## 1990–PRESENT

**Having replaced the *Dédalo* and its embarked first-generation Harriers with a new, purpose-built carrier and Harrier II fighters, the Spanish Navy is now introducing a new assault carrier.**

THE SPANISH NAVY'S replacement for the ageing *Dédalo* was the SNS *Principe de Asturias*. The new carrier was based on a US design for a Sea Control Ship. Although the US Navy lost interest in this small, multi-role carrier design, it was adopted by Spain, and the Bazán shipyard acquired rights for construction. The *Principe de Asturias* features a 12° ski jump, and is equipped to serve as a flagship for the Spanish Navy battle group.

Commissioned in 1988, the *Principe de Asturias* can embark up to 29 fixed- and rotary-wing aircraft, arranged as 17 in the hangar deck and 12 on the flight deck. For a typical mission, the air group might consist of eight Harriers, six Sea Kings, five AB212s, two SH-3(AEW)s and one or two Hughes 500s.

The original AV-8S (VA.1 Matador) has given way to the Harrier II, with greatly expanded operational capabilities. In 1983 Spain placed orders for 12 McDonnell Douglas AV-8Bs, which received the manufacturer's designation EAV-8B. In Spanish service, the designation VA.2 Matador is applied. The first examples arrived in Spain in 1987, and a new unit, 9a Escuadrilla, was stood up to operate them in the same year. A single two-seat TAV-8B was received in 2001 for training. In order to further expand the capabilities of the Harrier fleet, follow-on deliveries of a further eight aircraft were to Harrier II+ standard, incorporating a multi-mode AN/APG-65 radar that provides compatibility with the AIM-120 AMRAAM missile. These aircraft were received between 1966 and 1997, and also offer AGM-65 Maverick air-to-surface missile capability, Litening II laser targeting pod, and a forward-looking infrared sensor. The Harrier II+ modifications are also being integrated on the surviving eight EAV-8Bs, to produce a common standard. The final four 'Day Attack' EAV-8Bs are being upgraded by Cassidian, changes including the Pegasus 408A engine and improvements to the structure and avionics. When complete, the Spanish Navy will have a fleet of 16 multi-role Harrier II+ aircraft.

The Spanish Navy is in the process of inducting a new carrier to service. SNS *Juan Carlos I* embarked its first aircraft in February 2011, when SH-3D, Hughes

## Specifications

| | |
|---|---|
| Crew: 1 | Armament: One 25mm (0.98in) General |
| Powerplant: 1 x 105kN (23500lbf) Rolls-Royce | Dynamics GAU-12 Equalizer 5-barreled |
| F402-RR-408 vectored-thrust turbofans | Gatling cannon mounted under-fuselage; six |
| Maximum speed: 1070km/h (662mph) | under-wing pylon stations holding up to |
| Range: 2200km (1400 miles) | 5988kg (13,200lb) payload; four LAU-5003 |
| Dimensions: span 9.25m (30ft 4in); length | rocket pods (each with 19 CRV7 70mm |
| 14.12m (46ft 4in); height 3.55m (11ft 8in) | [2.75in] rockets); four AIM-9 Sidewinder or six |
| Weight: 10,410kg (22,950lb) loaded | AIM-120 AMRAAM air-to-air missiles; six |
| | AGM-65 Maverick air-to-surface missiles |

### ▼ Boeing (McDonnell Douglas) EAV-8B Harrier II+

*9a Escuadrilla, 2011*

Spain's radar-equipped Harrier II+ is compatible with the AIM-120 AMRAAM, seen here carried underwing, with Sidewinders outboard. The aircraft is also fitted with prominent under-fuselage aerodynamic strakes, which are attached when the 25mm (.98in) cannon pods are not fitted. For air-to-ground missions, the Harrier II+ can employ the Maverick missile.

▲ **Boeing (McDonnell Douglas) EAV-8B Harrier II+**

Armed with 227kg (500lb) 'dumb' bombs underwing, a Spanish Navy Harrier II+ prepares to take off from the *Principe de Asturias* during a live fire exercise. Spain introduced a rolling programme to bring all surviving members of its AV-8B community up to the same Harrier II+ standard, with multi-mode radar and other changes that include night vision goggle-compatible cockpit, embedded GPS, new navigation systems and radios, as well as radar-guided weaponry.

500 and AB212 helicopters landed on as part of initial trials. The vessel will also embark the Harrier II+s of 9a Escuadrilla. Configured primarily for amphibious assault operations and classed by the Spanish Navy as a Strategic Projection Ship, the carrier was commissioned in September 2010. Once in full operational service, *Juan Carlos I* will typically embark up to 30 helicopters or 10-12 Harrier IIs.

## Helicopter fleet

Current carrier-embarked rotary-wing types comprise the AB212, which has dispensed with its ASW and anti-ship role to undertake transport, electronic warfare and light attack duties, with 10 examples operational. The Hughes 500 (Model

369M) remains in use for training, although it also undertakes occasional liaison and calibration assignments. The SH-3D Sea King formerly in use has been replaced by the SH-3H, eight of which are configured for troop transport and search and rescue. The 'Hotel' was produced through conversion of existing SH-3D airframes during the late 1980s. The SH-3(AEW) conversion serves as an airborne early warning asset for the Spanish Navy, with three helicopters equipped with Searchwater radar.

| Arma Aérea de la Armada | | |
|---|---|---|
| Carrier-deployable units, 2011 | Rota | |
| | | Local designation |
| 3a Escuadrilla | AB212 | HA.18 |
| 5a Escuadrilla | SH-3/SH-3(AEW) Sea King | HS.9 |
| 6a Escuadrilla | Hughes 369M | HS.13 |
| 9a Escuadrilla | AV-8B/TAV-8B Matador II+ | VA.1A/B |

# Thailand

## 1997–PRESENT

**As flagship of the Royal Thai Navy, the carrier *Chakri Naruebet* serves in a prestigious role, although the retirement of the Harrier means it is now limited to helicopter operations.**

THE ROYAL THAI Navy ordered an aircraft carrier in 1991, the vessel being of German design, but ultimately being built by Bazán in Spain, in order to circumvent restrictions on German aircraft carrier exports. The resulting HTMS *Chakri Naruebet* was commissioned in 1997. The carrier is essentially similar to the Spanish Navy *Principe de Asturias*, although somewhat smaller.

Equipped with a 12° ski jump, the carrier was capable of operating V/STOL equipment, and for this purpose Thailand acquired seven former Spanish Navy AV-8S Harriers and a pair of two-seat TAV-8S trainers, these being delivered to 301 Squadron in 1996. Prior to receipt of the aircraft, RTN aircrew were trained on the type with the US Marine Corps

| Royal Thai Naval Air Division | |
|---|---|
| Carrier-deployable units, 2000 | U Tapao RTNAB |
| Carrier Air Wing 3 | |
| 301 Squadron | AV-8S/TAV-8S Matador |
| 302 Squadron | S-70B-7 Seahawk |

▼ *Chakri Naruebet*

The flagship of the RTN is seen in harbour, with AV-8S fighters on deck, together with some S-76 helicopters. In order to boost the serviceability of its first-generation Harriers, Thailand attempted to acquire additional airframes from US surplus and used these as a source of spare parts. When this deal fell through, the RTN was left with just a pair of operational Harriers by the late 1990s.

and at Rota in Spain. 301 Squadron was part of 3 Wing of the RTN, a new formation dedicated to operating carrier-capable aircraft. Prior to delivery, the Harriers were upgraded in Spain, and were provided with an air-to-air armament of AIM-9 Sidewinder missiles. Cluster bombs and unguided rocket pods could also be carried for attack and close support missions. By 1999, however, only one or two Harriers remained operational, leading to the type's withdrawal without replacement. Some thought was given to acquiring former Royal Navy Sea Harriers, but these plans came to nothing.

The only other aircraft type initially embarked in *Chakri Naruebet* was the Sikorsky S-70B Seahawk. The first of six S-70B-7s was received in 1997, to serve with 302 Squadron. Primarily equipped for ASW duties, the Seahawks are outfitted with dipping sonar, sonobuoys and Mk 46 lightweight torpedoes. In addition to the ASW mission, the Seahawk served as a SAR and plane-guard asset and is also used for liaison and transport missions between the carrier and the shore.

As initially commissioned, the air group of the *Chakri Naruebet* comprised a maximum of six Harriers plus up to six S-70Bs. A frequent visitor to the carrier was the S-76B, used for transport and search and rescue. The primary assigned roles for the carrier and its air group were support of amphibious assault operations, patrol and force protection around Thailand's coastline and Economic Exclusion Zone (EEZ), and humanitarian missions.

### Helicopter carrier

Following the retirement of the Harrier, the *Chakri Naruebet* became a dedicated helicopter carrier. In addition to the RTN types outlined above, the carrier can also support Royal Thai Army types, such as the CH-47D Chinook. Hangar space is limited to 10 aircraft, although additional capacity is available on the flight deck. Typical operations see the carrier embark an air group of 12 helicopters.

Most recently, the *Chakri Naruebet* has been used for disaster relief operations, a role in which it served during the Indian Ocean tsunami in 2004, and in the wake of floods in both 2010 and 2011. Other operations are limited by a lack of funding, which has seen the carrier frequently kept in dock at the naval base in Sattahip.

# United Kingdom
## 1990–PRESENT

**The Royal Navy emerged from the ASW-optimized environment of the Cold War with a powerful and flexible force of carriers, although the Navy lost its fixed-wing capacity in 2010.**

AFTER THE COLD War, the Royal Navy's three-strong carrier force saw action in the Balkans, initially in support of the no-fly zone over Bosnia from 1993. Throughout most of the course of the conflict in the former Yugoslavia, a carrier was on station in the Adriatic, and in 1995, Sea Harriers launched attacks against Serbian targets. By this stage, the Sea Harrier FA.Mk 2 had joined the carrier air group. Royal Navy carriers were similarly involved in policing the no-fly zone established over Iraq after the 1991 Gulf War. With three carriers in commission by the mid-1980s, the Royal Navy was able to maintain two ships in operational service at any given time. Initially, two squadrons of Sea Harriers were maintained by the FAA to serve on these ships, alongside ASW-tasked Sea Kings, reflecting the primacy of the anti-submarine tasking that had been critical during the Cold War.

### Updated Sea Harrier

A replacement for the Sea Harrier FRS.Mk 1 was initially developed as the FRS.Mk 2, before the service designation FA.Mk 2 was adopted. Equipped with Blue Vixen radar, the new version was capable of employing the AIM-120 AMRAAM air-to-air missile and these changes provided for a beyond visual range and look-down/shoot-down capability. Serving with No. 801 NAS, the Sea Harrier FA.Mk 2 saw its first operational employment over Bosnia in early 1995. In addition to 33 aircraft that were converted from

FRS.Mk 1s, a further 18 FA.Mk 2s were completed as new-build airframes for Nos 800 and 801 NAS.

After participation in operations in the Adriatic between 1993 and 1999, and enforcing the no-fly zone over southern Iraq, HMS *Invincible* was decommissioned in August 2005, leaving the Royal Navy with two carriers in service.

With the Sea Harrier FA.Mk 2 excelling in the air defence role, the decision was made to return Royal Air Force ground-attack Harriers to the Royal Navy's carriers, after having operated from HMS *Hermes* in the Falklands. A trial deployment was made by RAF Harrier GR.Mk 7s in 1994, and this paved the way for the creation of Joint Force Harrier (JFH), in 1998. Thereafter, RAF and Fleet Air Arm Harrier operations were combined, with joint shore bases at RAF Cottesmore and Wittering. As a result, the new-look carrier air group consisted of eight Sea Harriers, eight Harrier GR.Mk 7s, four Sea King AEW.Mk 7s and a pair of Sea King HAS.Mk 6s by the turn of the century. Rather than the previous ASW mission, the focus was now placed upon providing a rapid reaction force to crises anywhere around the globe.

JFH latterly divided its efforts between providing close air support from land bases in Afghanistan and providing carrier strike capability. In its ultimate form, the air group embarked in the 'Illustrious' class

was capable of conducting a range of missions including carrier strike, amphibious assault and ASW.

The primary combat air equipment was provided by the Harrier and the AgustaWestland (formerly EH Industries) Merlin. Two squadrons of each type would typically be supported by a pair of Sea King ASaC.Mk 7 (Airborne Surveillance and Control) helicopters. The Sea King ASaC.Mk 7 represents the latest incarnation of the airborne early warning Sea King, succeeding the AEW.Mk 7. Between 2002 and 2004, 13 Sea Kings, comprising 10 AEW.Mk 2s and three HAS.Mk 5s, were upgraded and re-designated as Sea King ASaC.Mk 7s, followed by two more Sea King HAS.Mk 6 conversions as attrition replacements. The latest model features the Cerberus mission system, Searchwater 2000 radar and the Joint Tactical Information Distribution System. Three Sea King ASaC.Mk 7s are routinely deployed to Afghanistan as part of Operation Herrick.

## ASW developments

Last of the illustrious line of ASW-configured Sea Kings was the HAS.Mk 6, with composite main rotors, a new tactical mission system, new sonar and magenetic anomaly detector. The definitive version was produced via conversion of the HAS.Mk 5 line, while a further five were acquired as new-builds. Replacing the Sea King HAS.Mk 6 in the ASW role

### ▼ BAe Sea Harrier FA.Mk 2

#### *No. 801 NAS, 1995*

Armed with up to four AMRAAMs (two are seen here under the fuselage, with Sidewinders underwing), and equipped with Ferranti Blue Vixen radar, the Sea Harrier FA.Mk 2 was a very capable air defence fighter. Seen wearing the chequered fin markings of No. 801 NAS, this aircraft is seen with undercarriage (including wingtip outriggers) deployed, and carries a bolt-on refuelling probe.

### Specifications

| | |
|---|---|
| Crew: 1 | 14.17m (46ft 6in); height 3.71m (12ft 2in) |
| Powerplant: 1 x 95.6kN (21,500lbf) Rolls-Royce | Weight: 11,884kg (26,200lb) loaded |
| Pegasus MK 106 vectored thrust turbofan | Armament: Two 25mm (.98in) Aden cannon wih |
| Maximum speed: At sea level with maximum | 150 rounds; five external pylons with |
| AAM load 1185km/h (736mph) | provision for AIM-9 Sidewinder, AIM-120 |
| Range: 185km (115 miles) | AMRAAM, and two Harpoon for Sea Eagle |
| Service ceiling: 15,545m (51,000ft) | anti-shipping missiles, up to a total of |
| Dimensions: span 7.7m (25ft 3in); length | 3629kg (8000lb) load |

## Specifications

Crew: 4

Powerplant: 3 x 1725kW (2312hp) Rolls-Royce
Turbomeca RTM322-01 turboshafts

Maximum speed: 309km/h (192mph)

Range: 1389km (863 miles)

Service ceiling: 4575m (15,000ft)

Dimensions: Rotor diameter 18.59m (61ft 0in);

length 22.81m (74ft 10in); height 6.65m
(21ft 10in)

Weight: 15,600kg (32,188lb) loaded

Armament: Five general purpose machine guns
(GPMG's); 960kg (2116lb) anti-ship missile
load, plus up to four homing torpedoes, depth
charges and rockets

### ▼ AgustaWestland (EH Industries) Merlin HM.Mk 1

#### HMS Norfolk, *1990*

The Merlin illustrated is the fifth pre-production aircraft, PP5, first flown in
October 1989 and which was used for early trials work aboard the frigate HMS
*Norfolk*, and later *Iron Duke*. It was fitted with full Merlin avionics and was also
used for sonobuoy and Stingray torpedo trials and was the second test airframe
for the RTM322. The operational Merlin began to be
delivered to the Royal Navy in December 1998, initially
equipping No. 700M NAS, an intensive flying trials unit.

is the Merlin HM.Mk 1, equipped with an
active/passive deployable array sonar, active/passive
sonobuoys, Stingray torpedoes and Mk 11 depth
charges. For surface search, the Merlin is equipped
with Blue Kestrel radar and an electro-
optical/infrared sensor turret. The Merlin entered
service in 1998, with 44 being procured for the FAA.

Survivors are to be upgraded to Merlin HM.Mk 2
standard by 2013, with updated cockpit, enhanced
mission systems and machine-gun. As the Merlin's
importance has increased, the last of the Sea King
HAS.Mk 6 helicopters were retired in 2010.

In order to complement the Merlin in the ASW
role, carriers can also embark the Westland Lynx,

### ▶ AgustaWestland Merlin HM.Mk 1

Reflecting the expanding
mission profile of the Merlin
HM.Mk 1, a boarding team
from the Type 23 frigate HMS
*Monmouth* performs a fast-
rope insertion on the flight
deck of a US Navy destroyer. In
the ASW role the Merlin
superseded the Sea King
HAS.Mk 6, and will eventually
replace both airborne early
warning and assault transport
versions of the Sea King.
Unlike the Sea King, the
compact Merlin can be
embarked in frigates.

## Specifications

Crew: 1

Powerplant: 1 x 96.7kN (21,750lbf) Rolls-Royce
Pegasus vectored-thrust turbofan

Maximum speed: 1065km/h (661mph)

Range: 277km (172 miles)

Service ceiling: 15,240m (50,000ft)

Dimensions: span 9.25m (30ft 4in); length
14.36m (47ft 1.5in); height 3.55m (11ft

7.75in)

Weight: 14,061kg (31,000lb) loaded

Armament: Provision for up to 4082kg (9000lb)
(short take-off) or 3175kg (7000lb) (vertical
take-off) of stores, including LAU-5003 rocket
pods, AIM-9 Sidewinder air-to-air missiles,
AGM-65 Maverick missiles and Paveway
laser-guided bombs

### ▼ BAe Harrier GR.Mk 7

**No. 4 Squadron, RAF, 1993**

After successful Harrier GR.Mk 3 operations from *Hermes* in the Falklands, and
successive exercises in 1984 and 1987, the RAF Harrier returned to carrier decks
in the form of the much more capable GR.Mk 7 variant. A first deck landing by the
type was recorded in June 1994, and regular deployments began
in late 1997.

typically used as a weapons platform to support the
Merlin's sensors. The Lynx is also used in the
Helicopter Delivery Service, transporting personnel
and spare parts, and for anti-surface warfare, armed
with a machine-gun and Sea Skua anti-ship missiles.
The latest variant of the Lynx is the HMA.Mk 8
Saturn, which will eventually be replaced by the all-
new Wildcat HM.Mk 1, first flown in 2009. At least
28 Wildcats will be provided for the FAA, becoming
operational in 2015.

Previously, the Harrier was expected to remain in
UK service until 2018. At one time it was expected that
all Harriers would be replaced by the Joint Combat
Aircraft, as the F-35 JSF is known in British parlance.
The JSFs were to operate from two new, large-deck
carriers, developed under the Future Aircraft Carrier
(CVF) programme, and likely to be named HMS
*Queen Elizabeth* and *Prince of Wales*. Unexpectedly, the
2010 Strategic Defence and Security Review (SDSR)
saw the Joint Force Harrier disbanded in December

2010, and HMS *Ark Royal* paid off with immediate
effect. By now, the JFH was operating the latest Harrier
GR.Mk 9 version, which equipped Nos 1 and 4
Squadrons and the Naval Strike Wing, No. 800 NAS.
This ultimate Harrier version incorporated provision
for the Paveway IV laser-guided bomb, Digital Joint
Reconnaissance Pod and Sniper targeting pod.

A final Harrier launch was made from the deck of
*Ark Royal* in November 2010, before the carrier
completed a final voyage, arriving back in
Portsmouth in December for decommissioning.

The SDSR decisions left a single carrier, HMS
*Illustrious*, in service, and this is now dedicated to
helicopter operations. The Royal Navy is already well
versed in helicopter operations from carriers, and
began to embark the Army Air Corps Apache
AH.Mk 1 attack helicopter in 2004–05, with the first
shipborne trials aboard the helicopter carrier HMS

## Specifications

Commissioned: 11 July 1980

Decommissioned: 3 August 2005

Displacement: 22,000 tons loaded

Length: 210m (689ft)

Beam: 36m (118.1ft)

Draught: 8.8m (28.9ft)

Propulsion: 4 x Rolls-Royce Olympus TM3B gas
turbines providing 75MW (97,000hp)

Speed: 52km/h (28 knots), 33km/h (18 knots)
cruising

Range: 13,000km at 33km/h (7000 nautical
miles at 18 knots)

Complement: 1051 (total); 726 Ship's
company; 384 Air Group personnel

Armament: 1 x Sea Dart SAM launcher with 22
missiles; 2 x 20mm (.79in) Phalanx CIWS, 2 x
single 20mm (.79in) AA guns

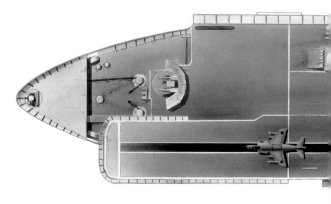

*Ocean*, followed by operations aboard *Ark Royal* from 2006. Other helicopter types increasingly embarked in carriers are the RAF Chinook and the Sea King HC.Mk 4, the latter a dedicated commando assault transport. All three types can be embarked during amphibious assault operations.

In addition to the assault ship *Ocean*, the sole vessel in its class, the Royal Navy fielded two landing platform docks in 2001, HMS *Albion* and *Bulwark*. While *Ocean* can accommodate 12 medium helicopters and six attack helicopters, the LPDs can each operate two helicopters at a time, with a third aircraft parked.

Once expected to acquire 138–150 JSFs, the UK will now purchase just 66 of the F-35C carrier variant rather than the previously planned STOVL F-35B. The two new carriers escaped the 2010 cuts, but although the first carrier will be equipped with catapult and arrester gear, the second will be kept in 'extended readiness', going into mothballs on completion. The move to the F-35C should ensure increased interoperability with the US and France, and the UK will eventually embark 12 F-35Cs on one CVF, which is due to enter service around 2020.

### Future rotorcraft

Other proposed new equipment includes the Maritime Airborne Surveillance and Control (MASC) programme, in which the Merlin will receive the Sea King ASaC.Mk 7 mission system and radar, to replace the Sea King in this role. The ASaC Merlin will also be joined by 27 former RAF Merlin HC.Mk 3s that will be transferred to the Royal Navy and adapted for shipborne operations. These helicopters will replace the Sea King HC.Mk 4 with the Commando Helicopter Force.

| 'Invincible' class air group development | |
|---|---|
| *Cold War ASW, circa 1980* | |
| Sea Harrier FRS.Mk 1 | 4–5 |
| Sea King HAS.Mk 5 | 9 |
| | |
| *Falklands War, 1982* | |
| Sea Harrier FRS.Mk 1 | 8 |
| Sea King HAS.Mk 5 | 9 |
| | |
| *Standard ASW, 1990s* | |
| Sea Harrier FA.Mk 2 | 8 |
| Sea King HAS.Mk 6 | 9 |
| Sea King AEW.Mk 2/2A | 3 |
| | |
| *Post-Cold War force projection, 2000s* | |
| Sea Harrier FA.Mk 2 | 8 |
| Harrier GR.Mk 7 | 8 |
| Sea King AEW.Mk 7 | 4 |
| Sea King HAS.Mk 6 | 2 |
| | |
| *Multi-mission, 2010 (Exercise Auriga)* | |
| Harrier GR.Mk 9A | 6 |
| Merlin HM.Mk 1 | 5 |
| Sea King ASaC.Mk 7 | 2 |
| Lynx HAS.Mk 3SGM | 2 |

▼ **HMS *Invincible* (R05)**

The lead ship of the 'Invincible' class is seen with Sea Harrier FRS.Mk 1s and Sea Kings spotted on deck. The armament includes the initial Sea Dart surface-to-air missile launcher, which later gave way to an enlarged and raised ski jump.

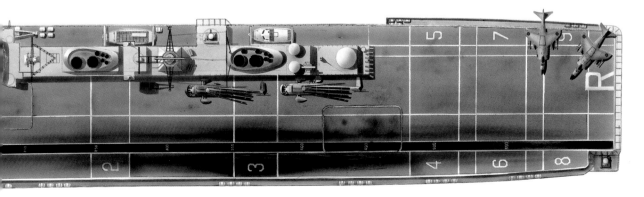

# United States

## 1990–PRESENT

**With its force of carriers one of the most visible signifiers of its military might, the US relies on carrier-based airpower and amphibious air assault assets for a range of global missions.**

SHORTLY AFTER THE end of the Cold War, the US Navy's carrier fleet found itself involved in America's largest military action since Vietnam. After Iraq's invasion of Kuwait in August 1990, US Navy carriers were soon on the scene, and by the time that Coalition air operations began in January 1991, six US Navy carriers were on station, four in the Red Sea and two in the Persian Gulf.

The Desert Storm campaign marked the final combat missions for the A-6 and A-7, as the F/A-18 emerged as the pre-eminent US Navy attack platform. Final operators of the venerable Intruder were VA-75 and VA-196, which gave up their last A-6Es in March 1997. The last two A-7E operators were VA-46 and VA-72, decommissioned in March 1991, immediately after they had seen their last action in the Gulf.

After Desert Storm, US Navy carriers remained on hand in order to police the Southern Watch no-fly zone over southern Iraq, before USS *Enterprise* and *Carl Vinson* launched air strikes against Iraq once more during the four-day Operation Desert Fox

offensive in December 1998. Desert Fox saw attack missions flown by both F/A-18Cs and F-14As, the latter having assumed an offensive role after surviving examples were equipped with 'Bombcat' software to add a new conventional attack capability. Meanwhile, the improved F/A-18C variant entered production in 1987, with deliveries following in 1989. A total of 137 of these variants were completed, major changes including a more expansive stores management and armament system, a more powerful mission computer and revised electronic warfare equipment.

### War in Yugoslavia

US Navy carrier aircraft were back in action over the Balkans during the 1990s. During Operation Deny Flight, US Navy aircraft operating from carriers in the Adriatic helped enforce the no-fly zone over Bosnia. The air campaign culminated in the attacks on Serbian targets prosecuted during Operation Allied Force during the Kosovo crisis in 1999. Once again, F/A-18Cs and F-14As, from USS *Theodore Roosevelt*, were responsible for most carrier-borne

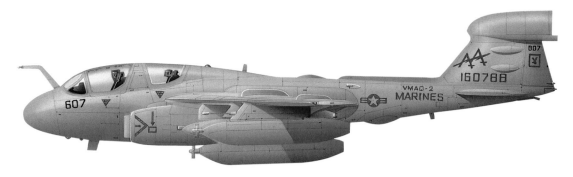

## Specifications

| | |
|---|---|
| Crew: 2 | Dimensions: span 16.15m (53ft 0in); length |
| Powerplant: 2 x 49.8kN (11,200lbf) Pratt & | 18.24m (59ft 0in); height 4.95m (16ft 3in) |
| Whitney J52-P-408 turbojets | Weight: 29,484kg (65,000lb) loaded |
| Maximum speed: 982km/h (610mph) | Armament: None on early models; retrofitted |
| Range: 1769km (1099 miles) | with external hardpoints for four or six AGM- |
| Service ceiling: 11,580m (38,000ft) | 88 HARM air-to-surface anti-radar missiles |

▲ **Northrop Grumman EA-6B Prowler**

*VMAQ-2, USS America, 1990*

This ICAP II Prowler was operated by VMAQ-2 of the US Marine Corps during operations against Libya in the late 1980s. The ICAP II variant incorporated improvements to the underwing jamming pods, allowing different frequency bands to be jammed simultaneously. The ICAP II version was also the first to add up to four AGM-88 HARM missiles, the Prowler's only offensive weapon.

## Specifications

Crew: 2

Powerplant: 2 x 49.8kN (11,200lbf) Pratt
& Whitney J52-P-408 turbojets

Maximum speed: 982km/h (610mph)

Range: 1769km (1099 miles)

Service ceiling: 11,580m (38,000ft)

Dimensions: span 16.15m (53ft 0in); length
18.24m (59ft 10in); height 4.95m (16ft 3in)

Weight: 29,484kg (65,000lb) loaded

Armament: A maximum load of 6804kg
(15,000lb) of offensive weapons carried on
four underwing hardpoints and one
centreline hardpoint

### ▼ Grumman KA-6D Intruder

#### VA-35, USS Saratoga, 1991–92

Wearing the 'Black Panthers' insignia of VA-35, this KA-6D tanker carries a typical
load of four external fuel tanks, plus a buddy refuelling store on the centreline
pylon. The latter was used in addition to the internal hose-and-drogue system,
which was located in the rear ventral position. The KA-6D also retained its
bombing capability, although the DIANE
equipment was deleted, limiting it to
daylight attack operations.

strikes, including suppression of enemy air defences, and aircraft operating from this carrier eventually recorded over 3000 combat sorties. By the late 1990s, the carrier air wing had evolved to include a squadron of 14 F-14s for air defence and strike escort, and three squadrons each of 12 F/A-18C/Ds for offensive missions (typically including one squadron provided by the US Marine Corps). A squadron of four E-2Cs provided airborne early warning and battle management capabilities, while a four-aircraft squadron of EA-6Bs served in the electronic protection role.

A four-aircraft squadron of S-3s provided surveillance, surface attack and in-flight refuelling capabilities. Lastly, a helicopter component consisted of a squadron of four SH-60Fs for ASW and a pair of HH-60Hs for plane-guard and special forces support. Carrier on-board delivery remained the preserve of the two assigned C-2As. It was with component structure similar to this that the US Navy provided a contribution to the invasion of Iraq in 2003, under Operation Iraqi Freedom.

By the turn of the century, the nuclear-powered carrier was dominant, with nine of the 12-carrier force being provided by CVNs. The major change in the composition of carrier air wings in the early 21st century has been the introduction of the Boeing F/A-18 Super Hornet, which has taken over some of the attack burden from the 'legacy' Hornet as well as replacing the F-14 in the fleet air defence role. The new century has also seen the emergence of a new class of nuclear-powered carrier, the 'Gerald R. Ford'

class, beginning with the name ship of the class, CVN-78, which will enter service in 2015.

The last of the F-14s included the definitive F-14D version, of which only 37 were completed. Compared to the F-14B, the F-14D added digital avionics, with the original AN/AWG-9 radar being upgraded to AN/APG-71 standard. The cockpit was compatible with night vision goggles, and new ejection seats were installed. The F-14D entered service in 1990 and was joined by a total of 18 F-14A jets that were upgraded to the same standard. Pending the availability of the ultimate F-14D model, an interim F-14A+ was fielded, before its designation

### Typical US Navy carrier air wing, Operation Desert Storm

| Carrier Air Wing 3 CVW 3 | |
|---|---|
| USS John F. Kennedy (CV-67) | 'Kitty Hawk' class |
| August 1990–March 1991 | |
| VF-14 | F-14A Tomcat |
| VF-32 | F-14A Tomcat |
| VA-75 | A-6E/KA-6D Intruder |
| VA-46 | A-7E Corsair II |
| VA-72 | A-7E Corsair II |
| VAQ-130 | EA-6B Prowler |
| VAW-126 | E-2C Hawkeye |
| HS-7 | SH-3H Sea King |
| VS-22 | S-3B Viking |

## Specifications

Crew: 1

Powerplant: 1 x 64.5kN (14,500lbf) Allison
TF41-A-2 turbofan

Maximum speed: 1123km/h (698mph)

Range: 1127km (700 miles)

Dimensions: span 11.81m (38ft 9in);
length 14.06m (46ft 1.5in); height 4.90m
(16ft 0.75in)

Weight: 19,050kg (42,000lb) loaded

Armament: One 20mm (.79in) M61 Vulcan

6-barreled Gatling cannon; four LAU-10
rocket pods for 127mm (5in) Mk 32 Zuni
rockets; two AIM-9 Sidewinder AAM, two AGM-
45 Shrike Anti-radiation missiles (ARM), two
AGM-62 Walleye TV-guided glide bombs, two
AGM-65 Mavericks, two AGM-88 HARM, two
GBU-8 electro-optically guided glide bombs;
up to 30 x 227kg (500lb) Mark 82 bombs or
Mark 80 series of unguided bombs; up to four
B28/B57/B61 nuclear bombs

### ▼ Vought A-7E Corsair II

*VA-72, USS* John F. Kennedy, *1991*

This A-7E is depicted as it appeared during Desert Storm, the Corsair II's combat swansong. The aircraft carries AGM-88 HARMs and Sidewinders for self defence. This particular aircraft, replete with mission markings on the nose, was flown by the executive officer of VA-72, Commander John Leenhouts. The squadron was assigned to CVW 3, alongside VA-46.

was changed to F-14B in 1991. The F-14B included the new General Electric F101 engine, improved cockpit displays, modified radar and other changes. The 'B' model served with five front-line squadrons of the Atlantic Fleet.

Another Tomcat variant was the F-14A(TARPS) with the Tactical Air Reconnaissance Pod System, which saw active service during Desert Storm. The original F-14A was withdrawn in 2003, leaving the F-14B and D to see out the Tomcat's service. Demonstrating its continued value, the F-14 was active to the last, with a last combat mission (and bomb drop) flown over Iraq in February 2006, by a pair of Tomcats from USS *Theodore Roosevelt*. On their return from combat operations, the last two front-line units, VF-31 and VF-213, retired their Tomcats, to resume service as Super Hornet operators.

With the retirement of the F-14 in 2006, the F/A-18 has been the US Navy's only front-line strike fighter. The Super Hornet has also assumed the in-flight refuelling role from the S-3B, when it began providing tanker capacity to the air wing in 2004. The Super Hornet began life as an evolutionary improvement of the 'legacy' Hornet, and a development contract was signed in 1992.

The first prototype, a single-seat F/A-18E, took to the air in 1995, and initial orders were placed a year later for both F/A-18Es and two-seat F/A-18Fs. Compared with its predecessor, the E/F boasts larger

wings, a stretched fuselage and engines of increased thrust. Successive orders have seen the US Navy sign up for a total fleet 515 F/A-18E/Fs, and 114 of the related EA-18G electronic warfare variant.

In terms of mission capability, the Super Hornet adds additional weapons stations, for a total of 11, and incorporates radar-absorbing materials and redesigned engine intakes to reduce its radar signature. An advanced electronic warfare self protection system is included, and weapons options are expanded. VFA-115 took the Super Hornet on its first operational cruise aboard USS *Abraham Lincoln* in 2001.

### Hornet upgrades

The 'legacy' Hornet continues to serve alongside the F/A-18E/F, and an upgrade programme has produced the F/A-18C+ configuration. This includes the Joint Helmet-Mounted Cueing System (JHMCS) and AIM-9X Sidewinder missiles, Multifunctional Information Distribution System (MIDS), colour cockpit displays, digital moving map, and revised countermeasures. Structural modifications are also made in order to extend service life. In order to wring some further operational use out of the F/A-18A, the F/A-18A+ upgrade was applied to 35 US Navy and 61 US Marine Corps aircraft in 2000–01. These jets were taken from the US Navy and Marine Corps Reserve and received C-model avionics, allowing them to employ precision-guided munitions and the AIM-120 AMRAAM air-to-air missile.

The S-3B Viking switched successfully from the Cold War ASW mission to emerge as a versatile sea control platform. During Desert Shield, the build-up to the 1991 Gulf War, S-3Bs undertook electronic surveillance missions in order to establish the electronic order of battle. During Desert Storm, they expanded their repertoire, attacking surface vessels, land-based air defence targets and launching decoys in support of strike packages. After service over the former Yugoslavia and again in Iraq in 2003, the S-3 made its final deployment in 2008 and the last front-line squadron was deactivated in 2009. After completing the type's final cruise aboard USS *George Washington*, the US Navy deployed four VS-22 S-3Bs to Al Asad AB in Iraq in July 2008. By this stage in the aircraft's career, its assigned role was intelligence, surveillance and reconnaissance, for which the Viking was equipped with AN/AAQ-25 LANTIRN targeting pods. VS-22, the final front-line S-3B operator, home-ported at NAS Jacksonville, Florida, deactivated in January 2009. Towards the end of its career the Viking was also adapted for intelligence gathering, when 16 S-3A airframes were converted to ES-3A Shadow standard. These aircraft served between 1993 and 1996 and saw their combat debut during Operation Deliberate Force over Bosnia in 1997. Another important role for the S-3B was as the US Navy's sole carrier-based in-flight refuelling tanker between the retirement of the final KA-6Ds in 1995, and the appearance of the Super Hornet.

The Super Hornet provides the basis for the US Navy's latest carrier-based jet, the EA-18G Growler. This will eventually replace the EA-6B in the electronic warfare role. The first unit to begin the transition to the EA-18G started to re-equip in January 2009. Ultimately, the last EA-6Bs should be retired from the front-line inventory by 2013. Using the airframe of the F/A-18F, the EA-18G adds the Prowler's existing AN/ALQ-99 radar jamming pods. Three such pods are normally carried, plus AMRAAM and HARM missiles.

AN/ALQ-218(V)2 antennae are carried in wingtip pods and around the fuselage, these again being adapted from systems used in the latest EA-6B Improved Capability (ICAP) III. The EA-18G's existing electronic warfare suite will in future be replaced by a new Next Generation Jammer. The Growler began operational testing in October 2008 and saw its combat debut with VAQ-132 during Operation 'Odyssey Dawn' over Libya in early 2011, the aircraft operating from land bases.

### ▼ Boeing (McDonnell Douglas) F/A-18C Hornet

**VFA-87, late 1990s**

Assigned to CVW 8, VFA-87 'Golden Warriors' first went to sea with the F/A-18C in March 1993, aboard USS *Theodore Roosevelt* (CVN-71), having previously operated the F/A-18A and A-7E. In 1993, the squadron supported Operations Deny Flight, Provide Comfort and Southern Watch, and in August 1995, aircraft from the unit were the first to strike Bosnian-Serb targets during Operation Deliberate Force. More recently, the squadron has seen active service in Operation Enduring Freedom in Afghanistan, and Operation Iraqi Freedom.

| Specifications | |
|---|---|
| Crew: 1 | Armament: One 20mm (.79in) M61 Vulcan |
| Powerplant: 2 x 48.9kN (11,000lbf) General | nose mounted 6-barreled Gatling cannon; |
| Electric F404-GE-402 turbofans | Rockets: Two 70mm (.75in) Hydra 70 rockets, |
| Maximum speed: 1915km/h (1189mph) | 127mm (5in) Zuni rockets |
| Range: 2000km (1250 miles) | Missiles: Provision for four AIM-9 Sidewinder, |
| Service ceiling: 15,240m (50,000ft) | four AIM-120 AMRAAM missiles; plus JDAM |
| Dimensions: span 12.3m (40ft 0in); length | precision-guided munition and Paveway laser |
| 17.1m (56ft 0in); height 4.7m (15ft 4in) | guided bombs |
| Weight: 16,770kg (36,970lb) loaded | |

The Prowler fleet has been active since the 1991 Gulf War, when it was a primary provider of electronic warfare support, as well as using its own HARM missiles to attack enemy air defence sites. In order to maintain the EA-6B's credibility until replaced by the Growler, the US Navy embarked on the ICAP III programme, based around upgrades to the AN/ALQ-99 radar jamming equipment.

### ▼ Lockheed S-3B Viking

**VS-24, USS John F. Kennedy, 1997**

Illustrated with undercarriage deployed, and with external fuel tanks underwing, this VS-24 Viking was the squadron's colourfully marked 'CAG bird'. VS-24 was the first unit to employ the Viking in combat, during Operation Desert Storm. The S-3B model added an improved forward-looking infrared sensor, enhanced radar and upgraded electronic support measures (ESM).

The airborne early warning role is also in the process of renewal, with the latest E-2Ds due to replace the current E-2C. Prior to fielding the all-new E-2D Advanced Hawkeye, the US Navy has been upgrading existing E-2Cs, with an ongoing programme of replacing avionics and electronics systems. This has resulted in four primary versions of the Hawkeye. The baseline standard is the E-2C+, while the E-2C Nav Upgrade features an improved navigation system and computer interface. The HE2K (Hawkeye 2000) brings improved avionics and computer-processing. Finally, the MCU-ACIS

### Specifications

| | |
|---|---|
| Crew: 4 | Dimensions: span 20.6m (68ft 8in); length |
| Powerplant: 2 x 41kN (9275lbf) General | 16m (53ft 4in); height 6.9m (22ft 9in) |
| Electric TF-34-GE-400B turbofan engines | Weight: 23,643kg (52,539lb) loaded |
| Maximum speed: 828.8km/h (518mph) | Armament: Up to 1781kg (3958lb) of AGM-84 |
| Range: 4232km (2645 miles) | Harpoon or AGM-65 Maverick missiles, |
| Service ceiling: 12,465m (40,900ft) | torpedoes, mines, rockets or bombs |

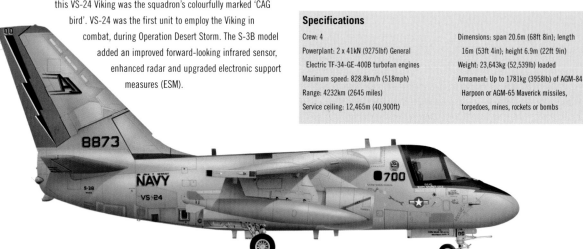

### Specifications

| | |
|---|---|
| Crew: 4 | Service ceiling: 10,363m (34,000ft) |
| Powerplant: 2 x 41kN (9275lbf) General | Dimensions: span 20.97m (68ft 8in); length |
| Electric TF34-GE-2 | 16.28m (53ft 4in); height 6.98m (22ft 9in) |
| Maximum speed: 833km/h (517mph) | Weight: 17,100kg (37,700lb) loaded |
| Range: 5121km (3182 miles) | Armament: none |

### ▼ Lockheed ES-3A Shadow

**VQ-5, USS Kitty Hawk, 1998**

Until its retirement on financial grounds in 1999, the ES-3A provided the carrier air wing with an organic electronic and communications gathering capability, and was outfitted for the task with advanced electronic surveillance and communications equipment, in addition to the standard AN/APS-137 radar and AN/ALR-76 ESM equipment. VQ-5 'Sea Shadows' was the West Coast operator of the ES-3A.

▲ **Northrop Grumman E-2C Hawkeye**

*VAW-126, USS* John F. Kennedy, *1995*

This VAW-126 'Seahawks' E-2C is illustrated with landing gear deployed, and as it appeared when operating as 'CAG bird' from USS *John F. Kennedy* (CV-67) in the early 1990s. By this time, the Hawkeye was operating in the Group II standard, with the AN/APS-145 Advanced Radar Processing System, improved computer processing, Link 16 and the Tactical Aircraft Mission Planning System (TAMPS).

**Specifications**

| | |
|---|---|
| Crew: 5 | Service ceiling: 9100m (30,000ft) |
| Powerplant: 2 x 3800kW (5093hp) Allison T56- | Dimensions: span 24.59m (80ft 7in); length |
| A-425 or -427 turboprop engines | 17.56m (57ft 7in); height 5.6m (18ft 3in) |
| Maximum speed: 552km/h (375mph) | Weight: 18,090kg (40,200lb) loaded |
| Range: 2824km (1525 miles) | Armament: none |

features the HE2K combat information system combined with the Nav Upgrade platform. All these 'legacy' E-2C variants use the AN/APS-145 radar system. A further Hawkeye upgrade adds new eight-bladed propellers, via the NP2000.

## Advanced Hawkeye

The E-2D made its first flight in August 2007, and the type will be better suited to the overland surveillance and battle management command and control missions, as well as the traditional airborne early warning role. The US Navy should receive 70 E-2Ds, the primary sensor of which is the AN/APY-9 multi-mode radar system. The first fleet squadron to receive the E-2D will likely be VAW-125 in 2013. Often overlooked, the C-2A Greyhound remains in service in the important carrier onboard delivery (COD) role. Indeed, such was the demand placed on the fleet of 17 production aircraft that follow-on orders were placed for a further 39 C-2As up to 1990. Outwardly similar to the original batch, the 'new' C-2As feature modernized avionics, more powerful T56-A-425 turboprops, structural improvements and a new auxiliary power unit.

## Joint Strike Fighter

The F/A-18A/C 'legacy' Hornet will be replaced by the F-35C carrier variant of the Lightning II Joint Strike Fighter, which is scheduled to achieve initial operational capability in 2016. Ultimately, 18 squadrons of F-35Cs will serve alongside 22 squadrons of F/A-18E/Fs, and 10 of EA-18Gs. In the meantime, the typical carrier air wing in 2011 incorporated one squadron of 11 F/A-18Fs, one squadron of 11 F/A-18Es, and two squadrons each of 11 F/A-18A+ or F/A-18C (sometimes including one USMC unit). Electronic warfare requirements were handled by four EA-6Bs or five EA-18Gs, while four E-2Cs served in the airborne early warning and control role. One squadron of 11 MH-60Rs and one squadron of eight MH-60S provided the rotary-wing component, while two C-2As were also attached, for a total of 67 or 68 aircraft.

The F-35C is the carrier version of the tri-service JSF, and the initial example, CF-1, was the last of the three variants to be rolled out, and made its maiden flight in June 2010. The carrier version is significantly different to the F-35 for the United States Air Force, with a wing of increased area, and strengthened undercarriage to cope with the rigours of carrier deck operations.

With the continuing war in Afghanistan, the US Navy has maintained a carrier on station in the Arabian Sea to support International Security Assistance Force (ISAF) troops. Typically, Carrier Strike Groups are rotated through the theatre every

## Specifications

**Crew:** 1

**Powerplant:** Two x 97.90kN (22,000lbf) thrust
General Electric F414-GE-400 afterburning
turbofan engines

**Maximum speed:** 1900km/h (1190mph)

**Range:** 722km (449 miles)

**Service ceiling:** 15,000m (50,000ft)

**Dimensions:** span 13.62m (60ft 1in); length
13.62m (44ft 9in); height 4.88m (16ft)

**Weight:** 29,900kg (66,000lb) loaded

**Armament:** One 20mm (.79in) M61A1 Vulcan
cannon; 11 external hardpoints for up to
8050kg (17,750lb) of ordnance

### ▼ Boeing F/A-18E Super Hornet
*VFA-122, NAS Leemore, 2003*

VFA-122 was the initial training unit for the Super Hornet and the first US Navy
unit to receive the type. The 'Fighting Eagles' is a shore-based outfit, at NAS
Leemore, California, where it serves as a Fleet Replacement Squadron for the
Hornet community. As well as F/A-18E/F Super Hornets, the unit also has 'legacy'
Hornets on strength, and is responsible for
training aviators and maintainers.

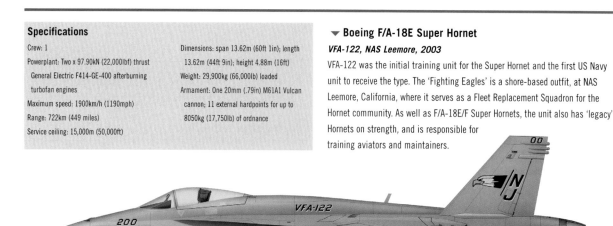

four to six months. Carriers operating in support of
ISAF can expect to launch as many as 70 sorties each
day under the auspices of Operation Enduring
Freedom, a single carrier being responsible for
between 30 and 50 per cent of daily air-to-ground
missions directed against insurgents in Afghanistan.

By 2009, the retirement of the US Navy's last
conventional carrier, USS *Kitty Hawk*, left 11
nuclear-powered carriers in service, with 10 'Nimitz'-
class vessels and the USS *Enterprise*. Ultimately, the
US Navy hopes to build 11 new 'Gerald R. Ford'-
class carriers by the middle of this century. Airpower
for the carriers is entrusted to 10 Carrier Strike
Groups (CSG) and Carrier Air Wings (CVW),
divided evenly between the Atlantic and Pacific
Fleets. Once the USS *Enterprise* decommissions at
the end of 2012, nine deployable carriers will remain,
pending the introduction of USS *Gerald R. Ford*.

Together with the emergence of the Super Hornet
as the most important carrier fighter, the US Navy is
in the midst of a programme to reorganize its
helicopter fleet. By the end of the first decade of the
21st century, a CSG typically included 13–15 rotary-
wing aircraft, comprising four SH-60Fs, three HH-
60Hs, four to six SH-60Bs and two MH-60S
helicopters. The Seahawk family had assumed its
position as the key rotary-wing type in US Navy
service as early as 1992, when the last example of the
SH-3D Sea King was retired. The SH-60F was
developed specifically for carrier-based, 'inner zone'
ASW operations, according to the 'CV helo'

requirement. Entering service in 1988, the SH-60F
superseded the SH-3 and carried dipping sonar in
place of the LAMPS III system used in the SH-60B.
The SH-60F first saw fleet service with HS-2 aboard
USS *Nimitz* in 1991.

Flown for the first time in 1988, the HH-60H was
a specialist search and rescue version of the Seahawk,
and could also be used to support special forces
operations. For its intended role, all ASW equipment
was removed, and a pair of machine-guns added for
self-defence. In addition, the electronic warfare
systems were improved, and additional fuel was
included. The HH-60H entered service with HCS-5

## Typical US Navy carrier air wing, 21st century

| Carrier Air Wing 9 CVW 9 | |
|---|---|
| USS *John C. Stennis* (CVN-74) | 'Nimitz' class |
| January 2009–July 2009, North Arabian Sea | |
| VFA-154 | F/A-18F Super Hornet |
| VMFA-323 | F/A-18C Hornet |
| VFA-146 | F/A-18C Hornet |
| VFA-147 | F/A-18E Super Hornet |
| VAQ-138 | EA-6B Prowler |
| VAW-112 | E-2C Hawkeye 2000 |
| HSC-8 | MH-60S Seahawk |
| HSM-71 | MH-60R Seahawk |
| VRC-30 (Det 4) | C-2A Greyhound |

▲ **Boeing (McDonnell Douglas) F/A-18C Hornet**
An F/A-18C Hornet assigned to the 'Ragin' Bulls' of VFA-37 launches from the USS *Harry S. Truman* (CVN-75), with three external fuel tanks and (empty) multiple ejector racks. Despite the arrival of the more capable Super Hornet, most carrier air wings will retain two squadrons of 'legacy' Hornets until the arrival of the F-35C Lightning II from 2016.

in 1989. In 2008 the composition of the carrier-assigned helicopters was rationalized as part of the US Navy Helicopter Master Plan, through the introduction of the new MH-60R and MH-60S helicopters, which are assigned directly to a CVW.

Where previously a single Helicopter Anti-Submarine Squadron (HS) would be supported by a number of detachments from Helicopter Anti-Submarine Squadrons Light (HSL), the CSG now calls upon a single Helicopter Maritime Strike Squadron (HSM), equipped with 11 MH-60Rs. Five of these helicopters normally operate from the carrier, with the remainder detached to other surface combatants. With the shift to HSM, the MH-60R is replacing the SH-60F/HH-60H of the Helicopter Anti-Submarine Squadrons as well as the SH-60B of the Helicopter Anti-Submarine Squadrons Light.

The HSM is complemented by another new type of unit, the Helicopter Sea Combat Squadron (HSC), which provides eight MH-60S helicopters. This new type has now entirely replaced the CH-46s

and UH-3s previously used in the role by the former Helicopter Combat Support Squadrons (HC). The HSC is a multi-role formation and as such can undertake search and rescue, combat search and rescue, logistics support, vertical replenishment and special forces support.

Reflecting the increasing importance of asymmetric warfare, the HSC is also expected to undertake anti-surface warfare and airborne mine countermeasures work. Since their logistics support role is central to their work, the HSC also deploys some of its aircraft (typically two) aboard an accompanying logistic support ship.

The Block III version of the MH-60S is the first to offer a robust strike capability, with stub wings that can carry up to eight AGM-114 Hellfire air-to-surface missiles, rockets and gun pods. A 7.62mm (.3in) GAU-17 Minigun can also be fitted to the door to provide suppressive fire. The new-look US Navy helicopter fleet will include 10 HSC and 10 HSM squadrons to be assigned to the 10 deployable CVWs by 2013.

A final US Navy carrier type was the single mine countermeasures support ship, USS *Inchon*, originally completed as an 'Iwo Jima' class helicopter carriers (LPH). In 1996 the ship emerged after a comprehensive refit, allowing it to embark a squadron of MH-53Es for the mine-countermeasures

## Specifications

Crew: 2

Powerplant: 1 x 120kN (27,000lbf) General
Electric F110-GE-400 turbofans

Maximum speed: 1988km/h (1241mph)

Range: 1994km (1239 miles)

Service ceiling: 16,150m (53,000ft)

Dimensions: span 19.55m (64ft 1.5in); length
19.1m (62ft 8in); height 4.88m (16ft)

Weight: 33,724kg (74,349lb) loaded

Armament: One 20mm (.79in) M61A1 Vulcan
rotary cannon with 675 rounds; external
pylons for a combination of AIM-7 Sparrow
medium range air-to-air missiles, AIM-9
medium range air-to-air missiles, and AIM-
54A/B/C Phoenix long range air-to-air
missiles

### ▼ Grumman F-14D Tomcat
#### VF-2, 1996

Depicted with a full air defence load-out of four AIM-54s under the fuselage, and a pair of AIM-7s and two AIM-9 missiles on the glove pylons, this F-14D is seen in the subdued colours of VF-2, which began to re-equip with this ultimate variant of the Tomcat in 1995. After transitioning to the F-14D, the 'Bounty Hunters' were assigned to the newly refurbished USS *Constellation* (CV-64). In July 2003, VF-2 was officially re-commissioned as VFA-2, thus beginning transition training to the F/A-18F Super Hornet.

mission. US Navy-operated, the MH-53E Sea Dragon is equipped with minesweeping gear, and eight of these helicopters were normally embarked aboard *Inchon*, before it decommissioned in 2002. Ultimately, the MH-53E is planned to make way for the versatile MH-60S in the airborne mine countermeasures role. When the 'Sierra' is adapted for the MCS role, the helicopter may also be based on the US Navy's new Littoral Combat Ships.

## Marine aviation

Second only to the carriers in terms of airpower capabilities are the US Navy's force of 'big-deck' amphibious assault ships. With the last of the helicopter carriers decommissioned in 1998, the US Navy has, since 2001, maintained 12 LHAs and LHDs as the centrepieces of a similar number of amphibious ready groups. By June 2001, seven 'Wasp'-class LHDs were in service alongside five 'Tawara'-class LHAs, although both types offer similar capabilities in terms of the air components. By the turn of the new century, the Aviation Combat Element (ACE) of each Marine Expeditionary Unit (MEU) comprised a reinforced squadron of 18 CH-46Es, augmented by four CH-53Es, four AH-1Ws, three UH-1Ns and six AV-8Bs.

While previously the Medium Helicopter Squadron (HMM) squadrons with their CH-46Es formed the backbone of the ACE, the introduction of the revolutionary MV-22B Osprey tilt-rotor means that the Marine Medium Tilt-rotor Squadron

(VMM) is increasingly forming the lynchpin of embarked USMC aviation.

Essentially, each MEU operates as a 'mini-Marine Corps', in which the ACE is one component that operates alongside the Ground Combat Element, the Command Element, and the Logistics Combat Element. The USMC maintains seven MEUs, arranged as three on each coast (the 22nd, 24th and 26th on the East Coast and the 11th, 13th and 15th on the West Coast) plus one forward-deployed in Japan (31st MEU). Each MEU can also utilize two KC-130 Hercules tankers that are usually stationed at their home base.

The MV-22B achieved initial operational capability in June 2007 and later that year made its first operational deployment to Iraq with VMM-263. In May 2009 the same unit made the type's first shipboard deployment as an ACE with the 22nd Marine Expeditionary Unit as part of the USS *Bataan* Expeditionary Strike Group. By 2017, Ospreys will be assigned to 19 active and four reserve squadrons, with two squadrons to convert to the type annually in order to achieve that aim.

Equipped for in-flight refuelling, the Osprey is capable of carrying 18 troops or up to 9072kg (20,000lb) of cargo. Following in the wake of the Osprey, further upgrade for the USMC comes in the shape of the AH-1Z and UH-1Y, replacing the AH-1W and UH-1N, respectively.

Meanwhile, the detachment of HH-46Ds formerly embarked for plane-guard duties have been replaced by the HH-60H and, more recently, the MH-60S.

The 'teeth' of the USMC aviation component is provided by a combined force of around 145 AV-8Bs and 235 F/A-18s. While the Harrier IIs are embarked in LHAs and LHDs, the Hornets make regular deployments aboard US Navy carriers, operating alongside US Navy 'legacy' Hornet units within mixed area air wings. The Marine Corps is the only front-line US operator of the two-seat 'Night Attack' F/A-18D, an all-weather attack aircraft that combines the advances of the F/A-18C together with accommodation for a back-seater who is provided with a fully missionized cockpit. The F/A-18Ds were the last 'legacy' Hornets built for the US military.

## Night attack Harrier

The AV-8B has been subject to a number of important upgrades during its service life. First, the AV-8B Night Attack upgrade that was first flown in 1987 added a forward-looking infrared sensor in a fairing above the nose, while the cockpit was made compatible with night vision goggles.

The AV-8B Harrier II+ was more significant, and was introduced from the 223rd production aircraft, in 1992. The Harrier II+ adds an AN/APG-65 multi-mode radar, while retaining the FLIR. Other changes include a wing outfitted with eight hardpoints. As

well as 27 Harrier II+ aircraft built as new, the modification has been made on existing 'day attack' AV-8Bs. The latest additions to the Harrier II fleet include compatibility with dual-mode laser-guided bombs (DMLGB) and relocation of the Litening targeting pod to the centreline station.

The USMC expects to retain its EA-6Bs until 2019, and these aircraft serve within four squadrons. The aircraft are being upgraded to ICAP III standard. USMC EA-6Bs have also made regular deployments aboard US Navy carriers. With the USMC planning to retain Prowlers longer than the US Navy, it has now begun its own aircrew training on the type.

The cornerstone of future USMC aviation is the F-35B short take-off and vertical landing (STOVL) variant of the Joint Strike Fighter. This is due to replace the existing fleet of F/A-18s, AV-8Bs and EA-6Bs, with a planned 420 aircraft to be acquired. Although the JSF programme has been subject to delay and cost increases, the USMC still aims to introduce the JSF to service with 21 operational squadrons, three fleet readiness squadrons, and one test and evaluation squadron. Depending on the continued progress of the JSF, the USMC could retire the AV-8B in 2021, followed by the F/A-18 in 2023.

The F-35B is the most complex of the three JSF versions, as a result of the Marine Corps' unique

### ▼ Boeing (McDonnell Douglas) AV-8B Harrier II

*VMA-214, 1993*

Seen as it appeared during the early 1990s, this AV-8B is of the Night Attack version, distinguished by the forward-looking infrared sensor above the nose. This aircraft is armed with a pair of AGM-65E Mavericks, two Mk 20 Rockeye II cluster bombs and Sidewinders. The 'Black Sheep' of VMA-214 were the first recipient of the Night Attack AV-8B, in September 1989. Although the unit was not active in Desert Storm, subsequent years saw the squadron take part in Operations Restore Hope, Southern Watch, Iraqi Freedom and Enduring Freedom.

### Specifications

Crew: 1

Powerplant: 1 x 97kN (22,000lbf) Rolls-Royce Pegasus F402-RR-408A turbofan

Maximum speed: 1070km/h (662mph)

Range: 1665km (1035 miles)

Service ceiling: 15,545m (51,000ft)

Dimensions: span 9.25m (30ft 4in); length 14.12m (46ft 4in); height 3.55m (11ft 8in)

Weight: 10,410kg (22,755lb) loaded

Armament: One General Dynamics GAU-12 Equalizer 25mm (.98in) 5-barreled Gatling cannon; six under-wing pylon stations holding up to 5988kg (13,200lb) payload; four LAU-5003 rocket pods (each with 19 CRV7 70mm (2.75in) rockets); four AIM-9 Sidewinder air-to-air missiles; six AGM-65 Maverick air-to-surface missiles; Paveway laser guided bombs or Mk 20 Rockeye II cluster bombs

▲ **Bell AH-1W SuperCobra**

*US Marine Corps, 1991*

Armed with TOW missiles, this SuperCobra, or 'Whiskey' Cobra is seen as it appeared during the 1991 Gulf War, for which a special sand-and-grey paint scheme was applied. A total of 96 new-build AH-1Ws were completed, together with many more conversions from earlier AH-1Ts. As well as the wire-guided TOW, the AH-1W version is capable of deploying the Hellfire, although TOWs and unguided rockets remain favoured for 'softer' targets.

**Specifications**

| | |
|---|---|
| Crew: 2 | 17.7m (58ft); height 4.19m (13ft 9in) |
| Powerplant: 2 x 1300kW (1742hp) General | Weight: 6690kg (14,750lb) loaded |
| Electric T700-GE-401C turboshaft | Armament: One 20mm (.79in) M197 Gatling |
| Maximum speed: 352km/h (218mph) | cannon; seven 70mm (2.75in) Hydra 70 |
| Range: 587km (365 miles) | rockets; eight 127mm (5in) Zuni rockets; |
| Service ceiling: 3720m (12,200ft) | eight TOW missiles; eight AGM-114 Hellfire |
| Dimensions: Rotor diameter 14.6m (48ft); length | missiles; two AIM-9 Sidewinder missiles |

requirement for STOVL capability. Use of a powerplant (either the Pratt & Whitney F135 or General Electric/Rolls-Royce F136 engine) that features an additional lift fan in the mid-fuselage also serves to increase weight, and reduce payload. The F-35B can carry a pair of 454kg (1000lb) stores plus two AMRAAMs internally, compared to the two 907kg (2000lb) weapons that can be carried internally by both the F-35A and C. The first F-35B, BF-1, made its maiden flight in June 2008. Despite progress made since then, the fate of the F-35B remains uncertain, especially with the Marine Corps indicating that it will likely acquire an unknown number of F-35Cs in order to support continued carrier air wing deployments.

## 'Huey' upgrades

Entering service in 1986, the AH-1W SuperCobra was a further development of the AH-1T. The AH-1W saw extensive service during the 1991 Gulf War, and remains the most important version of the AH-1 attack helicopter aboard US Navy assault ships. In addition to a three-barrelled M197 20mm (0.79in) cannon, the AH-1W can carry disposable armament in the form of Hellfire and TOW missiles, and unguided rockets. A wide range of missions fall within the AH-1W's operational spectrum, including close air support, offensive air support, armed escort, forward air control and reconnaissance. The UH-1Y Venom and AH-1Z Viper provide new equipment

for Marine Light Attack Squadrons. The 'Yankee' and 'Zulu' share 84 per cent common parts including four-bladed main and tail rotors and the engines. Much of the airframe is new, and revised avionics include 'glass' cockpits. While the 'Zulu' retains the General Electric T700-401 engines of the AH-1W, the UH-1Y uses more powerful T700-401C engines. Both the UH-1Y and AH-1Z will eventually be cleared to use the Advanced Precision Kill Weapon System, a laser-guided 70mm (2.75in) rocket.

Subject to protracted development, the upgraded UH-1Y attained initial operational capability in August 2008. By January 2009 UH-1Ys of HMLA-267 were embarked in USS *Boxer*, marking the type's first deployment. The USMC ultimately aims to field 160 UH-1Ys within 10 active squadrons and one reserve squadron.

The AH-1Z attack helicopter, which was first flown in December 2000, is being produced via the upgrade of 'Whiskey' Cobras, and is also being manufactured as a new-build. The AH-1Z achieved initial operating capability with HMLA-367 at MCAS Camp Pendleton, California, in February 2011, after the squadron began operating the type in September 2010.

At this stage, plans called for the remanufacture of 131 AH-1W helicopters to AH-1Z configuration plus a further 58 new-build aircraft, providing the Marine Corps with a total of 189 AH-1Zs. The AH-1Z is slated to achieve full operational

## Specifications

Crew: 4

Powerplant: 2 x 1416kW (1900hp) General
Electric T700-GE-401-C engines

Maximum speed: 296km/h (183mph)

Range: 463km (287 miles)

Service ceiling: 3580m (12,000ft)

Dimensions: Rotor diameter 16.4m (53ft 9in);

length 19.8m (64ft 10in); height 3.8m
(12ft 5in)

Weight: 9967kg (21,973lb) loaded

Armament: 7.62mm (.3in) or 12.7mm (.5in)
crew-served machine guns; AGM-114 Hellfire
anti-surface missiles and Mk54 lightweight
torpedoes

### ▼ Sikorsky MH-60R Seahawk

*HSM-71, 2008*

Home-ported at NAS North Island, California, HSM-71 'Raptors' was the US Navy's first operational Helicopter Maritime Strike Squadron, and was established in October 2007. The squadron made its maiden deployment with the *John C. Stennis* Carrier Strike Group in January 2009. Weapons options for the 'Romeo' include torpedoes and Hellfire missiles, the latter seen here carried on the stub pylons.

capability in 2020. Under its latest plans, the USMC will ultimately field 15 AH-1Z Vipers and 12 UH-1Y Venoms within each Light Attack Helicopter Squadron.

The designated replacement for the heavy-lift CH-53E is the CH-53K, development of which was approved in October 2005. Although based on a similar airframe, the CH-53K will offer twice the lift capacity of the CH-53E. The USMC has a

requirement for 200 CH-53Ks, and these are due to replace CH-53D/Es with 10 active duty squadrons, one reserve squadron and one test squadron. The CH-53K is scheduled to achieve initial operational capability in 2017, with full operational capability to follow in 2023. Compared to the CH-53E and previous variants, the latest CH-53K utilizes an advanced structure, with composite cockpit and cabin sections.

## Specifications

Crew: 1 or 2

Powerplant: 2 x 1150kW (1541hp) General
Electric T700-GE-401C turboshaft
engines

Maximum speed: 304km/h (189mph)

Range: 230km (130 miles)

Service ceiling: 6100+m (20,000+ft)

Dimensions: Rotor diameter 14.88m (48ft

10in); length 17.78m (58ft 4in); height 4.5m
(14ft 7in)

Weight: 8390kg (18,500lb) loaded

Armament: Two external stations for 70mm
(2.75in) Hydra 70 rockets; two pintle mounts
for 7.62mm (.3in) M240D machine guns,
12.7mm (.5in) BMG GAU-16/A machine guns,
or 7.62mm (.3in) GAU-17/A Gatling guns

### ▼ Bell UH-1Y Venom

*HMLAT-303, Marine Corps Base Camp Pendleton*

Successor to the UH-1N Twin Huey with the USMC is the 'Yankee', or UH-1Y Venom, which is immediately recognizable on account of its four-bladed main and tail rotors. Stationed at Camp Pendleton, California, Marine Light Attack Training Squadron 303 'Atlas' provides training on the UH-1Y and AH-1Z as part of Marine Aircraft Group 39 (MAG-39) and the 3rd Marine Aircraft Wing (3rd MAW).

# List of Abbreviations

| | | | | |
|---|---|---|---|---|
| AAM | air-to-air missile | | MAW | Marine Aircraft Wing |
| ACE | Aviation Combat Element | | MCAS | Marine Corps Air Station |
| AEW | airborne early warning | | MDAP | Mutual Defence Assistance Programme |
| AMRAAM | Advanced Medium-Range Air-to-Air Missile | | MEU | Marine Expeditionary Unit |
| ASV | anti-surface vessel | | NAF | Naval Air Facility |
| ASW | anti-submarine warfare | | NAS | Naval Air Station (US); |
| CAG | Carrier Air Group | | | Naval Air Squadron (UK) |
| CAM | Catapult Armed Merchantman | | NATO | North Atlantic Treaty Organization |
| COD | carrier onboard delivery | | PLAN | People's Liberation Army Navy |
| CSG | Carrier Strike Group | | RAF | Royal Air Force |
| CTOL | conventional take-off and landing | | RAN | Royal Australian Navy |
| CV | aircraft carrier, conventionally powered | | RCN | Royal Canadian Navy |
| CVA | attack carrier | | RTN | Royal Thai Navy |
| CVB | aircraft carrier, large | | SAR | search and rescue |
| CVAN | attack carrier, nuclear powered | | STOBAR | short take-off but assisted recovery |
| CVE | escort carrier | | STOVL | short take-off and vertical landing |
| CVL | aircraft carrier, small | | USMC | United States Marine Corps |
| CVS | anti-submarine carrier | | VAQ | Electronic Attack Squadron |
| CVN | aircraft carrier, nuclear powered | | VAW | Carrier Airborne Early Warning Squadron |
| CVW | Carrier Air Wing | | VFA | Strike Fighter Squadron |
| Det | Detachment | | VFC | Fighter Composite Squadron |
| ECM | electronic countermeasures | | VMA | Marine Attack Squadron |
| ESM | electronic support measures | | VMAQ | Marine Electronic Warfare Squadron |
| EW | electronic warfare | | VMFA | Marine Strike Fighter Squadron |
| FAA | Fleet Air Arm | | VMFA(AW) | Marine (All-Weather) Strike Fighter Squadron |
| FAB | *Força Aérea Brasileira* (Brazilian Air Force) | | VMMT | Marine Medium Tilt Rotor Squadron |
| FLIR | forward-looking infrared | | VQ | Fleet Air Reconnaissance Squadron |
| HARM | high-speed anti-radiation missile | | VR | Fleet Logistic Support Squadron |
| HC | Helicopter Combat Support Squadron | | VRC | Fleet Logistic Support Squadron (Composite) |
| HM | Helicopter Mine Countermeasures Squadron | | VS | Sea Control Squadron |
| HMH | Marine Heavy Helicopter Squadron | | V/STOL | vertical/short take-off and landing |
| HMLA | Marine Light Attack Helicopter Squadron | | VTOL | vertical take-off and landing |
| HMM | Marine Medium Helicopter Squadron | | | |
| HS | Helicopter Anti-Submarine Squadron | | | |
| HSC | Helicopter Sea Combat Squadron | | | |
| HSL | Helicopter Anti-Submarine Light Squadron | | | |
| HSM | Helicopter Maritime Strike Squadron | | | |
| IJN | Imperial Japanese Navy | | | |
| LHA | amphibious assault ship — general purpose | | | |
| LHD | amphibious assault ship — multi-purpose | | | |
| LPH | landing platform helicopters | | | |
| MAC | merchant aircraft carrier | | | |
| MAD | magnetic anomaly detection | | | |
| MAG | Marine Aircraft Group | | | |

# Index